Tourism and Geographies of Inequality

Slum tourism is a controversial pastime rising in popularity on a global scale. Known as 'slumming', it has been practised since Victorian times. In recent years, slum tourism occurs in more and more cities of the Global South. Township tourism across South Africa, favela tourism in Rio de Janeiro and slum tourism in Mumbai have grown to mass tourism dimensions.

This volume provides a collection of studies that shed light on the geographies of inequality in slum tourism from historical, sociological, political and anthropological perspectives. By connecting slum tourism to debates over the ethics and aesthetics of travel, volunteering, second homes and cross border mobility, the chapters provide ample ground for an understanding of slum tourism as transversal terrain in which questions of global equity come to the fore.

Based on unique and in-depth research from across the globe, the collection forms an indispensable resource for scholars and students of tourism and the geographies of inequality as well as those interested in questions of representation and tourist experience.

This book was originally published as a special issue of *Tourism Geographies*.

Fabian Frenzel is a Lecturer at the School of Management, University of Leicester, UK. His research interests converge in the political implications of travel and mobility. As a postdoctoral Marie Curie Fellow at the University of Potsdam he has investigated slum tourism in Africa, India and Brazil.

Ko Koens is a Lecturer at the Academy of Hotel and Facility Management, NHTV Breda University of Applied Sciences, The Netherlands. His main research interests are sustainability, entrepreneurship and social dilemmas in tourism and hospitality.

Tourism and Geographies of Inequality

The New Global Slumming Phenomenon

Edited by
Fabian Frenzel and Ko Koens

Routledge
Taylor & Francis Group

LONDON AND NEW YORK

First published 2015 by Routledge

2 Park Square, Milton Park, Abingdon, Oxon, OX14 4RN
605 Third Avenue, New York, NY 10017

Routledge is an imprint of the Taylor & Francis Group, an informa business

First issued in paperback 2020

Copyright © 2015 Taylor & Francis

British Library Cataloguing in Publication Data
A catalogue record for this book is available from the British Library

ISBN 13: 978-1-138-79559-4 (hbk)
ISBN 13: 978-0-367-73968-3 (pbk)

Typeset in Times New Roman
by RefineCatch Limited, Bungay, Suffolk

Publisher's Note
The publisher accepts responsibility for any inconsistencies that may have arisen during the conversion of this book from journal articles to book chapters, namely the possible inclusion of journal terminology.

Disclaimer
Every effort has been made to contact copyright holders for their permission to reprint material in this book. The publishers would be grateful to hear from any copyright holder who is not here acknowledged and will undertake to rectify any errors or omissions in future editions of this book.

Contents

Citation Information

The chapters in this book were originally published in *Tourism Geographies*, volume 14, issue 2 (May 2012). When citing this material, please use the original page numbering for each article, as follows:

Chapter 6

Mobile Imaginaries, Portable Signs: Global Consumption and Representations of Slum Life
Uli Linke
Tourism Geographies, volume 14, issue 2 (May 2012) pp. 294–319

Chapter 7

Glimpses of Another World: The Favela *as a Tourist Attraction*
Thomas Frisch
Tourism Geographies, volume 14, issue 2 (May 2012) pp. 320–338

Chapter 8

Encounters over Garbage: Tourists and Lifestyle Migrants in Mexico
Eveline Dürr
Tourism Geographies, volume 14, issue 2 (May 2012) pp. 339–355

Please direct any queries you may have about the citations to
clsuk.permissions@cengage.com

Slum Tourism: Developments in a Young Field of Interdisciplinary Tourism Research

FABIAN FRENZEL* & KO KOENS**

*School of Management, University of Leicester, Leicester, UK
**International Centre for Research in Events, Tourism and Hospitality, Leeds Metropolitan University, Leeds, UK

ABSTRACT *This paper introduces the Special Issue on slum tourism with a reflection on the state of the art on this new area of tourism research. After a review of the literature we discuss the breadth of research that was presented at the conference 'Destination Slum', the first international conference on slum tourism. Identifying various dimensions, as well as similarities and differences, in slum tourism in different parts of the world, we contest that slum tourism has evolved from being practised at only a limited number of places into a truly global phenomenon which now is performed on five continents. Equally the variety of services and ways in which tourists visit the slums has increased.*

The widening scope and diversity of slum tourism is clearly reflected in the variety of papers presented at the conference and in this Special Issue. Whilst academic discussion on the theme is evolving rapidly, slum tourism is still a relatively young area of research. Most papers at the conference and, indeed, most slum tourism research as a whole appears to remain focused on understanding issues of representation, often concentrating on a reflection of slum tourists rather than tourism. Aspects, such as the position of local people, remain underexposed as well as empirical work on the actual practice of slum tourism. To address these issues, we set out a research agenda in the final part of the article with potential avenues for future research to further the knowledge on slum tourism.

Introduction

This Special Issue of *Tourism Geographies* deals with the concept of slum tourism, which has been receiving increased attention in academic research after its (re)emergence at the end of the twentieth century. Amidst a proliferation of case studies, the emerging field of slum tourism now faces the challenge of addressing the definition of its scope and consequently its main conceptual questions. This is particularly true in respect of the many overlaps that exist between slum tourism research and related concepts and aspects of critical tourism research. We hope the Special Issue can assist in getting to grip with these challenges. It finds its origin in the conference *'Destination Slum! – Reflections on the production and consumption of poverty in tourism'*, which was held in Bristol from 9–11 December 2010. The current article serves as an introduction to the subject and aims to provide a backdrop for the following papers. After a concise critical examination of research on slum tourism to date, we discuss the development of the conference and its purpose. We then reflect on the papers presented at the conference and provide an overview of the seven papers that now form this Special Issue. While the papers echo many of the themes that are found in the literature on slum tourism, they also point towards the development of new approaches and an expansion of the field. In the last section we discuss omissions in the current literature and outline potential fruitful approaches to the topic and directions for future research.

Assessment of Previous Research on Slum Tourism

Slum tourism has been addressed explicitly in tourism literature since it (re-)emerged as a distinct niche of tourism in the last three decades, although it has been punctually mentioned, however, for example by MacCannell's (1976) comments on ghetto tours in 'The Tourist'. The academic debate follows very vocal discussions in the realm of journalism, which focused on the moral ambiguities surrounding 'slum tourism'. Academics were quick to dismiss many of the journalist accounts as problematic. Selinger and Outterson (2009: 3) commented critically: 'Perpetuating one-sided polemics, they fail to satisfy the demands of communal justification. Furthermore, most contributors to poverty tourism discourse do not comment on whether other people already have advanced similar, if not identical, views'. Ethical concerns, however, remain one mayor topic also in the academic discussions, albeit often in a more differentiated and case-based manner.

Initially most reflections focused on two main cases of slum tourism in the global South: township tourism in South Africa and *favela* tourism in Brazil. The phenomenon of township tourism in the major urban centres of South Africa gained attention in the 1980s. Township tours, developed to educate white local policymakers on the situation in the townships, became increasingly popular among so-called 'struggle junkies' – political tourists interested in the fight against apartheid (Dondolo 2002). Since the end of apartheid this nucleus of township tourism has developed massively. It is now seen as a major source of potential economic revenue and government policy supports the channelling of tourism flows into townships. While no figures exist for South Africa as a whole, it is estimated that every year up to 300,000 people visit the townships around Cape Town, showing the importance of tourism at least on a regional level (Rolfes 2009).

Authors have emphasized the role of township tours in representing the 'new South Africa'. According to Ramchander (2007), townships not only stand as places of poverty and crime, but also evoke the courage of black South African struggle for equal democratic rights. Marginality continues to be an important feature of post-apartheid South Africa as political history, lifestyle and the culture of people in townships are successfully commoditized and marketed in the tours. At the same time people from the townships have difficulty in profiting from the increasing tourism flows (Rogerson 2004). Such reflections on the ethics of township tourism can be seen as closely connected with a broader tourism research that deals with ways in which marginalized groups are subjected to the tourist gaze (Urry 2002).

The other major global slum tourism destination can be found in Rio de Janeiro where the *favelas* – particularly 'Rocinha' – attract large groups of tourists. *Favelas*, like townships, have a specific history as areas of urban poverty in the Brazilian context (Cardoso *et al.* 2005). They were predominantly associated with negative signifiers, such as poverty and, later, drug trade and violence. *Favela* tourism started during the Rio 1992 Earth Summit, when so many delegates were interested in visiting the *favelas* that local tour operators started offering stand-alone '*favela* tours'. Since then they have become a popular destination, with around 480,000 tourists visiting per year (Freire-Medeiros 2009).

Tourism has arguably played an important role in changing the image of the *favela* positively. In the townships the initial tours started with the political motive of showing the impoverished situation in the townships and this still forms the basis of most tours today (Butler 2010). Tourism in the *favelas* has always been aimed more at representing a rather positive imaginary. Some of these positive signifiers have been associated with the *favela* before the arrival of tourism. *Favelas* were represented as places of 'authentic' culture, for example samba music and dance, such as in Marcel Camus' film 'Orpheu Negro' from 1959 (Jaguaribe & Hetherington 2004). Freire-Medeiros (2009) has indicated that tourism has played an important role in the creation of what she calls the travelling 'trademark *favela*', a global imaginary of the *favela* reproduced increasingly in films, video games, night clubs and parties around the world. The 'travelling *favela*' has itself induced new flows of tourism to the *favelas*. It can be argued slum tourism takes place in the context of other modes of representation of slums and presumably much can be learned from exploring the semantics of these different modes (Linke 2012; Frisch 2012).

The most prominent example of the expanding development of slum tourism may be found in Mumbai. Its tourism development dates back to 2006 when an English/Indian-owned tour operator started the tours after taking inspiration from *favela* tourism in Rio de Janeiro and it has rapidly established itself as another 'big ' slum tourism destination(Freire-Medeiros 2009; Meschkank 2010; Dyson 2012). A link has also been made to film tourism research in respect of 'Slumdog Millionaire' and the subsequent increase in slum tourism in Mumbai (Mendes 2010). Other more recent work on slum tourism has taken place in Kenya where evidence suggests slum tours of the 'Kibera' slum date back to the global World Social Forum (WSF) meeting in 2007. Quite parallel to the initial occurrence of tourism in the *favelas*, delegates attending an international conference of civil society actors lined up for tours offered into Kibera during the WSF. These tours have now been turned into a lucrative business by at least five operators targeting mainstream tourists (Mowforth & Munt 2009).

Slum tourism research has proven to be 'undisciplined', much like tourism research in general (Tribe 1997). A wide range of disciplines have dealt with the phenomenon and it has been discussed from a variety of theoretical angles. The academic field of slum tourism research is comprised primarily of case studies. By nature these are unique and it is not always easy to directly transfer concepts, ideas and theoretical angles. Rolfes (2009) has pointed to the differences that matter between tourism in townships, *favelas* or other kinds of slums. While the definition of a slum according to the UN Habitat is 'a heavily populated urban area characterised by substandard housing and squalor' (United Nations Human Settlements Programme 2003), these areas all originate in particular historical conditions and hence form distinct social and political spaces. Presumably then, forms of tourism to these areas also differ. Furthermore, researchers have equally pointed to the fact that generalizations do not stop on the level of the 'global' slum, but continue in more local denominations. A *favela*, as Freire-Medeiros (2009) has argued, is not like any other *favela*. Townships equally differ, as do their possibilities for different forms of tourism (Koens 2012).

At the same time it is evident that the increasing number of case studies has led academic slum tourism debates to a certain level of comparative and conceptual reasoning. The occurrence of new cases has made a comparative approach towards a more thorough understanding of slum tourism even more salient, as parallels and, indeed, mutual influences between locations become more obvious. Flyvbjerg (2006) has argued how a range of case studies can be the backbone of good theorizing. Such a development appears to be starting to take place within slum tourism research now.

A way of addressing conceptual questions has been to evoke a historical dimension of slum tourism. The poor attracted rich visitors long before the advent of 'modern slum tourism'. Koven (2004) has pointed to the practice of 'slumming', a nineteenth-century Victorian past time. Similar historical studies have been conducted for Harlem and Chicago and for the Bronx (Conforti 1996; Anbinder 2001; Dowling 2009; Heap 2009) but also for continental Europe (Welz 1993; Steinbrink 2012) follows up on the expansion of slum tourism research in his contribution to this Special Issue by identifying different periods of slum tourism towards the development of what he calls 'global slumming' in the present.

Seeing slum tourism as a business transaction, the questioning of the exchange is at the heart of quite a few conceptual attempts. Freire-Medeiros (2009; 2011), amongst others, has evoked the concept of commodification to discuss *favela* tourism. Commodification of poverty is here understood as a way of capitalist value creation. For Freire-Medeiros (2009: 586), this is exceptional, as she notes:

[A]ltough under capitalism every single thing may be turned into a commodity, [Marx states that] there is one thing which can never be bought or sold: poverty, for it has no exchange value. The fact is that at the turn of the millennium, poverty has been framed as a product for consumption through tourism on a global scale.

The more general notion of commodification has been discussed intensely in tourism literature, also in relation to questions of authenticity (Hannam & Knox 2009). Critically, commodification can be seen as a differentiation between use value and exchange value. Use value is considered as socially embedded value while exchange value of the commodity is abstracted from the social context of its use. The question that remains is what is being commodified in slum tourism or, in other words, what is the slum tourism product? Is it really the slum itself and the imaginaries associated with it? Asking the tourists, research has established that poverty is the most important quality that tourists associate with slums. One can follow logically that this is what they come to see when they do a slum tour (Rolfes *et al.* 2009). Analysing the discourses of justification that tourists employ to explain their visits, it has been shown that mere curiosity to see poverty is rarely stated as a reason to visit slums, presumably because such a curiosity would be considered morally problematic and voyeuristic.

Scrutinizing the specific role of intermediaries, such as tour operators and guides, Butler (2010), Rolfes (2009) and Meschkank (2010) all argue they fulfil a significant role in creating a transformative narrative, a re-interpretation of poverty into something that is more easily told and sold. In this sense the poverty of Mumbai's Dharavi slum – an expectation of the tourist – is transformed by the tour into the experience of entrepreneurial spirit, ingenuity and diligence. In tours in Cape Town poverty is translated to historical injustice as well as ethnic and cultural uniqueness, while in Rio's *favela* tours poverty translates into community and solidarity. The way slum tourism is packaged with a particular focus on the way representations are crafted by professionals in the field seems to be a fruitful future avenue for research that deals with the ethical aspects of this phenomenon. Slum tourism representational techniques and their critique can be studied also in reference to reflections of 'literary slumming', the constructions and representations of poverty and slums in novels, films, video games, urban design and art (Williams 2008). These questions were discussed widely in the conference and contributions to this Special Issue by Dovey and King (2012) and Dyson (2012) touch upon it. Crossley's (2012) article provides a further link focusing on a second transformation that is present in the slum–tourism exchange: the transformation that concerns the tourist subject.

Quite a few conceptual approaches have addressed the question of the slum tourist's subjectivity. Slum tourism in South Africa, Rio de Janeiro and Nairobi was initiated by politically motivated tourists. Their demand for the slum, often voiced in the name of awareness and political transformation, created the initial set up of slum tour infrastructure, used later by larger cohorts of more mainstream tourists for whom the experience is packaged and somewhat mass produced. This development mirrors a more general pattern of tourist consumption and comes with differentiation processes that are clearly visible in slum tourism. Researchers have shown how slum tourists, often aided by intermediaries, construct their own experience as more authentic, morally superior and more valuable than those of other slum tourists (Freire-Medeiros 2009). Consumerist distinction, as Bourdieu (1984) has shown, employs aesthetic judgement to defend class positions. Slum tourism, as a highly ambiguous form of consumption, seems to evoke consumerist distinction based on moral and political judgement. To avoid replicating the distinctions tourists make about their slum tours, it is worthwhile referring Koven's (2004: 9) definition of slumming:

> I have made mobility, not fixity, central to my definition of slumming. I use slumming to refer to activities undertaken by people of wealth, social standing, or education in urban spaces inhabited by the poor. Because the desire to go slumming was bound up in the need to disavow it, my history of slumming includes the activities of men and women who used any word except slumming – charity, sociological research, Christian rescue, social work, investigative journalism – to explain why they entered the slums. My definition of slumming depends upon a movement, figured as some sort of 'descent' across urban spatial and class, gender and sexual boundaries.

Such generalizing allows linking slum tourism research to established areas of reflection on the role of poverty in the construction of the middle class traveller, for example, backpacker subjectivity. In this vane, Hutnyk (1996) has shown how backpackers construct themselves as 'better travellers' by engaging in charity in Calcutta. At the same time Calcutta is constructed as a place of poverty, which enables and justifies the charitable intervention. Rebuking the moral and political high ground those travellers may claim, critical researchers have also discussed volunteer tourism and justice tourism in respect of the images that these practices produce of the people visited. Critique has been voiced against the post-colonial character of the underlying discourses and imaginaries (Simpson 2005). Salazar (2004) has pointed out how 'development tourists' were often less interested in the development of the places they visited than their own development. This indicates a potential expansion of slum tourism research into the research of development and social movement practice when dealing with the context of high global mobilities and political tourism (Pezzullo 2007; Frenzel *et al.* 2011). In this Special Issue it is Crossley's (2012) contribution, in particular, that sheds new light on this question.

A further expansion of slum tourism research involves linking it to the more pragmatic questions of poverty relief through tourism. This question is paramount in research of tourism in the developing world. Is it at all possible for tourists to make any difference and, if so, in what way? In the 1970s optimism was great that tourism could form a tool, a 'passport' for development, a claim that first triggered a lot of development activity but was soon questioned by empirical research (De Kadt 1979). More detailed research on the benefits of slum tourism has particularly taken place with regards to the townships in South Africa and is less positive. Scheyvens (2007) has questioned whether tourism can provide economic empowerment for the township communities and Rogerson (2004) has – in respect of Soweto – identified problems, such as limited demand and limited training of communities in dealing with tourists, as major obstacles to benefits of slum tourism for the townships. The question he asks concerns the potential of small businesses to provide development paths in townships.

We argue that slum tourism researchers could benefit from a deeper critical reflection of the debates surrounding community-based tourism (CBT) and pro-poor tourism (PPT). Within CBT approaches, poverty is often part of the tourism product and poverty reduction the main rationale. CBT has been criticized for being rolled out as a catch-all programme of neo-liberal development agencies, without much regard for local specific contexts or economic viability. Ruiz-Ballesteros and Hernuandez-Ramuriez (2010) criticize CBT by stating it created a niche market for a particular type of tourist rather than helping the poor. There is a dearth of critical empirical studies on CBT in Africa but Dixey (2008) found that donor CBT projects in Zambia were unsustainable and warns that this can perpetuate underdevelopment and argues that CBT remains a privileged solution. She concludes that even if lessons learnt are assimilated and community tourism enterprise development is more viable, CBT will remain on the periphery of tourism development and have very limited potential for poverty reduction.

CBT is considered a form of PPT, defined as tourism that generates net-benefits to the poor (Ashley et al. 2001: 2). However, the emphasis of PPT is not on creating new tourism products more beneficial for the poor. PPT approaches have emphasized the need not to create new tourism products for poverty alleviation, but rather making existing (mass) tourism offerings more beneficial to the poor (Ashley & Haysom 2006). PPT approaches have been criticized on the basis of offering limited historical and conceptual grounding and doing little more than legitimizing existing tourism practice with only minor changes (Harrison 2008). In an effort to rebuke this critique, proponents have argued that PPT chooses to focus on pragmatics and that even small improvements could be seen as a way forward (Goodwin 2008).

We believe slum tourism research can shed new lights on these debates by showing the importance of the global and local context in which tourism develops. Also it can help shift the focus away from the primarily quantitative and economic definitions of poverty that arguably underlie some of this research. Poverty cannot be limited to the lack of material resources and, hence, poverty alleviation should not only focus on 'net benefit' or material income (Tomlinson et al. 2008). Slum tourism research might offer insights towards the development of qualitative criteria of poverty alleviation as existing research indicates the role tourists may play in giving recognition to urban communities that are stigmatized in their own societies (Freire-Medeiros 2009). At the same time such research needs to be wary of the fact that tourism can have a negative impact if the complexity and heterogeneity of communities are not taken into account sufficiently (Van der Duim *et al.* 2006).

Before we turn to a deeper reflection of how the conference and the papers in this Special Issue have contributed to an expansion of current slum tourism research, let us state that this overview of the existing literature has been partial and limited. We hope to have shown some of the central debates in the field so far and we have also pointed towards the way in which this research can be expanded and further developed. In the next section we will reflect on the contributions from the conference and discuss in more detail the other papers of this Special Issue.

Reflections on the Destination Slum Conference

In this part of the article we reflect on the papers as they were presented at the conference '*Destination Slum! – Reflections on the production and consumption of poverty in tourism*'. We investigate contributions of the papers but also comment on areas that received less attention and maybe need further investigation. The conference itself was enabled by an early career researcher grant provided by the University of the West of England to one of the authors (Fabian Frenzel) and marked the official launch of the international slum tourism network (Slum Tourism Network 2010). Speaking on behalf of the entire organizational committee, we would like to express our gratitude to all presenters and attendees for the great discussions and the organizational team for their support. The fact that it was possible to organize a conference solely involving slum tourism is indicative of the recent growth of interest in this subject. A total of 24 papers were presented at the 'Destination Slum' conference, seven of which are highlighted in this Special Issue. Most of the other papers are published in an edited volume (Frenzel *et al.* 2012). Both publications form a comprehensive reflection of the state of the art of research in slum tourism, while also pointing towards omissions and future avenues for research. A full list of papers presented at the conference is shown in Table 1.

The presented papers exemplified the interdisciplinary nature of slum tourism and included theoretical and empirical reflections using or combining approaches from anthropology, business and management studies, economics, geography, history, psychology and sociology. The majority of papers were qualitative in nature, while quantitative approaches were largely limited to descriptive statistics, reflecting the youth of the field and exploratory nature of much of the research. Half of the papers involved case studies, while the other half primarily approached slum tourism from a conceptual perspective. This contrasts somewhat with the general literature on slum tourism where most research is based on case studies. Few authors presented comparative research on different slums, although mutual grounds were often

Table 1. Papers presented at the 'Destination Slum' conference

Author	Title	Affiliation
João Afonso Baptista	Conceptual Poverty (Eradication) in 'Community-Based Tourism'	Institute of Ethnology, Martin-Luther-University, Halle, Germany
Kanika Basu	Slum Tourism: For the Poor by the Poor	Housing & Urban development Corporation, New Delhi, India
Shelley Ruth Butler	Curatorial Interventions in Township Tours: Two Trajectories	McGill University, Montreal, Canada
Thomas F. Carter	Stalking the Phantoms of Nostalgia: The Dynamics of Tourism in Habana Vieja, Cuba	Chelsea School, University of Brighton, UK
Emilie Crossley	'Poor but Happy': Negotiating Poverty in a Volunteer Tourism Setting	School of Social Sciences, Cardiff University, UK
Natália De' Carli & Mariano Pérez Humanes	What is Shown and What is Hidden: Favelatour and the Aesthetic Dimension of Poverty	Federal University of Pernambuco; Architecture Department at the University of Seville, Spain
Yannan Ding	'Happy City': beyond the sarcasm toward urbanism in a developing city	Department of Geography, KU Leuven, Belgium
Kim Dovey & Ross King	Informal Urbanism and the Consumption of Slums	Melbourne School of Design, University of Melbourne, Australia
Eveline Dürr	Slum Tourism and Transnational Lifestyles: A Case Study from Mexico	Institut für Ethnologie, University of Munich, Germany
Peter Dyson	Slum Tourism: Representing and Interpreting 'Reality' in Dharavi, Mumbai	Emmanuel College, Department of Geography, University of Cambridge, UK
Bianca Freire-Medeiros	*Favela* Tourism: Listening to Local Voices	Getulio Vargas Foundation (Fundação Getulio Vargas), Rio de Janeiro, Brazil
Thomas Frisch	Glimpses of Another World: The Favela and its Transformation from a 'Social Exclusion Area' into a Touristic Attraction	University of Salzburg, Austria
Ko Koens	Competition, Co-operation and Collaboration in Township Tourism: Experiences from South Africa	International Centre for Responsible Tourism, Leeds Metropolitan University, UK

(Continued on next page)

Table 1. Papers presented at the 'Destination Slum' conference *(Continued)*

Author	Title	Affiliation
Karol Kurnicki	Breaking Through the Imaginary. Slum Tourism as a Search for Urban Authenticity.	Jagiellonian University, Kraków, Department of Sociology, Poland
Uli Linke	Mobile Imaginaries, Portable Signs: The Global Consumption of Iconic Representations of Slum Life	Department of Sociology and Anthropology, Rochester Institute of Technology, USA
Moustafa A. Mekawy	Improving Egyptian Slums' Conditions Through Responsible Tourism Activities	Menoufiya University- El-Sadat City, Egypt
Julia Meschkank	Slumming in Mumbai: Dharavi and the Tensions between Different Constructions of Reality	Department of Geography and Regional Science, University of Potsdam, Germany
Louis Rice	Slum Genealogy	University of the West of England, UK
David Picard	The Poor Fisherman and his Wives: Ecotourism and the Cultivation of Poverty in the Zanzibar	University of Lisbon, Portugal
Andy Seaton	Travels with an 'Amateur Casual' : Slumming with James Greenwood in Late Nineteenth Century London	University of Bedfordshire, UK
Jasna Stefanovska	Learning from Topaana: Lessons from a Neighbourhood Where the Other 1% Lives	Faculty of Architecture, Ss. Cyril and Methodius University, Skopje, Macedonia
Malte Steinbrink	Doing the Slum: Geographical Reflexions on Poverty Tourism from an Historical Perspective	Institute of Geography & Institute of Migration Research and Intercultural Studies (IMIS), University of Osnabrück, Germany
Danielle Taana Smith	Gangster Tourism: Representations of 'The Ghetto' in the Era of Global Security	Rochester Institute of Technology, USA
Lina Tegtmeyer	But What About the Music?	Graduate School for North American Studies, Freie Uniformität Berlin, Germany
Kisnaphol Wattanawanyoo	Poverty Tourism in Old Historical Bangkok	School of Architecture and Design, King Mongkut's University of Technology Thonburi, Thailand

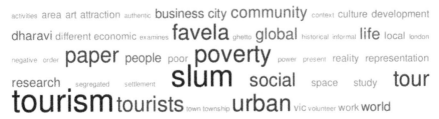

Figure 1. Tag cloud describing the words most often used in abstracts submitted to 'Destination Slum! – Reflections on the production and consumption of poverty in tourism'.

found in discussions following presentations. The outcomes of these discussions were enlightening and we would like to invite more research in this direction.

The geographical spread of the papers presented was impressive and showed slum tourism needs to be seen as a global phenomenon rather than restricted to certain parts of the (developed) world. Researchers from six continents presented their work on different forms of slum tourism in Africa, Asia, Europe, North and South America. Ten papers out of 24 focused on the townships in South Africa, the *favelas* in Brazil and Dharavi slum in India (Figure 1); these are the areas that have received by far most attention in academic literature up till now. Other presentations focused on tourism in deprived urban areas elsewhere, such as ghetto's in the US, the Ashwa'iyyatt in Egypt and Chinese 'villages in cities', while case studies from Cuba, Mexico, Thailand, Mozambique and Macedonia also were presented.

A number of papers dealt with tourism in a setting that may not directly be viewed as a slum. An example of this is Linke's (2012) contribution that discusses the way slum imaginaries are used in tourism in the 'global North'. Other examples in the current issue come from Crossley (2012) and Duerr (2012) and deal with tourism in a more rural setting. Although possibly better labelled poverty tourism, they provide enlightening findings that are relevant for tourism in urban slums as well and demonstrate how loosely related these two types of tourism are. Indeed, it suggests that at least some forms of slum tourism may be seen as a type of poverty tourism.

Even though one of the defining characteristics of slum tourism appears to be poverty, the presentations showed that slums are not uniform entities. There are great social differences even within some of the ones visited by tourists and it is increasingly difficult to distinguish (parts of) slums from other more affluent suburbs. One example that was mentioned at the conference is 'Rocinha', the most famous tourist *favela*, of which the lower slopes nowadays are highly developed (as represented by the presence of a McDonalds), which has led local government to actually no longer classify it as a *favela*. Such developments have not only practical consequences for slum tourism providers who need to adapt their narratives or for tourists expecting to see only abject poverty. They should also remind slum tourism researchers to critically reflect their conceptual understanding of poverty and slum tourism.

Nearly all authors acknowledge in one way or another the ethical issues surrounding slum tourism dilemmas. Most papers focused their attention on the way slums are represented and consumed. Particular ethical implications seem to derive from the visual experience in which poverty depends on existing and often problematic signifiers, for example dirt. In a way, certain tours seem to search for images of dirt. As Duerr (2012) shows in this Special Issue, this can go as far as making a rubbish dump into a tourism sight. Ethical problems also arise when slums are visually signified through the race and ethnicity of their inhabitants as, for example, the case of US ghetto tourism seemed to indicate.

Conference presentations focused primarily on slum tours in which the visual experience was emphasized particularly. The extensive images and films to support findings during many presentations highlight the importance of visual aspects of slum tourism on these tours. Although increasing numbers of accommodation and catering businesses become involved in slum tourism, these developments received little attention. Furthermore, it was noted that there was a distinct lack of research that involved the ideas and perceptions of local people. Only a limited number of papers investigated the production of slum tourism and ways in which local businesses get involved. The lack of research on these issues might have practical reasons. Language and cultural barriers between (often) foreign middle-class researchers and local people make such research (particularly empirical) much more challenging than research on tourists. Almost all conceptual papers dealt with issues of representation, yet few discussed local concerns, even though when dealing particularly with issues of representation it is evidently important to take local concerns into account.

Overview of Papers Presented in the Special Issue

Turning to the individual papers that can be found in this Special Issue, we have tried to highlight certain work that reflects what was discussed at the conference and provides new insights into the concept of slum tourism. Starting with Steinbrink (2012), he reflects upon current globalized poverty tourism trends from a historical perspective. He notes how the emergence of different forms of tourism over time can be seen as a construction and reflection of the society from which they originate. He takes the reader on a trip through the history of slumming, starting in London in Victorian times and following it, as it moved with British tourists, into the United States in the late nineteenth century. He notes how slums always have been constructed to represent 'the other side' and 'place of the other', not only in an economic, but also in a cultural sense. Changes in society (e.g. globalization) can be seen as the precedent for the current manifestation of slum tourism. Steinbrink finishes by discussing how this affects tourists who relate themselves and their identity to those who are visited.

Crossley (2012) focuses on the role of poverty in the making of tourists' subjectivities. Taking a psychosocial perspective, she presents findings from a longitudinal research project that deals with the ways in which volunteer-tourists experience and negotiate poverty. Poverty, she argues is perceived as 'threatening' when it provides a challenge for Western materialistic lifestyles and identities. This conflicts with their needs for presenting the self in a positive light when engaging in volunteer work. Tourists deal with this by creating neutralizing conceptions for the poverty they encounter, for example by viewing impoverished communities as 'poor but happy'. Such coping mechanisms act as barriers and prevent the intimate engagement that is seen as being exemplary of volunteer and slum tourism. This mitigation limits the potential of poverty to shock, move and change people's perspective and may lead to objectification and stereotyping.

Dyson (2012) further develops the concept of representation and interpretation in his investigation of slum walking tours in Dharavi, India. The tours position themselves to represent 'reality' to counter the 'fake' or 'fictional' negative images that dominate Western representations of slums. He explicates the difficulties of such a perspective and notes that representations are always subjective, conditional and uncertain. His analysis of the different interpretations of 'reality' by tourists sheds further light upon these issues by discussing how tourists use their agency to rationalize, interpret and comprehend what is offered to them in different ways. The article concludes that while the tours partially change tourist perceptions, the ability to transform the negative image of slums is restricted by the very techniques they use to position the slum as the archetype of 'reality'.

Exploring the dilemmas and contradictions of the imaginary and representation of informal settlements in in Asia, Dovey and King (2012) tackle the aesthetics of slum tourism. While slum tourism involves the creation of a brand-like attraction of informal settlements as part of a city's image, city authorities generally see slums as having negative symbolic capital and place identity and try to hide them. Slum tourism creates a paradoxical situation, where the flows of tourists to these areas are desired yet may foster urban imaginaries radically different from the ones cities and countries normally want to project. It is in this tension that they see the transformative potential of slum tourism. The attraction of slums appears to be not formal beauty, but anxiety and awe of being overwhelmed by informality. This may have the potential of re-considering political and moral positions.

Linke (2012) takes a more critical stance when she explores ways in which the iconic representations of shantytowns are produced for transnational consumption. In her insightful paper she shows how representations of the slum are taken out of their context and are recycled and consumed in tourism elsewhere. Competing representations of urban poverty are manufactured based on aesthetics and symbolic and affective means. Core images are detached from social life and globally mobilized for the use of artistic exhibits, fashion, social movements and private agents. Slums are represented in a decontextualized and typified way and consumed by those that can afford to refashion their social identity using these representations.

In his paper on tourism in Rocinha, Rio de Janeiro, Frisch (2012) explores the process through which the *favela* has been turned from a social problem into a tourist attraction. He argues tourism takes up the *favela*'s rich symbolic potential and is both depending on as well as contributing to existing discourses. Of particular importance here are visual elements of the *favela*. In a critique on current tourism, the dominance of external agents and lacking local participation is seen as denying residents a role as thinking, independently acting subjects. He concludes current *favela* tourism does not go beyond a form of 'negative sightseeing'.

The difficult relationship between tourists and the local population is also explored by Duerr (2012). She relates slum tourism to the concept of transnational mobilities in the case of a town in Mexico where expats from the US are involved in organizing tours to garbage dumps. The tours offer tourists the opportunity to visit a poor local community of people who dwell on the garbage site, living from recycling. The stated aims of the tours are to educate and support these local communities. Duerr frames the tours in the complex North American–Mexican relationship, which is often shaped by power imbalances and uneven economic conditions. She highlights the role of transnational brokers in the production of slum tourism as a potential field of further comparative research. Her conclusion is that despite potentially good intentions, the tours provide only limited space for local people to take ownership of how they are represented, while the tourists and expats benefit either in their desire for 'authentic' experiences or in creating a nexus of meaning in which they might try and position and legitimize themselves as foreign residents *vis-à-vis* the local community.

Avenues for Future Research

The papers in this Special Issue cover extensive ground and they provoke as many questions as they answer. We will take a look at some of these questions. In this section we aim to describe some possible avenues for future research on slum tourism. Furthermore we try to single out what we think are crucial issues for future debate and have identified several points that come out of this from our perspective.

On the basis of the papers presented at the conference, it would appear that slum tourism is moving from individual and descriptive case studies towards more con- ceptual and theoretical work. This development is commendable and we hope it will continue. However, most conceptual work is limited to issues of representation and other areas of research are still investigated mainly from a case study perspective.

The increase in slum tourism research in different areas around the world has, until now, resulted in little research comparing and contrasting findings. To further conceptual questions and to expand knowledge in the field we would argue future research needs to address the difficulties that result from comparing cases and to embark on a comparative research agenda. This concerns, for example, the entry of the public sector as a stakeholder taking an active part in the development of slum tourism enterprises. In Rio de Janeiro, for example, recent developments have shown a whole wave of public sector interventions into the business in the name of urban regeneration and economic empowerment of the poor (Tourism Review

2010). These are similar to the frameworks in which the public sector has supported the development of township tourism in South Africa since a decade ago (Rogerson 2005).

More significantly this support of the public sector in Rio comes after initial scepticism over the practices of slum tourism from various state agencies. Slum tourism in Mumbai still is regarded with not dissimilar scepticism and has evoked what seems to be vociferous condemnation in the Indian public realm (Dyson 2012). This shows some similarities to the initial reactions of certain parts of the Brazilian and South African public and might be a characteristic of early stages in the development of slum tourism. In all cases the rejection of slum tourism seems to originate in the respective middle and upper classes, while the residents affected by slum tourism tend to sanction it. Following on from this observation it might be worthwhile exploring a process character of slum tourism development. To what extent does it follow the route observed in the South African case and how can these differences be related to differing social contexts. Rio seems to be poised for a reflection on the gradual transformation of attitudes by the middle classes and political elites and research to be published by Bianca Freire-Medeiros (2012) will shed new light on the phenomenon.

The majority of papers implicitly or explicitly investigated slum tourism as a phenomenon of gazing at the 'exotic and economically poor'. When viewed from this perspective such slum tourism research can be classified as part of the larger discourse of poverty tourism. However, such a perspective does create a bias towards international slum tourism in developing countries and appears to be insufficient to describe domestic, cultural and/or political tourism in slums. For these forms of slum tourism, a definition based on geographical boundaries would seem more suitable, even if such an approach has its own limits (how does one delineate a 'slum'). Extended depictions of what constitutes slum tourism appear to have their merits and difficulties and may be used to investigate different aspects of the phenomenon.

Several papers dealt with slum tourism as the commodification of poverty. However, it seems that it is not necessarily poverty itself that is commodified but rather the potentially transformative experience of poverty that is characteristic of slum tourism. Such a transformation can take two forms: either the tourist's knowledge and understanding of urban poverty or the actual conditions of poverty that the slum tours promise to transform. In this sense slum tourism is sold as a way to alleviate poverty and could be discussed in the context of the recent emerging field of philanthropic travel and more broadly business ethics and corporate social responsibility. Further contributions are needed to improve understanding of the nature of transformations and transactions that form the core of the business of slum tourism. Here future research could profit from an engagement with literature that theorizes value creation and problematizes the predominantly quantitative outlook of studies that attempt to assess tourism's and slum tourism's contribution to poverty alleviation. At the same time such approaches are useful in reminding us how slum tourism is at heart an economic process, in which a variety of global and local actors are involved.

The lack of attention to how the slum tourism chain is organized and, in particular, to ways in which local businesses participate, makes it difficult to understand the impact of slum tourism on local communities. The little research that has been done on this matter by Frisch (2012) in the current issue and Koens (2012) suggests these issues are complex, with local participation influenced by power imbalances.

This brings us to our final avenue for further research. We note that the local perspective is relatively unknown. Research thus far has focused on the perspectives of slum tourism operators and tourists. Reactions of local people as well as the interaction with other local businesses have been reflected upon much less, a point made by Bianca Freire-Medeiros in the conference and reiterated in her recent work on the issue (Freire-Medeiros 2012). Whilst there may be practical reasons for this, the lack of knowledge on this matter seems one of the most important gaps in our knowledge today and this requires further investigation.

References

Anbinder, T. (2001) *Five Points: The 19th-century New York City Neighborhood that Invented Tap Dance, Stole Elections, and Became the World's Most Notorious Slum* (New York: Free Press).

Ashley, C., Goodwin, H. & Roe, D. (2001) *Pro-poor Tourism Strategies: Expanding Opportunities for the Poor* (London: ODI).

Ashley, C. & Haysom, G. (2006) From philanthropy to a different way of doing business: strategies and challenges in integrating pro-poor approaches into tourism business, *Development Southern Africa*, 23(2), pp. 265–280.

Bourdieu, P. (1984) *Distinction: A Social Critique of the Judgement of Taste* (Cambridge, Mass.: Harvard University Press).

Butler, S. R. (2010) Should I Stay or Should I Go? Negotiating Township Tours in Post-apartheid South Africa, *Journal of Tourism and Cultural Change*, 8(1–2), pp. 15–29.

Cardoso, A., Elias, P. & Pero, V. (2005) *Spatial Segregation and Labour Market Discrimination – The Case of Rio's Favelas* (Coventry: IER).

Conforti, J. (1996) Ghettos as tourism attractions, *Annals of Tourism Research*, 23(4), p. 830.

Crossley, É. (2012) Poor but happy: Volunteer tourists' encounters with poverty, *Tourism Geographies*, 14(2), pp. 235–253.

Dixey, L. M. (2008) The unsustainability of community tourism donor projects: Lessons from Zambia, in: A. Spenceley (Ed.) *Responsible Tourism: Critical Issues for Conservation and Development*, pp. 323–343 (London: Sterling VA: EARTHSCAN).

Dondolo, L. (2002) *The Construction of Public History and Tourism Destinations in Cape Town's Townships: A Study of Routes, Sites and Heritage*, Cape Town: University of the Western Cape.

Dovey, K. & King, R. (2012) Informal urbanism and the taste for slums, *Tourism Geographies*, 14(2), pp. 275–293.

Dowling, R. M. (2009) *Slumming in New York: From the Waterfront to Mythic Harlem Reprint* (University of Illinois Press).

Dürr, E. (2012) Encounters over garbage: Tourists and lifestyle migrants in Mexico, *Tourism Geographies*, 14(2), pp. 339–355.

Dyson, P. (2012) Slum tourism: Representing and interpreting 'reality' in Dharavi, Mumbai, *Tourism Geographies*, 14(2), pp. 254–274.

Flyvbjerg, B. (2006) Five misunderstandings about case-study research, *Qualitative Inquiry*, 12(2), pp. 219–245.

Freire-Medeiros, B. (2009) The favela and its touristic transits, *Geoforum*, 40(4), pp. 580–588.

Freire-Medeiros, B. (2011) I went to the city of god': Gringos, guns and the touristic favela, *Journal of Latin American Cultural Studies*, 20(1), pp. 21–34.

Freire-Medeiros, B. (2012) *Touring Poverty* (London: Routledge).

Frenzel, F., Böhm, S., Quinton, P., Spicer, A., Sullivan, S. & Young, Z. (2011) Comparing alternative media in North and South: The cases of IFIWatchnet and Indymedia in Africa, *Environment and Planning A*, 43(5), pp. 1173–1189.

Frenzel, F., Koens, K. & Steinbrink, M. (Eds) (2012) *Slum Tourism Poverty, Power and Ethics* (London: Routledge).

Frisch, T. (2012) Glimpses of another world: The *Favela* as a tourist attraction. *Tourism Geographies*, 14(2), pp. 320–338.

Goodwin, H. (2008) Pro-poor tourism: a response, *Third World Quarterly*, 29(5), pp. 869–871.

Hannam, K. & Knox, D. (2009) *Understanding Tourism: a Critical Introduction* (London: Sage).

Harrison, D. (2008) Pro-poor tourism: a critique, *Third World Quarterly*, 29(5), pp. 851–868.

Heap, C. (2009) *Slumming: Sexual and Racial Encounters in American Nightlife, 1885–1940* (Chicago: Chicago University Press).

Hutnyk, J. (1996) *The Rumour of Calcutta: Tourism, Charity, and the Poverty of Representation* (London: Zed Books).

Jaguaribe, B. & Hetherington, K. (2004) Favela tours: indistinct and mapless representations of the real in Rio de Janeiro, in: M. Sheller & J. Urry (Eds) *Tourism Mobilities: Places to Play, Places in Play*, pp. 155–166 (London: Routledge).

de Kadt, E. (1979) *Tourism – Passport to Development?: Perspectives on the Social and Cultural Effects of Tourism in Developing Countries* (New York: Oxford University Press).

Koens, K. (2012) Competition, cooperation and collaboration; business relations and power in township tourism, in: F. Frenzel, K. Koens & M. Steinbrink (Eds) *Slum Tourism Poverty, Power and Ethics*, pp. 105–123 (London: Routledge).

Koven, S. (2004) *Slumming: Sexual and Social Politics in Victorian London* (Princeton, NJ: Princeton University Press).

Linke, U. (2012) Mobile imaginaries, portable signs: Global consumption and representations of slum life, *Tourism Geographies*, 14(2), pp. 294–319.

MacCannell, D. (1976) *The Tourist: A New Theory of the Leisure Class* (New York: Schocken Books).

Mendes, A. (2010) Showcasing India unshining: Film tourism in Danny Boyle's Slumdog Millionaire, *Third Text*, 24(4), pp. 471–479.

Meschkank, J. (2010) Investigations into slum tourism in Mumbai: poverty and the tensions between different constructions of reality, *GeoJournal*, 76(1), pp. 7–62.

Mowforth, M. & Munt, I. (2009) *Tourism and Sustainability: Development, Globalisation and New Tourism in the Third World*, 3rd ed. (London: Routledge).

Pezzullo, P. (2007) *Toxic Tourism: Rhetorics of Pollution, Travel, and Environmental Justice* (Tuscaloosa: University of Alabama Press).

Ramchander, P. (2007) Township tourism – blessing or blight? The case of Soweto in South Africa, in: G. Richards (Ed.) *Cultural Tourism: Global and Local Perspectives*, pp. 39–67 (New York: Haworth Press).

Rogerson, C. M. (2005) Unpacking tourism SMMEs in South Africa: structure, support needs and policy response, *Development Southern Africa*, 22(5), pp. 623–642.

Rogerson, C. M. (2004) Urban tourism and small tourism enterprise development in Johannesburg: The case of township tourism, *GeoJournal*, 60(1), pp. 249–257.

Rolfes, M. (2009) Poverty tourism: theoretical reflections and empirical findings regarding an extraordinary form of tourism, *GeoJournal*, 75(5), pp. 421–442.

Rolfes, M., Steinbrink, M. & Uhl, C. (2009) *Townships as Attraction: An Empirical Study of Township Tourism in Cape Town* (Potsdam: Universitaetsverl. Potsdam).

17

Ruiz-Ballesteros, E. & Hernuandez-Ramuriez, M. (2010) Tourism that empowers?, *Critique of Anthropology*, 30(2), pp. 201–229.

Salazar, N. B. (2004) Developmental tourists vs. development tourism: A case study, in: A. Raj (Ed.) *Tourist Behaviour: A Psychological Perspective*, pp. 85–107 (New Delhi: Kanishka Publishers).

Scheyvens, R. (2007) Exploring the tourism–poverty nexus, *Current Issues in Tourism*, 10(2), pp. 231–254.

Selinger, E. & Outterson, K. (2009) *The Ethics of Poverty Tourism*, Boston School of Law Working Papers. Available at http://www.bu.edu/law/faculty/scholarship/workingpapers/documents/SelingerEOuttersonK06-02-09.pdf (accessed 12 December 2012).

Simpson, K. (2005) Broad horizons?: Geographies and pedagogies of the gap year, Doctoral dissertation, University of Newcastle upon Tyne.

Slum-Tourism Network (2010) *The International Slum Tourism Network*. Available at http://slumtourism.net (accessed 12 December 2012).

Steinbrink, M. (2012) 'We did the slum!' – Urban poverty tourism in historical perspective, *Tourism Geographies*, 14(2), pp. 213–234.

Tomlinson, M., Walker, R. & Williams, G. (2008) Measuring poverty in Britain as a multi-dimensional concept, 1991 to 2003, *Journal of Social Policy*, 37, pp. 597–620.

Tourism Review (2010) *Rio Offers a New Tourist Attraction – A Tour to the Slums*. Available at http://www.tourism-review.com/rio-top-tour-welcome-to-the-slums-news2405 (accessed 8 August 2011).

Tribe, J. (1997) The indiscipline of tourism, *Annals of Tourism Research*, 24(3), pp. 638–657.

United Nations Human Settlements Programme (2003) *The Challenge of Slums: Global Report on Human Settlements, 2003* (London: Earthscan Publications).

Urry, J. (2002) *The Tourist Gaze*, 2nd ed. (London: Sage Publications).

Van der Duim, R., Peters, K. & Akama, J. (2006) Cultural tourism in African communities: a comparison between cultural Manyattas in Kenya and the cultural tourism project in Tanzania, in: M. Smith & M. D. Robinson (Eds) *Cultural Tourism in a Changing World: Politics, Participation and (Re)Presentation*, pp. 104–123 (Clevedon, UK: Channel View Publications).

Welz, G. (1993) Slum als Sehenswuerdigkeit. 'Negative Sightseeing' im Staedtetourismus, in: D. Kramer & R. Lutz (Eds) *Tourismus-Kultur, Kultur-Tourismus*, pp. 39–55 (Muenster: Lit-Verlag).

Williams, C. (2008) Ghettourism and voyeurism, or challenging stereotypes and raising consciousness? Literary and non-literary forays into the favelas of Rio de Janeiro, *Bulletin of Latin American Research*, 27(4), pp. 483–500.

Notes on Contributors

Dr Fabian Frenzel is a lecturer at the School of Management, University of Leicester. His main research interests are the political implications of international tourism and mobility. He has done empirical research on *favela* tourism in Rio de Janeiro, asking whether tourism has played a role in empowering *favela* communities. He is a founding member of the international slum tourism network.

Ko Koens is a PhD researcher at the International Centre for Research in Events, Tourism and Hospitality at Leeds Met University. His research deals with small tourism businesses involved in township tourism around Cape Town. He aims to gain an understanding of the ways in which these small tourism businesses function and how they link up with the existing tourism market. He is a founding member of the international slum tourism network.

'We did the Slum!' – Urban Poverty Tourism in Historical Perspective

MALTE STEINBRINK

Institute for Geography & Institute for Migration Research and Intercultural Studies (IMIS),
University of Osnabrück, Osnabrück, Germany

ABSTRACT *Slum tourism in the Global South is a relatively new phenomenon. The tourist gaze at the poverty of the Others is long established, though. This paper is concerned with the genesis of urban poverty tourism. By placing the phenomenon of slumming in the wider realm of the social upheavals in Victorian London and early twentieth century USA, the historical review first explains its dependency on the social context determining its emergence and evolution. Secondly, slum tourism is shown to be adequately understood only if seen as part of modern city tourism. Thirdly, it is demonstrate that the* culturalization of poverty *attains special significance in slum tourism. Fourthly, the history of slum tourism is shown to have implications for understanding present-day slum tourism in the Global South, using South Africa as an example. The article is designed to be a first step towards understanding the conditions, forms and consequences of globalization of slum tourism and the process of constructing the* global slum *as a universal type of tourist destination.*

Introduction

Tourism lives on what is different. Its economic implications alone urge it to constantly create new products and open up new segments on the market. Tourism always looks for new places, inventing *sights* and *sites* which are then marked and marketed as tourist attractions. The fact that tourism needs innovations for purposes of self-preservation is by no means new. What is interesting, however, is to take a look beyond this pure logic of market mechanisms in order to find out *how*, *why* and *with what implications* places of tourism are socially constructed.

The emergence of a new trend in tourism, too, always gives rise to reflection on why it emerges precisely at a particular point in time and in a particular social context. Since the 1990s, one such new trend has been observable in long-distance international tourism, a development which has been spreading rapidly on a global basis and which, at first sight, might look surprising; and that is 'slum tourism' in the Global South. In spite of strong criticism coming from the international media, visits to poor urban areas in big cities in the South are unmistakably gaining in importance both in terms of tourism and in economic terms. How can this development be explained? How and with what consequences are slums constructed as destinations worth touring during a holiday?

In an increasing number of big cities in the Global South, poor urban settlements are marketed for tourism. This slum tourism takes place primarily in the form of guided tours – be they bus, jeep or walking tours. The slum tours already constitute an important item in the range of offers made by the urban tourism industry. For example, a slum tour has now become part of the standard programme of a visit to Cape Town or Johannesburg; and a tour of Rocinha, Rio de Janeiro's largest *favela*, is, today, one of the tourist's must dos, just as strolling at the beach of Ipanema and climbing the Sugar Loaf. Estimates suggest an annual 300,000 or so tourists embarking on slum tours in Cape Town (AP 2007) and approximately 40,000 in Rio (Freire-Medeiros 2009). These figures indicate that slum tourism is already a highly professionalized business in South Africa and Brazil. But slum tours have also been meeting with increasing interest in other countries of the Global South, both among tourists and providers, who see a huge growth potential in this branch of tourism. For example, organized slum tours are executed, *inter alia*, in the poor areas of Manila (Philippines), Jakarta (Indonesia), Cairo (Egypt), Buenos Aires (Argentina), Nairobi (Kenya), Mazatlán (Mexico), Bangkok (Thailand) and Windhoek (Namibia).

A current example is India, where slum tourism is noticeably expanding at present. A driving force for this development has been the huge media attention in the wake of eight-times Oscar-awarded Hollywood Film *Slumdog Millionaire* (2009), which is acted against the backdrop of Dharavi, the largest slum in Mumbai (Hannam & Knox 2010; Meschkank 2011).

The new phenomenon of slum tourism in the Global South not only reminds us that tourism lives on what is novel and different; it suggests, at the same time, that new trends in tourism are never created out of nothing. They draw upon more or less known images and ideas about unfamiliar and distant regions and their inhabitants. They have recourse to stocks of standardized long-standing ascriptions that arise in discursive processes occurring both within and outside tourism. Tourism seeks for discursive connectivity, reproduces these ascriptions and creates new meanings, while reacting to social structures and their changes. Allegedly new forms of tourism almost always have historical forerunners with which they link semantically and from which their specific repertoire of offers develops. For example, tourism in 'Europe's Cultural Capitals' or cultural sightseeing tours organized by companies like the German firm Studiosus can be traced back to the 'Grand Tour', the educational tours of the nobility in the sixteenth to eighteenth centuries (cf. Adler 1989). Similarly, contemporary mass seaside tourism has a long history, which began from the 'discovery of the coast' in the eighteenth and nineteenth centuries and led, via Brighton as the archetype of the seaside resort, to the 'global beach' (Löfgren 1999) as a present-day global-universal destination type (cf. also Shields 1991).

Today's slum tourism in the Global South has forerunners, too. This paper seeks to illustrate how 'long-established' modes of constructing, presenting and perceiving slums as places worth touring find their way into the current practice of poverty tourism. Hence, the reconstruction of the roughly 150-year-old tradition of this form of tourism is not only of interest with regard to the illustration of the history of the development of tourism; it can also provide valuable clues to an understanding of today's forms and modes of constructing slums as 'places of tourism' (Pott 2007). If we assume that the *tourist gaze* (Urry 1990) at poverty is long established (at least in its essential features), then current poverty tourism as such will be less astounding than the dynamism of its global spread. An overriding goal of research on slum tourism, then, would consist in grasping the conditions, forms and consequences of its globalization. The present paper, which is primarily concerned with the genesis of poverty tourism, is designed to be a first step towards understanding the process of constructing the *global slum* as a global-universal type of tourist destination.

In this paper, a brief presentation of the recent phenomenon – drawing upon the example of township tourism in South Africa – will be followed by a closer look into the long-standing tradition of slum tourism. By attempting to place the phenomenon in the wider realm of the social and cultural upheavals happening in each of the periods studied, the historical review seeks, first, to explain its dependency on the social context determining its emergence and evolution. Secondly, it will become clear that slum tourism can be adequately understood only if seen as part of modern city tourism. Thirdly, the historical review will demonstrate that and how the *'culturalization'* of poverty attains special significance in slum tourism. Fourthly, the closing remarks indicate in what respects the insights gained from the historical review can be drawn upon for enquiries into present-day slum tourism in the Global South.

Slumming in the Global South: the Example of Township Tourism in South Africa

'Township tourism' is South Africa's version of the new global phenomenon of poverty tourism. It is meant to serve here as an example to start from in my analytical concern with the phenomenon.

The economic significance of international tourism for South Africa has increased considerably since the end of apartheid. The number of international arrivals in the country rose from 3.6 million in 1994 to 9.1 million in 2007 (Steinbrink & Frehe 2008). In terms of its significance for South Africa's GNP, the tourism sector has, meanwhile, even outdone gold mining, which has for long been the backbone of that country's national economy. It is expected that tourism's economic importance will continue to grow even in the future, thanks to the 2010 football world cup (cf. Haferburg & Steinbrink 2010).

Generally speaking, the tourist industry sees the country's tourism potential in its landscape and natural beauty (national parks, impressive mountain landscapes, beaches, vineyards, etc.). However, following the end of apartheid, *township tourism* has been developing as a new branch of the tourism industry – a development which has little to do with the traditional sights. Township tourism is organized mainly in the form of guided bus tours which run through selected townships. The tour destinations are the urban residential areas of those population groups formerly classified as 'non-white', residential areas which emerged during the era of the apartheid regime and which were planned on the basis of that regime's inhuman racist ideology. It is the poorest strata of the population that live in the townships. The majority of the 'black' city dwellers still live there – and, largely, still under deplorable living conditions.

Township tourism had forerunners during the apartheid era, but in its recent form it started in the early 1990s. The first township tours were conducted to Soweto (*South Western Township*) in Johannesburg. At the time, township tourism was a kind of niche tourism for politically interested travellers who wanted to visit Soweto as a place symbolizing oppression and the anti-apartheid struggle, their aim being to see the sites of resistance and the houses in which symbolic figures, such as Nelson Mandela and Bishop Tutu, used to live. It was from there that township tourism evolved rapidly, expanding over the whole of South Africa as a phenomenon of urban tourism. An ever-increasing number of international travellers – predominantly from Britain, Germany, The Netherlands and the USA – travelled through the townships and informal settlements of different historical origins and sizes during their holidays in South Africa. In the process, historical and political aspects which had initially been the focus shifted to the background (Rolfes *et al.* 2009).

According to official data, over 300,000 tourists participated in organized tours in Cape Town in 2006 (AP 2007). This is almost 25 percent of the total annual number of overseas international visitors. Apart from the trip to the Table Mountain, the trip to Cape Point, the visit to the Waterfront and a wine tour, township tourism is among the 'things to tick off the list' while visiting Cape Town. Township tourism is a booming business. More and more tour operators are pushing their way into the market. In Cape Town, roughly 50 different tour operators can be identified. Meanwhile, an increasing number of big travel agencies operating on an international or a supra-regional basis now also include township tours in their – otherwise rather conventional – range of products. Township tourism has thus developed into a phenomenon of mass tourism in South Africa (cf. Rolfes & Steinbrink 2009).

To understand the phenomenon of slum tourism, it appears useful to first discuss the question of what the slum actually 'is' – not from a social-scientific perspective or from the perspective of town planning, but from the viewpoint of tourism. In order to find out what tourists look for in the slums, the question as to what they expect to find there would suggest itself. (*They want to see what they expect to see!*) It appears plausible to assume that the attractiveness of slums as tourist destinations is

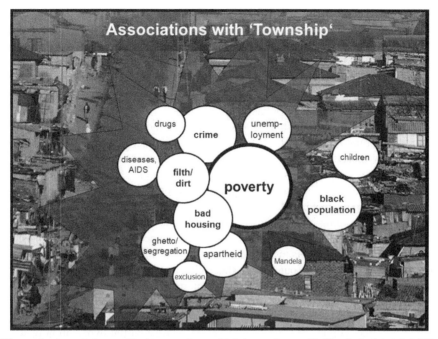

Figure 1. Associations with the term 'township' (according to Rolfes & Steinbrink 2009; author's own representation).

directly connected with the images, conceptions and associations the tourists have of the places they intend to visit; in the case of South Africa, this would mean their image of the township.

What images, then, do tourists have of the townships? This question constituted the focus of a study project conducted in Cape Town in 2007. Questions were put to 179 tourists, immediately before embarking on a township tour, on what they associated with the term 'township' (cf. Rolfes *et al.* 2009).

The results reveal that negative associations dominate the picture (see Figure 1). 'Township' is associated with crime, squalor, drugs, poor housing conditions, apartheid, unemployment, etc. The most frequently mentioned association by far was 'poverty'. 'Poverty' is in the centre of the semantic field evoked by the term 'township'. Meschkank (2011: 55) obtains very similar results in her study of tourism in Dharavi/Mumbai: 'If you ask the tourists participating in a Dharavi tour what they expect to see, the most common answer is: poverty'. It is, therefore, appropriate to understand township tourism as a kind of *poverty tourism*.

Yet, 'poverty' does not characterize this form of tourism sufficiently. For – as in the case of many other forms of tourism – 'spatialization' plays a central role in endeavours that make it possible to visualize and experience poverty and, thus, in the construction of urban tourism as a whole. Poverty's territorial localization makes it possible for it to be expected, planned and visited for purposes of tourism. Consequently, the tours are conducted to certain areas, to city districts categorized as townships, as *favelas* or, generally, as slums. It is in these areas that poverty is located; this is where poverty can be expected and experienced – the slum is the 'place of poverty'. The term 'slumming' explained further below, therefore, describes this form of poverty tourism very precisely.

The results of the studies stated above are, understandably, startling, since they do contradict common notions of what tourists do during their holiday. True, gazing at poverty may indeed lead to the striven-for 'distance away from everyday life'; yet, the wish to see 'something else' as expressed in the common holiday motives usually refers to something nice, beautiful and relaxing. In contrast thereto, township tourism seems to correspond to what MacCannell (1976) calls 'negative sightseeing': a kind of social bungee jumping in which the predominantly bourgeois thrill-seekers – driven by a lust for *angst* (cf. Welz 1993: 48) – seek to experience the social depth. The slum tours seem to permit tourists to fathom out the possible drop height sensuously (using their eyes, ears and noses), but without themselves actually running the risk of a hard landing (Steinbrink & Frehe 2008). But I doubt that the lust for the socio-voyeuristic thrill and the wish to experience a 'safe danger' or an 'insulated adventure' (Schmidt 1979) is sufficient to grasp this phenomenon of tourism analytically. This element of 'controlled risk' (Freire-Medeiros 2009) is only a very partial explanation of what motivates tourists to visit impoverished urban areas.

Here, the question immediately arises as to the origin of this tourist gaze at the poverty of Others. How has the tourist interest in the slum developed historically? What traditions of spatializing observation and interpretations exist in the collective memory of the tourists? How, then, is it conceivable that 'places of poverty' have become 'places of tourism' (Pott 2007)?

A Review of the History of Slumming

The concept of 'slumming' has described a particular social practice for one and a half centuries; in this practice, members of wealthy population groups visit residential areas of poor urban groups in their leisure time. The origins of this practice lie in the metropolises of the North, especially in Britain and the USA, where modern (urban) tourism also evolved.

The 'slum' has always symbolized the 'dark', the 'low', the 'unknown' side of the city; it has always been a projection surface. From the bourgeois perspective, the poor urban areas have constantly been constructed as areas containing 'the Other'. Accordingly, visiting a slum for leisure purposes has always been done in the wish to experience the Other. However, what was identified as being 'the Other' varied from one historical period to another and depended on the respective social context in which it existed.

Victorian London: The Cradle of Slumming

The practice of slumming has its roots in nineteenth-century London. It was from there that the phenomenon started, and it did so, as will be seen later, in a very Victorian-Anglican manner.

London – at the time, the politically and economically most powerful city in the world and capital of the world-encompassing British Empire – developed into a demographic colossus in the nineteenth century. Its population grew from one million to six million within one hundred years. Its urbanization rates, which were due primarily to rural exodus and immigrations from Ireland, were just as enormous as was the gap between the rich and the poor. In the course of urbanization and industrialization, the social classes were separated geographically in a typically European east–west divide. The blatant urban segregation pattern appeared like the spatial configuration of the deeply split social order of the time.

Originally 'slum' was a slang expression which referred to individual lodgings, then to backyards ('back slums') and later to whole urban quarters (Mayne 1993). The etymological origin of the word is controversial. The *Oxford Dictionary of Etymology* describes it as a word of unknown origin, but presumes a 'gypsy' origin (Hoad 1996). Cassidy (2007), however, presupposes an Irish origin (*s'lom* [pron. s'lum], the Irish meaning being 'is bare, is naked, is poor'). Davis (2007: 26) refers to the *Vocabulary of the Flash Language* by Vaux (1912), according to which slum means something like 'swindle' or 'criminal machinations' (translations based on German version (2007) of *Planet of Slums* (2006)). According to Dyos *et al.* (1982), it was Cardinal Wiseman who turned the term 'slum' into a term of the standard language from around 1820 onwards. Dyos *et al.* (1982) point out that Wiseman was often quoted in British newspapers in that time, slowly leading to the wider popular use of the term 'slum' for a more general description of destitute urban housing conditions (ibid). Since the mid of the 19th century, certain poor settlements in the USA, France and India were also labelled as slums (Davis 2007: 26).

London's rapid growth resulted in the fact that its inhabitants no longer knew every part of their city from personal experience. An 'imaginative geography' of the city thus emerged in parallel with the clear spatial separation between the rich and the poor. From the viewpoint of the top of the vertical hierarchy of London's social structure, the slums of the East End represented the dark 'abyss'. One needs only to take a glance at Peter Keating's collection of social reports (Keating 1976) from that time to notice how often the word 'abyss' occurs in the titles alone. The slum, according to this observation, labels the place of the physical, social, economic and moral abyss and of the threatening fall into the bottomless pit.

In the perception of London's middle and upper classes, the East End slums were 'places of the unknown Other'. The existence of these places alone was a cause for concern and fear in society. The fears, however, were not only about sanitary and hygienic conditions and the threat of epidemics (in particular, cholera). Rather, there were also social worries about the decline of civilization and the loss of public control. This gave rise to an image of the East End as another world – chaotic, uncivilized and horrifying. In other words, the slum represented the materialized anti-thesis to the bourgeois order of the Victorian era (Frank 2003: 53).

The nineteenth century was the period of colonial voyages of discovery, and the deletion of white spots on the world map was a British passion at that time. In Victorian London, the East End was often referred to as the 'dark continent' (cf. Frank 2003: 54f.; Lindner 2004) – the same designation used for Africa.

> As there is a darkest Africa, is there not also a darkest England? ... May we not find a parallel at our doors and discover within a stone's throw of our cathedrals and palaces places of similar horrors to those which Stanley has found in the Equatorial forest? (Booth 1890: 11–12).

By analogy with the colonial voyage of discovery, the explorer's spirit, too, awoke in the city, the aim of which was to discover 'the distant' in 'the near-by' ('at our doors', 'within a stone's throw'). There was an awakening of interest in social expeditions into the abysmal depths of the *urban terra incognita*.

The first people to go on these 'social expeditions' were clergymen, such as William Booth, founder of the Salvation Army, journalists and social reformers. In their reports, they tended to present themselves as explorers who ventured, dead-tired, into the bottomless social swamp. Their reports established a new literary genre – the exploratory social reportage. In their writings, the social reporters decisively influenced and shaped the discourse on the East End, and the prevailing image of its inhabitants.

To the wealthy of London, the slums were, on the one hand, a threatening strange world. On the other hand, however, the slums promised adventures and formed the projection space for the wildest of fantasies. Frequently wrapped in the cloak of concern, welfare and charity, more and more private benefactors in the middle of the century were setting off for the 'undiscovered land of the poor'. Early forms of slum tours were already encountered here. At the time, the discovery tours to London's East End were guided by police officers in civilian attire, journalists and clergy (Figure 2).

These upper-class visits in the East End were called 'slumming' as early as around 1850 (cf. Koven 2006). The term 'slumming' is, therefore, almost as old as the term 'slum' itself. Koven (2006: 6–10) notes that from the outset, the term slumming was mostly used with a scornful to explicitly derogatory connotation by members of the upper class, who, for their part, did not indulge in this practice. 'Slumming, the word and the activity associated with it, was distinguished historically by a persistent pattern of disavowal. It was a pejorative term ... ' (Koven 2006: 8). The curiosity about the slum that finds expression in the slumming activity did indeed evoke suspicion from the very beginning, particularly in regard to the motivation of the so-called *slummers* (i.e. those who practised slumming). Behind the lofty intentions

Figure 2. Slum tour in Victorian London. *Source*: Koven (2006: 15).

transmitted outwardly, other, less noble, motives were suspected, motives of which the slummers should obviously have been ashamed.

This suggests that more was associated with the slum – the place of the 'unknown Other' – than just the difference in economic terms. There was more to slums than their characterization as places of poverty. For there were also association chains linked to 'poverty' which stretched into fields that lay outside the economic sphere. It can be shown that 'slum' and 'poverty' have experienced a semantic coupling resulting from the talk about the 'omnipresence of filth and dirt' (cf. Lindner 2004: 20). An indication of how closely 'slum' and 'dirt' are connotatively connected is given by the observation that at the turn of the century, the term 'slum' was often rendered in German as *Schlammviertel* ('mud quarter') (cf. Spiller 2008 [1911]).

The words 'filth' and 'dirt' lie at the point where two chains of association deriving from slum and poverty intersect (Figure 3). Both chains of association lead directly into corporeality – in particular, into the lower zones of the body: through cholera, a serious form of diarrhoea, into the anus, and through lust, into the genitals. The Victorian era was a period in which corporeality was denied and concealed in the bourgeois milieu. It thus becomes clear that 'dirt' indeed is by no means only a

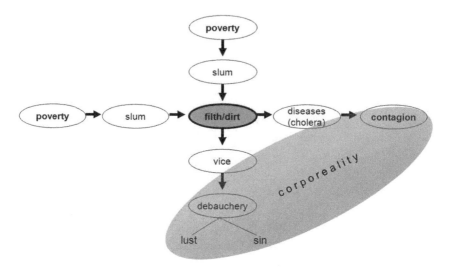

Figure 3. Poverty, slum and dirt as a close semantic association. *Source*: author's representation.

hygienic category and that it has always been a moral category, too, which refers to something indecent and repugnant.

In the middle- and upper-class discourse over the slum, an almost direct equation of the poor sanitary conditions with a state of moral decay took place. Through the close semantic relation between 'poverty', 'dirt' and 'sin', the poverty concept also became subjected to moralizing and, through the assignment of poverty to certain areas, a connection was finally established between urban topography and morality, which was tantamount to the construction of a *moral topography* of the city.

The slums apparently strongly provoked the dirty fantasies of London's bourgeoisie, its 'belief' in moral standards notwithstanding. From the middle-class point of view, poverty and slums have stood not only for misery and disease, but also for eroticism, licentiousness and sexual savagery. Little wonder, then, that the slums, in the eyes of London's society, which was shaped by rigid moral expectations and inflexible social rules, were areas of both gloomy threat and erotic curiosity: slums were places of moral decay and places of libidinal liberty (cf. Lindner 2004: 19ff.).

This explains indeed why the non-slummers often imputed filthy motives to the slummers. And it also explains why the *professional* or *altruist slummers* (the clergy, social reformers, benefactors, etc.) made repeated attempts to distinguish themselves from the *casual* or *leisure slummers* to avoid being thrown into the same 'pot of mud', in view of their noble motives (cf. also Koven 2006).

In the second half of the nineteenth century, however, slumming increasingly developed into a more 'purpose-free' leisure-time activity of London's higher classes.

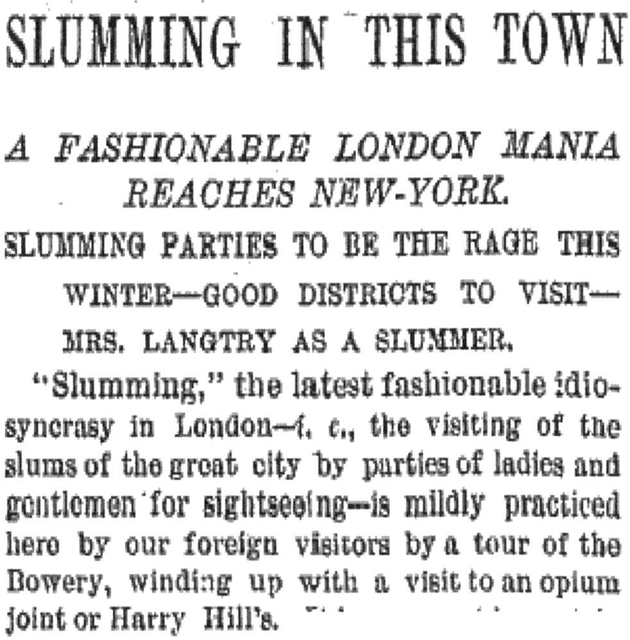

SLUMMING IN THIS TOWN

A FASHIONABLE LONDON MANIA REACHES NEW-YORK.

SLUMMING PARTIES TO BE THE RAGE THIS WINTER—GOOD DISTRICTS TO VISIT— MRS. LANGTRY AS A SLUMMER.

"Slumming," the latest fashionable idiosyncrasy in London—*i. e.*, the visiting of the slums of the great city by parties of ladies and gentlemen for sightseeing—is mildly practiced here by our foreign visitors by a tour of the Bowery, winding up with a visit to an opium joint or Harry Hill's.

Figure 4. 'Slumming in this Town'. *Source: New York Times* (14 September 1884).

Amusement shifted into the centre of things and the 'lust for vice', as well as interest in the 'immoral Other', became more clearly visible. The new phenomenon had hardly gained contours as a leisure-time entertainment, when its globalization began. Slumming was now making its way 'across the pond'.

'Let's Go Slumming in the USA'

In the USA, the phenomenon of slumming emerged for the first time in New York in the 1880s. Figure 4 shows a cutting from an 1884 issue of the *New York Times*. The journalist who wrote this newspaper article described slumming as "the [latest] rage", as a London peculiarity and new fashion ("a fashionable London Mania"; "the latest fashionable idiosyncrasy in London") imported to New York by well-to-do tourists from England. Additionally, he prophesied that this extravagant fashion would develop into a hype amongst the New Yorkers– and he was later proven right.

The idea of slumming fell on fertile ground in the USA. However, its social breeding ground in the USA differed from that in Victorian England. The phenomenon, therefore, did develop differently in America. Following the first appearance of slumming in the 'New World', a process of change was evolving which was very interesting in regard to the genesis of poverty tourism as a whole. In the social context of the

USA in the early twentieth century, the element of moral difference remained char-acteristic of slumming (Dowling 2007; Heap 2009) but, successively, other markers of difference became more dominant in the construction of the slum as the 'place of the Other'. This change in the construction of 'the Other' localized in the slum will be the subject of our further discussion.

Touristification of slumming – urban heterogeneity as a tourist attraction. Although slumming in London already comprised certain elements of tourism – e.g. Koven (2006) indicates that Victorian Travel Guidebooks recommended visits to charitable institutions in the East End – it was in New York that one could actually speak of the 'touristification' of slumming.

The occurrence of slumming in the USA was directly linked with the development of international (urban) tourism. As indicated in the above-quoted *New York Times* article (see Figure 4), it was the tourists from England who carried the idea of slumming in their mental luggage. And now, the ladies and gentlemen from London wanted to visit the poorer areas in New York (e.g. Bowery, Five Points), too, during their sightseeing tours. Here, then, for the first time, the element of a regionalizing (cultural) comparison, which is typical of (urban) tourism, appears on the scene. Urban tourism is fundamentally based on the spatial differentiation between *here* and *there*. For the fact that cities become places worth touring is based on a spatially indicated expectation of difference (cf. Pott 2007: 113). Consequently, the first slum tourists from London compared 'their' London East End with the Lower East Side in Manhattan:

> A quite well-known young English Noble, returning from a tour of the east side the other night with some friends, observed over his brandy and soda: 'Ah, this is a great city, but you have no slums like we have. I have been in rickety condemned buildings that it was absolutely dangerous to go through! Found six families living in one miserably ventilated cellar – 24 persons, 10 of them adults, living in one room. No such slums here!' (*New York Times*, 14 September 1884).

It was through the practice of slumming that poor urban areas first became tourist sights which were then drawn upon for comparisons between the tourist's own city with the one visited. In other words: it was in New York that the tourist's comparative gaze, in search of the differences between 'own city' and the destination, first designed the slum as an urban tourist attraction.

Slumming in the USA developed in such a way that the slummers could give in to their tourist curiosity without being ashamed of doing so. Entertainment intentions were professed more openly; the tourists were now in a position to cast off the moral cover without having any qualms. Compared to slumming in London, slumming in New York at the end of the nineteenth century was no longer about social reformist matters; it was rather about showcasing and experiencing slums as interesting tourist sights.

For the first time, too, even the guidebooks at the time recommended routes for walking tours in the cities, which passed through various working-class areas (cf. Keeler 1902; Ingersoll 1906). Shortly before the turn of the century, the first tour companies were established in Manhattan, Chicago and San Francisco; these companies specialized in guided slum visits, both reproducing and altering the slum semantics that had emerged in London. Due to the commercialization of slum tours, slumming became open to a broader range of customers. More and more city tourists from other parts of the USA were now participating in slum tours. Slumming had become an integral part of urban tourism (Cocks 2001: 174ff.).

The strong interest taken in slumming in the cities of the USA was closely linked with the image of the *cosmopolitan metropolis* simultaneously evolving in that era. This image comprised the notion of an internal heterogeneity of the city, of the inner-urban juxtaposition of the unequal, the co-existence of backwardness and modernity, and of wealth and poverty. America's cities quite symbolically exemplified the concept of the cosmopolitan city. Urban tourism took up this idea, and in its modes of representation, it reproduced the discursive connection between largeness, density, strangeness, heterogeneity and urban cosmopolitanism: city tourism marketing and image campaigns pursued the aim of presenting the internal differences within the cities in order to highlight the cosmopolitan character of the urban destinations. In the process, the thematized differences were spatially assigned to different parts of the city. The commercial slum visits, too, were explicitly referred to particular city quarters, thus emphasizing the schema of spatial classification. Another reason, therefore, why the slums were also seen as 'sights worth visiting' was that they were conceived of as an expression of the city's internal heterogeneity, of the wealth of contrasts of city life, and of its cosmopolitan diversity. In this way, the slums and slum tours contributed towards making the city as a whole an attractive tourist destination.

'Culture' is the dominant mode of observation in urban tourism and, indeed, a defining feature of urban tourism as a specific form of tourism in its own merit (as opposed to seaside tourism, hiking and many other forms of tourism) (cf. Pott 2007: 109ff.). Since slumming became an integral element of modern urban tourism in America, the two comparative perspectives discussed – the heterogenizing perspective, which emphasizes the internal diversity of the city (*this one here* vs. *that one there*), and the comparative perspective (*tourist's own town* vs. *town visited*) – can be understood as variants of the tourists' cultural observation schema. And, indeed, culture is explicitly referred to precisely when the heterogenizing schema which focuses on inner-urban spatial differences is being applied in the context of slumming. The next section will examine this aspect more closely.

Ethnicization of slumming – the immigrant quarter as a tourist attraction. The representation of America's metropolitan tourist destinations emphasized the spatial juxtaposition of different cultures within the city. The special focus was on ethno-cultural differences. This discursive framework did also structure the slumming phenomenon in urban tourism (cf. Conforti 1996; Dowling 2007; Heap 2009). Thus, it was in the American version of slumming that 'ethnicity' became a dominant category. The slumming tours, which had evolved in different cities all over the States after the turn of the century, predominantly went to the urban enclaves of the new immigrant groups from Eastern and Southern Europe, and from Asia. This led to the development of a phenomenon that Cocks (2001) calls 'ethnic slumming'. The destination slum was now constructed as a 'place of the ethno-cultural Other'.

It is revealing to look at this ethnicization of slumming against the social background at the time of its emergence. Ethnic slumming evolved in a period in which the significance of 'racial' and 'national' categories was undergoing rapid and fundamental changes in the political system of the USA. Between 1880 and 1920, there were millions of immigrants from Eastern and Southern Europe and from Asia entering the USA. This brought about feelings of disquiet among the so-called White Anglo-Saxon Protestants (WASPs). Many felt threatened by this wave of immigration, and they assumed that the non-Protestant groups (Catholics, Jews and adherents of Asian religions) were less capable of being integrated in American society than were the old immigrant groups from Northern and Western Europe.

It was at that time that public approval of the idea of 'racial equality' was undergoing a noticeable decline. In particular, the former slaves and their descendants were excluded from participation in political life; in the Southern States, legislation was adopted ensuring their residential segregation and the deprivation of their rights and, in the rest of the country, this was wrongfully practised as well (Cocks 2001: 187). On the whole, nationality and racial classifications were relevant categories with regard to access to jobs and housing. Racism and xenophobia shaped many sectors of society, including urban development (Cocks 2001). This led to the emergence of the well-known immigrant colonies (e.g. Little Italy, Chinatown, Judea and Russian Quarter) in the big cities of the USA, quarters that were often characterized by poor urban housing conditions and economic poverty.

For tourism, on the other hand, these places became exotic, colourful attractions (cf. Conforti 1996). The segregated quarters were presented as picturesque and aesthetically complementary to the modern parts of the city. Perceiving them as a natural part of the modern metropolis brought about some relief from the everyday discourse over immigrants and their unsettling otherness.

The then prevailing concept of culture, which was also relevant to tourism, constituted a combination of modernist-evolutionist and racist thinking. The notion of 'race' comprised both biological and (unalterable) cultural particularities. According to this notion, the respective 'races' and their 'natural modes of life' represent hierarchical stages in the process of human evolution. White Americans as well as Northern and Western Europeans, the notion suggests, are at the very top of the evolutionary ladder, followed by Eastern and Southern Europeans, Asians, 'American Indians' and – at the very bottom of the ladder – the Blacks. Culture and cultural forms of expression – from literature to handicraft and music, and to lifestyle, world view and ways of social interaction – were interpreted as expressions of race and/or national origin. This notion permitted the tourists to see the living and working conditions of the different immigrant groups as expressions of a 'cultural identity'. To them, the immigrant-quarters dwellers functioned as bearers of their respective cultures. Whatever they did was interpreted as a cultural expression of their 'unalterable nature' (cf. Cocks 2001).

The tourist representation of the different immigrant quarters – take the example of San Francisco's Chinatown – focused on the 'cultural identities' of the inhabitants and accentuated their cultural otherness. The representations in tourism largely fell back on stereotypes and homogenizing ascriptions in order to meet the tourists' expectations as regards observable differences and thus to fulfil their quest for authenticity.

The ethnic categorization and essentialization of social reality in the context of urban tourism contributed to the legitimization of the social and economic disparities. Observed within the cultural schema, the immigrant groups were symbolically assigned to their place – both spatially (i.e. within 'their' quarters) and socially (i.e. at the margins of society). Along with the presentation and interpretation of observable differences as cultural (and quasi-natural) differences, the social inequalities were deproblematized. The slum was no longer regarded as a manifestation of socio-structural conditions of inequality, but as an expression of the cultural configuration of a modern American metropolis.

It follows that the display of the American city for purposes of urban tourism by no means presented it as a materialized symbol of the assimilation of various immigrant groups in American society. On the contrary, what it presented was a relatively unconnected form of coexistence. The ideology of the social melting pot had become fragile anyway. With the presentation of immigrant quarters as picturesque elements of a loose conglomerate of single cultural spaces, slumming fulfilled a relieving function: it masked the problem-related assimilation discourse which was omnipresent in bourgeois political discussions and in the media – in favour of the observation of the colourful, exotic places of the 'ethnic Other' (Figure 5).

Apart from international tourists, it was the bourgeois WASPs who visited the immigrant quarters. The WASPs regarded America as the most modern of all countries and the American people as culturally superior. To them, the inhabitants and cultures of the slums were in contradistinction to their own culture. They considered the slum dwellers and their cultures backward, irrational and paralysing to progress. Modern Americans, the WASPs believed, did not adhere to superstition, but practised science, and their culture was characterized not by tradition and stagnation, but by rationality and progress.

Yet, at the turn of the century, modernity and progress were certainly viewed critically, too. The pace at which the built environment was changing gave rise to feelings of insecurity among many Americans, just as the change in values and the

"Picturesque Costumes"   "Chinese Fortune Teller"

Figure 5. Colourful postcard: Chinatown, San Francisco. *Source:* Curt Teich Company *c.* 1930 (www.flickr.com/photos/28061667@N08/4313630505/; accessed 3 May 2010).

crumbling of old certainties did. The pressure of progress and of having to advance at all costs was also experienced as a burden. This led to the emergence of new emotional longings within America's middle class, for example the yearning for a pre-modern world, for warmth, deceleration and communal togetherness (cf. Conforti 1996). The slum visits served this purpose. The immigrant quarters were turned into sights on which these nostalgic yearnings could focus. The quarters symbolized a 'way of life' which seemed to be more strongly filled with social meaning than the modern everyday life of the tourist in a cold and sterile American society determined by market rationalism and individualism. The slumming tours thus helped to give the living conditions in the segregated city districts an idyllic character. Hence, they intensified the trend towards romanticizing urban poverty (cf. Cocks 2001).

The destination slum produced by the early form of urban tourism in Europe and North America was thus adapted, on the one hand, to the image of the modern, heterogeneous city. However, with its romantic connotations, it also served, at the same time, as a place of desire for tourists, permitting them to experience a pre-modern world of a bygone era. The culturalization of the slum, with the described homogenization, essentialization and idyllicization of social conditions, looked like a legitimization of the social and economic disparities within American society. *Ethnic slumming*, therefore, does not mean the reduction of social distance; in effect, it always means its creation and reaffirmation.

Conclusion: Global Slumming, the Global Slum and Othering in Tourism

The review illustrates that my initial observation of a *new* practice of tourism in Cape Town, Rio de Janeiro and Mumbai is only correct to a limited extent. There is no doubt that poverty tourism has been spreading with a remarkable dynamism in many countries of the Global South since the 1990s. Yet, this phenomenon only represents the most recent stage in the 150-year-old history of tourist slumming.

The present globalization of this form of tourism, which for long was confined to the big cities of the North, can be understood as a change in, and as a further stage of development of, slum tourism on a global scale. A continuation of slum tourism is ensured by the fact that essential elements of its earlier forms are incorporated into its current practice (see Table 1). Visiting and experiencing *poverty*, which is territorially assigned to certain city areas ('slums'), has remained the goal of slum tourism. This kind of *spatialization* serves to concretize and visualize poverty. The examples from London and the USA demonstrate that the slum was always construed and experienced as 'the other side of the city' and as the 'place of the Other'; at the same time, they illustrate that this 'Other' had always been a lot more than just the 'economic Other'. Therefore, the *culturalization* of poverty is essential to slum tourism. While in the townships of today's South Africa the tourist gaze is focused on 'African culture', seeking to find a *culture of locals* (or a *culture of locality*) orientated to a sense of community and attachment to locality, in Victorian London, poverty was addressed moralizingly in the discursive context of a *culture of licentiousness*. And in the USA of the late nineteenth and early twentieth centuries, it is culturalization that was practised as *ethnicization* in the slum tours.

In spite of the continuity one may observe, the reconstruction of the genesis of slum tourism also clearly reveals changes in the phenomenon. What is regarded as 'the Other worth visiting' and how the cultural mode of observation assumes concrete shape varies from social context to social context. The coding of the cultural schema with its dominant distinction between 'the moral' and 'the immoral', which was very relevant in the case of London, changed when slumming was touristified in the American context. Moral aspects still played an important role in American Slumming (Dowling 2007; Heap 2009), but the focus of the culturalizing tourist gaze shifted towards the immigrant cultures, which the tourists (most of them WASPs) observed as pre-modern in a bid to distinguish them from their own culture. The destination 'slum' was presented as the 'place of the ethnic pre-modern Other'. One still comes across both codings of the cultural schema (*moral/immoral* and *modern/ethnically pre-modern*) in present-day slum tourism in the Global South (see Rolfes & Steinbrink 2009; Rolfes 2010; Meschkank 2011). Both codings (and there may be more) have entered the semantics of recent slumming. Today, however, there seemingly is a new dominant coding: the distinction between '*the global*' and '*the local*' (see Figure 5).

In a summarizing comparison, we could, therefore, contrast *Moral Slumming* in London's East End of the nineteenth century and *Ethnic Slumming* in the USA of the early twentieth century on the one hand, with today's form of slumming on the other. In the further development of slum tourism in times of a world-encompassing long-distance mass tourism, it is not only a global extension of the phenomenon that is taking place. The distinctions made between *North* (origin of the tourists) and *South* (slums as the destinations of the tourists) are also gaining considerably in importance. This includes the distinctions between the *global* ('global village')

Table 1. The essential elements of slum tourism through the ages

		Periods and places of slumming		
		East End (London): nineteenth century	China Town, Little Italy (NYC, San Francisco: early twentieth century)	Township, *favela*, slum (Johannesburg, Rio, Mumbai; early twenty-first century)
Social contexts of emergence	Society (as a whole)	Industrialization, class society, colonization/British Empire, denial of corporeality/prudery	Migration/'New World', modernization, Fordism	Globalization, world society, post-colonialism
	Nation/region	See above, urbanization, rural–urban migration, social reforms/welfare	Modern America. national identity/national history, melting pot/assimilation, discrimination/racism	e.g. in South Africa: post-apartheid, transformation
	City	Urban growth, segregation/slum development, epidemics/cholera, sanitation	Internal migration and segregation of African Americans, urban migrant colonies	Global competition of cities, persistence of ethno-economic segregation patterns, urban growth, informality
	Urban tourism	('social/erotic voyage of urban discovery')	Urban tourism as a mass phenomenon	International tourism in developing countries as a mass phenomenon, urban tourism in developing countries, urban destination management
Mode and medium of tourist construction	Culturalization of poverty	Culture of 'licentiousness'	Immigrant cultures	– African/Brazilian/Indian culture – ('authentic') culture of locality
	Dominant coding of the cultural schema	moral/immoral	modern/premodern	global/local
	Spatialization of poverty (slum as . . .)	Place of the immoral Other	Place of the pre-modern Other	– Local place in the globalized world – Place of (cultural) distance in the 'global village'
Type		*Moral slumming*	*Ethnic slumming*	*Global slumming*

and the *local* (slums as places of cultural distance in the global village), as well as between the globalized tourist from the *North* and the local slum dweller in the *South*. Does the 'destination slum' represent a *yearning for locality* in a globalizing world? Is the 'destination slum' a place to visit in order to experience the world's cultural diversity threatened by the homogenizing forces of globalization ('McDonaldization') and global tourism ('Disneyfication')? In that sense it appears appropriate to speak of *Global Slumming* in today's context. Current examples of slum tourism in Africa (Rolfes & Steinbrink 2009; Rolfes 2010), Asia (Meschkank 2011) and Latin America (Freire-Medeiros 2009) and their representation in commercials and we-blogs give evidence. They can be interpreted as indications of the process that the new global/local observation schema, together with the historical semantic elements of slum constructions, are developing world-wide into a universal destination type – the *Global Slum*.

'Global slumming' and 'global slum' are still fairly imprecise terms. However, the future analysis of the processes and constructions they denote can, indeed, build on the reconstruction of the genesis of slum tourism. In addition to the results already summarized, the review also draws attention to the fact that slum tourism, from its appearance in New York onwards, can be interpreted as an integral element of modern *urban tourism*. Furthermore, the accounts on slumming in London and New York show that the construction of 'the Other' has always been based, and continues to be based, on stereotyping. The tourism-specific localization of the Other in the slum (re-)produces a homogenizing and essentializing perspective. The tendency towards the deproblematization and depoliticization of social inequalities arising from the culturalist gaze practised and exercised in early forms of slum tourism is still observable in recent forms. Moreover, I have repeatedly called attention to the dependence of the forms of slum tourism and modes of observation on social contexts. For the analysis of current township tourism in South Africa, for example, this would mean examining the forms of tourism against the background of a functionally differentiated globalized world society, of social transformations taking place in South Africa in the post-apartheid era, of the competition of cities in the global marketplace, etc. (see Table 1).

There is a further finding that seems important in connection with the necessary social contextualization of the analysis of tourism, since it reveals some promising potential as a frame of reference. I will look into it very briefly here. The reconstruction of slum tourism documented in this article not only illustrates the variability of the slum tourist construction of 'the Other' and/or of the 'place of the Other'; it equally reminds us that this – like any other construction of the Other – refers to the identity of the tourists themselves and the process of its construction (as the other side of 'the Other'). In this sense, slumming can be interpreted as a part of a self-constituting 'Othering' (Reuter 2002). The destination slum, which emerges through the spatialization of the self-constituting Other at the 'other place' (the place of 'the Other'), functions as a medium of Othering and thus as a medium of the construction of the tourist's own identity. Regardless of whether 'the Other' localized in the slum is repudiatingly (e.g. as 'the frightening Other') or positively connoted (e.g. as 'the exotic, attractive Other'), the slum remains a *medium of self-reflexive Othering*. The slum functions as a symbol turned space, as 'the foreign' to which 'the tourist's 'own' is related, be that by comparing or by contrasting – no matter whether 'the Other' is seen as cold and threatening or warm and romantic. The demarcation line remains untouched, as it is a precondition for the tourist's experience of identity.

If we consider current slum tourism against the background of globalization, and if we relate it to the contemporary horizon of a world society, then it would make sense to study the recent slumming phenomenon as part of a *global Othering* process. For, in contrast to its historical forerunners, slumming in the Global South is evidently no longer merely about 'the other side of the city' or about intra-societal heterogeneity, but, additionally – and perhaps essentially – about the 'other side of the world'. This brings the self-constituting process of constructing a *'world-societal Other'* to the foreground.

A *postcolonial perspective*, therefore, suggests itself for the in-depth analysis of contemporary slum tourism in the south. The cultural theory of Postcolonial Studies offers different valuable approaches to a critical look into the origin and effects of representations of 'the Cultural', 'the Other' and 'the Foreign', or of 'the Culturally Hybrid' which emerges through cultural contact. Although postcolonial theories have successfully proven their analytical usefulness in various disciplines, international tourism research has made relatively little use of them so far. This is astonishing, given the fact that tourism from *'the West'* has been (re-)producing considerably powerful representations of *'the Rest'* (cf. Hall 1992). Thus, as regards future research on slumming, the question is now spotlighted of whether, in what respects and with what consequences slum tourism in the Global South is embedded in postcolonial discourses.

Acknowledgements

I would like to express my gratitude to Prof. Dr. Andreas Pott (University of Osnabrück) for his very important contributions and for the most valuable comments on an earlier version of this paper. And I would like to thank Michael Ayamba Asu for his help with translations and editing.

References

Adler, J. (1989) Origins of sightseeing, *Annals of Tourism Research*, 16, pp. 7–29.

AP (2007) Township Tourism booming as visitors want to see "real" South Africa, *USA Today*, January 9. Available at http://www.usatoday.com/travel/destinations/2007-01-04-south-africa-township-tourism_x.htm (accessed 10 June 2010).

Booth, W. (2008[1890]) *In Darkest England and the Way Out* (Charleston: Bibliobazaar).

Cassidy, D. (2007) *How the Irish Invented Slang: The Secret Language of the Crossroads* (Edinburgh: AK Press).

Cocks, C. (2001) *Doing the Town. The Rise of Urban Tourism in the United States, 1850–1915* (Berkeley: University of California Press).

Conforti, J. M. (1996) Ghettos as tourism attraction, *Annals of Tourism Research*, 23, p. 842.

Davis, M. (2007) *Planet der Slums* (Berlin: Assoziation A.)

Dowling, R. M. (2007) *Slumming in New York: From the Waterfront to Mythic Harlem* (Illinois: First Illinois Paperbacks).

Dyos, H. J., Cannadine, D. & Reeder, D. (1982) *Exploring the Urban Past: Essays in Urban History* (Cambridge: Cambridge University Press).

Frank, S. (2003) *Stadtplanung im Geschlechterkampf. Stadt und Geschlecht in der Großstadtentwicklung des 19. und 20. Jahrhunderts* (Opladen: Leske&Budrich).

Freire-Medeiros, B. (2009) The favela and its touristic transits, *Geoforum*, 40(4), pp. 580–588.

Haferburg, C. & Steinbrink, M. (Eds) (2010) *Mega-Event und Stadtentwicklung im globalen Süden. Die Fußballweltmeisterschaft 2010 und ihre Impulse für Südafrika* (Frankfurt a. M.: Brandes & Apsel).

Hall, S. (1992) The West and the rest: Discourse and power, in: S. Hall & B. Gieben (Eds) *Formations of Modernity*, pp. 275–320 (Cambridge: Polity Press).

Hannam, K. & Knox, D. (2010) *Understanding Tourism* (London: Sage).

Heap, C. (2009) *Slumming: Sexual and Racial Encounters in American Nightlife, 1885–1940*. (Chicago: University of Chicago Press).

Hoad, T. F. (1996) 'Slum', in: *The Concise Oxford Dictionary of English Etymology. Encyclopedia.com.* Available at http://www.encyclopedia.com (accessed 10 February 2009).

Ingersoll, E. (1906) *Handy Guide to New York City* (Chicago: Rand, McNally).

Keating, P. J. (1976) *Into Unknown England, 1866–1913: Selections From the Social Explorers* (Manchester: Manchester University Press).

Keeler, C. (1902) *San Francisco and Thereabout* (Kessinger Publishing).

Koven, S. (2006) *Slumming. Sexual and Social Politics in Victorian London* (Princeton: Princeton University Press).

Lindner, R. (2004) *Walks on the Wild Side. Eine Geschichte der Stadtforschung* (Frankfurt: Campus).

Löfgren, O. (1999) *On Holiday. A History of Vacationing* (Berkeley: University of California Press).

MacCannell, D. (1976) *The Tourist. A Theory of Leisure Class* (New York: Schocken Books).

Mayne, A. (1993) *The Imagined Slum. Newspaper Representation in Three Cities* (Leicester: Leicester University Press).

Meschkank, J. (2011) Investigations into slum tourism in Mumbai: Poverty tourism and the tensions between different constructions of reality, *GeoJournal*, 76, pp. 47–62.

Pott, A. (2007) *Orte des Tourismus. Eine raum- und gesellschaftstheoretische Untersuchung* (Bielefeld: Transcript).

Reuter, J. (2002) *Ordnungen des Anderen. Zum Problem des Eigenen in der Soziologie des Fremden* (Bielefeld: Transcript).

Rolfes, M. (2010) Poverty tourism: Theoretical reflections and empirical findings on an extraordinary form of tourism, *GeoJournal*, 75(5), pp. 421–442.

Rolfes, M. & Steinbrink, M. (2009) Raumbilder und Raumkonstruktionen im Township-Tourismus. Studierende erforschen Townshiptouren in Kapstadt/Südafrika, in: M. Dickel & G. Glasze (Eds) *Vielperspektivität und Teilnehmerzentrierung – Richtungsweiser der Exkursionsdidaktik*, pp. 123–140 (Berlin: LIT Verlag).

Rolfes, M., Steinbrink, M. & Uhl, C. (2009) *Townships as Attraction. A Case Study on Township Tourism in Cape Town* (Potsdam: Universitätsverlag).

Schmidt, C. (1979) The Guided Tour: Insulated adventure, *Urban Life*, 7(4), pp. 441–467.

Shields, R. (1991) *Places on the Margin. Alternative Geographies of Modernity* (London: Routledge).

Spiller, E. (2008 [1911]) *Slums. Erlebnisse in den Schlammvierteln moderner Großstädte* (Wien: Czernin Verlag).

Steinbrink, M. & Frehe, K. (2008) Townshiptourismus in Kapstadt: To go or NO GO, *Praxis Geographie*, 12, pp. 38–43.

Urry, J. (1990) *The Tourist Gaze. Leisure and Travel in Contemporary Societies* (London: Sage).

Welz, G. (1993) Slum als Sehenswürdigkeit – 'Negative Sightseeing' im Städtetourismus, in: Kramer, R. & Lutz, D. (Eds) *Tourismus-Kultur, Kulturtourismus*, pp. 38–43 (Hamburg: LIT Verlag).

Poor but Happy: Volunteer Tourists' Encounters with Poverty

ÉMILIE CROSSLEY
Cardiff University, Cardiff, UK

ABSTRACT *This article explores how young volunteer tourists encounter and negotiate poverty in rural Kenya. Using a longitudinal psychosocial methodology, I demonstrate how poverty can be conceptualized as a threatening 'object' to volunteer tourists, inducing unconscious anxiety by challenging Western materialistic lifestyles and identities. Volunteer tourists negotiate this anxiety in three ways: by transforming poverty into a source of moral redemption; by allowing poverty to become subsumed into a seductive, exotic landscape so that it can be admired and consumed; and by constructing impoverished communities as 'poor but happy'. It is argued that these neutralizing constructions act as barriers, preventing the intimate engagement with communities that volunteer tourism promises and lessening the potential of poverty to shock, move and even change those who come into contact with it.*

Introduction

In recent years, tourism researchers have become increasingly interested in understanding the manifold links between tourism and poverty. Examples from within this diverse field include work on pro-poor tourism, where tourism is considered as a mechanism for alleviating poverty (Hall 2007), explorations of the relationship between tourism and post-colonialism (Hall & Tucker 2004) and poverty tourism or 'poorism' – the latest market niche which involves travel to poor parts of the world and even tours of slums (Freire-Medeiros 2011). This last area of work presents an interesting departure from traditions that have looked into the systemic workings of tourism in relation to poverty, instead pointing directly at the tourists themselves who are demanding impoverished places as their holiday destinations. In this sense, poverty tourism has affinities with the more established practice of volunteer tourism; the only real divergence between the two being the level of tourist involvement in trying to reduce poverty. Given this growing trend, it is now more important than ever to consider tourism at the level of tourist subjectivity, so that we can understand the motivations and desires that lead people to travel to poor parts of the world and the responses that tourists have to their encounters with poverty.

In this article, I want to consider a variety of tourism that brings people from Western countries into contact with poverty through the creation of volunteer projects in Third World countries. By claiming to provide an ameliorative function in poor communities, volunteer tourism clearly engages with the pro-poor tourism agenda, and the personal involvement of tourists as consumers of holidays in poor places and, supposedly, agents of change makes this an interesting area for the exploration of tourist subjectivities in encounters with poverty. The growth of volunteer tourism stems in part from the alternative and sustainable tourism movements instigated in the 1970s and early 1980s, which also bore comparable and intersecting niche markets, such as community tourism and ecotourism (Pearce 1992; Wearing 2001). According to Lyons and Wearing (2008: 6), alternative tourism 'reconfigures the tourist destination as an interactive space' where agency, creativity and intersubjective encounter replace the passive, 'Othering' gaze of more conventional touristic practices, and they situate volunteer tourism as a 'contested' form within this broad category. The addition of volunteer labour to this reconfigured space sets up volunteer tourism as a potentially ethical model for travel to poorer parts of the world; one that stresses sustainability, reciprocity (bringing benefits to host communities and guests alike), instigates a different form of touristic practice that avoids objectifying other people and places, and contains the potential to foster a sense of altruism and social responsibility (McGehee & Santos 2005; Wearing & Wearing 2006; Lyons & Wearing 2008).

Despite volunteer tourism's facilitation of the movement of (largely) affluent tourists to poor parts of the world, there has been limited engagement within academia concerning volunteer tourists' responses to poverty, with most studies attempting to adopt a more holistic approach to capturing the volunteer tourism 'experience' (e.g. Wearing 2001; Broad 2003; McIntosh & Zahra 2007). Providing an interesting exception, however, Simpson's (2004) work on the pre-university gap year has produced some worrying findings regarding young volunteer tourists' comprehension of poverty. Simpson (2004: 688) found that volunteers were unwilling to accept that poverty, as they had witnessed in 'developing' countries, was a feature of Western society and, instead, went to great lengths to differentiate these two spaces:

> rather than finding commonality between the developed and developing worlds, students are emphasizing difference and establishing a dichotomy of 'them and us'. Poverty is allowed to become a definer of difference, rather than an experience shared by people marginalized by resource distribution. Poverty becomes an issue for 'out there', which can be passively gazed upon, rather than actively interacted with.

Such a discursive distancing, or spatial Othering, may not only prevent volunteer tourists from developing a nuanced, politicized appreciation of the problem of poverty, but may also create an obstruction to the development of empathy with local people. Simpson also found evidence of the romanticization of poverty, as volunteer tourists tended to portray materially deprived societies as happy with their ways of life and as adequately compensated for their poverty by emotional, spiritual or community 'wealth'. Even when poverty was acknowledged by Simpson's participants as being negative, it seemed to induce no feelings of concern or guilt in them, nor any sense of urgency to act to resolve the problem, which seems perplexing given their role as volunteers. Instead, the volunteers expressed how observing poverty had made them feel 'lucky' and enabled them to develop greater 'appreciation' for their own situation and wealth (Simpson 2004: 688).

In a very different take on encounters with poverty, Zahra and McIntosh (2007) set out to explore the emotional and cathartic experiences of young volunteer tourists by speaking to people about memories of their trip a number of years after having volunteered. Their research claimed that confrontations with poverty and human suffering were particularly powerful catalysts that generated experiences of a depth and significance not found within mainstream tourism. They observed that, 'Suffering provoked emotive reactions including sentimental outbursts of grief, tears, action, giving away money, and even escape' (Zahra & McIntosh 2007: 117). The volunteer tourists' emotional reactions were also coupled with intellectualizations of a similar ilk to those found in Simpson's (2004) work, with talk again of the happiness, resilience and the spiritual wealth of poor communities. However, despite these fascinating findings, Zahra and McIntosh (2007) and Simpson (2004) provide no theoretical explanation of why encounters with poverty should induce emotionality or lead to particular representations of poor communities, thus leaving our comprehension of these phenomena incomplete.

Given the diverse terrain of intellectual, emotional and behavioural responses to poverty in volunteer tourism that the above studies allow us to glimpse, the potential for research into these topics has clearly not been exhausted. This article attempts to complement existing work in this area by presenting a psychosocial exploration of volunteer tourists' subjectivities. I begin by setting out the theoretical foundations for understanding subjectivity psychosocially, emphasizing the roles of 'defence' and 'investment' in the spatial practices of volunteer tourists, before turning to a discussion of the psychosocial, longitudinal methodology used in this research. The paper then presents a selection of my research findings, demonstrating how poverty undergoes various defensive transformations through volunteer tourist subjectivities, becoming a source of redemption and an authentic, exotic object that can be consumed. This analysis builds on Simpson's (2004) work by showing how volunteers are simultaneously invested in poor communities' happiness and suffering, creating a set of dilemmatic responses. I consider these findings in the context of volunteer tourism's supposed shift from a tourism of passivity and 'gazing' to one of intimacy and reciprocity (Wearing 2001; Wearing & Wearing 2006), arguing that the responses to poverty documented may not only prevent volunteer tourists from being affected by and gaining a deeper awareness of the hardship suffered by others, but may also act as broader barriers to engagement with host communities.

Researching Tourist Subjectivities

In recent years, the growing diversification of tourist practices, and particularly the expansion of the 'new tourisms', has challenged tourist studies to reconsider the fundamental notion of who counts as a 'tourist' and how this figure can be theorized and researched (Franklin & Crang 2001; McCabe 2005). Volunteer tourism provides a particularly interesting example of such diversification as it draws the subject into a complex and often contradictory arena, attempting to fuse work with leisure, travel with integration into a community and the hedonism of mainstream tourism with a sense of philanthropy and ethical conduct. Yet attempts to study this practice have been constrained by an unwillingness to engage with theory, leading to a body of literature which is highly descriptive of, in particular, volunteer tourists' motivations, experiences and values. This sort of descriptivism has been noted as a problem across many areas of tourism studies (Britton 1991; Mowforth & Munt 1998; Kingsbury 2005). However, given the widely accepted metaphorical significance of the tourist in social theory (Dann 2002) and the more specific importance of the volunteer tourist as an instantiation of contemporary ethical discourses, I suggest that it is necessary to think more creatively about how we can open up new interdisciplinary spaces in order to devise convincing theorizations of tourist subjectivity.

Previous engagements with tourists 'in the flesh' (Desforges 2000) have exemplified various dimensions through which tourist subjectivity is constituted and practised. Such work has shown us how tourists discursively construct holiday destinations (e.g. MacCannell 1976; Urry 1990; Young 1999; Bærenholdt *et al.* 2004), how identities are built in intimate connection with visited places (e.g. Dixon & Durrheim 2000; McCabe & Stokoe 2004) and how mobilities and experiences in spaces of tourism form narrative resources that feed into broader biographies and provide tourists with cultural capital that can be brought back home (e.g. Neumann 1992; Desforges 2000; Noy 2004). However, whilst the methods employed in these bodies of work proficiently capture many features of tourist subjectivity, others may be getting overlooked or may not be considered as legitimate objects of study within broadly social constructionist approaches. Here I am alluding to such things as tourists' desire for places, fantasies of travelling, enjoyment whilst away or feelings of sadness or even guilt for travellers visiting poor communities. These aspects of tourist subjectivity intersect with and, to some extent, are regulated by discursive and narrative structures and yet, I argue, cannot be fully understood through a solely discursive framework because of their emotional, experiential and potentially unconscious basis.

As a complement to this existing work, I want to suggest that psychosocial studies holds great potential for grasping elements of tourist subjectivity that other approaches may elide. Psychosocial studies can be conceived of as a body of work which attempts to theorize subjectivity and identity in ways that avoid the pervasive dualisms entrenched in social research; these include divisions between agency/structure, individual/society, personal/collective and mind/body (Henriques *et al.* 1984; Frosh 2003). As in discursive psychology, psychosocial researchers try to understand the discursive formation of subjectivity through talk, text and interaction, conceptualizing subjects non-dualistically as simultaneously enabled and constrained by the discursive resources and practices available to them (Wetherell 1998; Wetherell & Edley 1999). However, for many this analytical strategy is insufficient for explaining why subjects maintain particular identity positions even when these may produce contradictions and be problematic for them (Edley 2006). Thus, psychosocial theorists appeal to a range of extra-discursive elements to complement and enhance their theorizations, including explorations of affect, embodiment and psychodynamics (Cromby 2005; Frosh & Baraitser 2008). According to the psychosocial approach, then, the subject is a complex configuration of interpermeating psychic and social processes, which results in a unique but inherently social 'arena of personal subjectivity' (Frosh *et al.* 2003).

To further refine this concept of the psychosocial, I want to briefly explore two salient aspects of subjectivity which become available to research through this approach and suggest how each might be applied to the study of tourist subjectivities. First, tourists must be considered as what Hollway and Jefferson (2000) call 'defended subjects', who develop complex and often spatially expressed mechanisms to ward off anxiety that poses a constant threat to the integrity and functioning of the Self. Hollway's work (1989; Hollway & Jefferson 2000) draws on Kleinian theory to conceptualize such unconscious defence mechanisms as intersubjective processes, which pass between people and are intrinsically relational rather than operating within each individual. This theorization allows defences to be interpreted as dynamic and social forces, thereby avoiding psychological reductionism. The concept of defence may be particularly relevant to the study of difficult encounters in tourism, such as tourists being confronted by poverty through volunteer tourism or travel to slums, as these encounters may be particularly anxiety provoking.

The second concept is that of 'investment', which refers to the conscious and unconscious 'reasons' behind a subject's adoption of particular subject positions and use of certain discourses (Frosh & Saville Young 2008). These 'reasons' may arise from a variety of sources, such as social positioning, personal biography, emotions and defence mechanisms, and incorporating these elements into analyses provides psychosocial researchers with a way of 'thickening' and enriching interpretations of personal narratives (Frosh & Saville Young 2008: 110). Investment can help us to think about why tourists take up identity positions, as opposed to just how, and allows motivations for travelling to be interpreted more creatively (Frosh *et al.* 2003). For example, an investment in the position of 'volunteer tourist' may arise partly from desires and fantasies of travelling to remote and unusual destinations in poor parts of the world, and may also involve defensive reasons, such as assuaging the anxiety generated by the prospect of travelling to these poor areas as an affluent Western traveller. Utilizing such psychosocial concepts, therefore, reveals new dimensions of tourist subjectivity whilst also providing bodies of theory that can be drawn upon to go beyond mere description.

Method

The present research aimed to investigate the experiences and subjectivities of ten young British people, aged 18 to 24 years, who were about to undertake a structured volunteer programme in Kenya of between one and three months in duration. The programme, offered by a commercial provider, involved a mixture of environmental conservation and community projects run in rural locations experiencing high levels of socio-economic deprivation, alongside more mainstream touristic activities, such as safaris and days on the beach. In order to become familiar with the programme and to interview my participants, I joined the group (which comprised nearly fifty people in total) in Africa for a month's overt participant observation in July 2010. During this time I kept a daily reflexive field diary, recording the day's events, thoughts and feelings I had about the activities, noteworthy topics of conversation within the group, reflections after interviews, and my dreams. I hoped that as well as providing me with a more detailed understanding of volunteer tourism, this firsthand involvement would help to bring out personal meanings that (consciously or not) I was bringing to the research context (Birkeland 2005); thus providing material that could be used to deepen my reflexive practice and enrich the interpretation of data.

In its methods this research sought to go beyond the conventional qualitative modes of enquiry in the field, in which volunteer tourists' experiences are most commonly captured either through conversations held in the ethnographic site (e.g. Broad 2003; Simpson 2004; Gray & Campbell 2007) or using retrospective interviews following a volunteer placement (e.g. Wearing 2001). Whilst being a popular method in the study of travel narratives, particularly regarding changing conceptions of self and identity as a result of youth travel (Neumann 1992; Desforges 2000; Noy 2004), retrospective interviews produce representations of the past refracted through the present and such accounts will inevitably contain omissions and exaggerations of certain elements. Therefore, in an attempt to transcend these 'snapshot' approaches, a longitudinal methodology was used that would allow me to conduct repeated in-depth narrative interviews with the participants across a period of approximately eleven months. Interviews took place prior to, during and twice after the volunteer tourism placement, allowing me to examine how opinions, aspirations, identities and experiences fluctuated, metamorphosed and were actively negotiated by participants through time. This resulted in a total of 40 interviews, each lasting between 15 and 90 minutes, although for the purposes of this article only material from the first two waves of interviews will be drawn upon.

The interviews were designed to elicit narratives about the participants' lives and their involvement in volunteer tourism. In keeping with the psychosocial theorization of subjectivity outlined above, a format was used that would allow narratives to emerge relatively undirected by the interviewer so that links and disjunctions in the interviewee's speech could be examined for evidence of unconscious or emotional associations (Hollway & Jefferson 2000; Cartwright 2004). Each digitally audio-recorded interview started with a broad, open-ended question and subsequent questions were guided mainly by the flow of the participant's narrative, asking for elaborations and further reflections at various points. After exhausting this process, a small number of additional questions relating to theoretically or thematically salient areas were posed. The second, third and fourth wave of interviews were used to explore new material based on events that had occurred since our last conversation, as well as following up themes from previous interviews.

After the interviews had been transcribed verbatim and anonymized, the analysis commenced with a basic discursive/narrative reading before attempting to explain participants' investments in particular identity or attitudinal positions by exploring unconscious or affective mechanisms. Together with this psychosocial reading, I tried to explore spatio-temporal patterns made apparent by the longitudinal generation of data, such as the fulfilment or frustration of desires expressed by participants before departing for their trip and the retrospective framing of experiences in Kenya. Finally, I used data from my reflexive field diary to enable comment on volunteer tourist practices that were either not mentioned in the interviews or did not feature substantially in them. Where data are shown as part of the analysis below, excerpts are labelled by, for example, (Amy 1, 18:11), which denotes the first interview with Amy starting at 18 minutes 11 seconds in (see Appendix for transcription conventions).

Psychosocial Dynamics of Volunteer Tourism

In this analytical section I want to show the potential of using a psychosocial approach to interpret volunteer tourist subjectivities. This approach allows us to understand how responses to poverty in tourism are not simply intellectual or emotional products of the individual, but are expressive of powerful forces and dynamics occurring at the nexus of socio-cultural forms and lived, unique subjectivities. Using this framework, and by tracing the shifts in participants' accounts across time and space, I will show how volunteer tourists negotiate the poverty that they encounter and demonstrate how it is necessary to take into consideration the defensive and desirous functions of tourist subjectivities in order to adequately interpret their responses. In addressing these elements of volunteer tourist subjectivities, this research explores previously uncharted terrain in tourism geography.

The following data were selected because of their relevance to a theoretical interest in poverty which, although framing the research in its rationale and interpretation, did not drive the line of questioning during the interviews. The findings are presented in three sections representing the various responses to poverty that emerged from the participants' narratives. These focus on poverty as a force for internal moral transformation, as an exotic feature of the Kenyan landscape and as a dismissible element of the lives of the 'happy poor', respectively. The three responses featured in the majority of participants' accounts, although their occurrence and level of elaboration varied between participants. For example, whilst gaining appreciation through encountering poverty was cited by two-thirds of participants as a motivation for their travels, fewer followed this through in subsequent interviews. However, it should be stressed that the purpose of this analysis is not to establish the norms of volunteer tourist subjectivities, but rather to explore the forms of subjectivity made available by this context.

Redemptive Poverty

Poverty is a potentially problematic 'object' for young volunteer tourists to deal with. For those embroiled and invested in a culture that celebrates affluence, materialism and consumption, poverty signifies lack, failure and Otherness. Yet the frequent media exposure it receives makes poverty and the suffering it brings unavoidable for the general public, lodging it permanently in the Western psyche. Volunteer tourists who choose to travel to and work with poor communities are placing themselves in a situation where they must confront the realities of how other people live, but although the tourists have come as helpers and want to feel positive about the impact their labour is making, I argue that poverty remains unsettling and threatening to them. In this first analytical section I want to explore how volunteer tourists negotiate and resolve the threat that poverty presents for them by seeking personal transformation in the form of a gained sense of 'appreciation'. This aspiration is traced from before our departure for Africa through to later stages when 'appreciation' has supposedly been attained.

Nearly all of the volunteer tourists I spoke to stated in their first interview that they wanted to develop a greater sense of 'appreciation', 'perspective', 'respect' or 'gratitude' through travelling as a volunteer to Kenya. In their accounts, this pursuit of 'appreciation', which I feel is the term that captures most accurately the sentiment being expressed, took one of two forms in relation to materialism. In the first version, 'appreciation' would allow the volunteer tourists to recognize the good fortune of their material wealth, as shown in the following passage taken from the first interview with Amy:

> *Émilie*: What are the different things that you're hoping to get out of, of going?
> *Amy*: Um (.) think to kind of have a bit more respect for kind of everything that I own at the moment. [*Émilie*: Hmm] 'Cause I mean I've got a new iPod, a new phone, a new camera ... Um, just kind of a bit more appreciation for everything, um 'cause I recognize that what I have is, you know, really great

like, I shouldn't be so (*laughs*) like down in myself and thinking you've got nothing when actually (.) you've got so much more than a lot of people have (Amy 1, 18: 11).

For Amy, encountering poor people lacking in possessions promises to add personal value to her own things and legitimizes her veneration of materiality in the form of giving thanks for what she has. In contrast, the excerpt from Lisa's interview, below, demonstrates a different permutation of the 'appreciation' discourse in which she seeks, or expects, a refutation of Western materialism, echoing findings from Zahra and McIntosh (2007) and Zahra (2011):

Émilie: What sort of different view (.) on things [*Lisa*: Yeah] what d'you, what sort of view d'you mean?
Lisa: Um, I dunno like (.) like kind of the materialistic side of things like that (.) you like here you, you don't really (.) you take for granted like what you have and then [*Émilie*: Hmm] I think a lot of it's gonna be (.) to do with coming back with a different perspective on it, just [*Émilie*: Hmm] thinking it's just stuff it doesn't matter (Lisa 1, 27: 32).

Discursively, or performatively, the accounts given by Amy and Lisa provide justifications for their desire to travel to Africa that exceed the pure hedonism associated with mainstream tourism products; 'appreciation' has connotations of moral betterment that sit well within the ethical framework of volunteer tourism. However, I believe that more is going on in these accounts than simply the positive presentation of Self. The pursuit of 'appreciation' also provides a defensive function for young volunteer tourists. Poverty presents a challenge to the lifestyles, materialism and indulgences of affluent Western subjects and can therefore induce feelings of guilt or unconscious anxiety as the Self is threatened by this spectre. By seeking 'appreciation', volunteer tourists are able to demonstrate an acknowledgement of poverty whilst also preserving their present lifestyle and Self. By dissolving ignorance and replacing this with gratitude, 'appreciation' becomes an ethical end in itself, allowing volunteer tourists to resume their lives back in the West in the knowledge that they have undergone a personal, internal transformation. This removes the onus for volunteer tourists to maintain efforts to combat poverty once they have returned home and because this is a modification of the Self rather than of the Other it is a much more easily attainable resolution.

We can see this process in action by following Lisa as she undergoes this transformation. Here, Lisa is recounting an emotional experience she has recently had at a local primary school, where she had what she describes as 'a bit of a mental breakdown' after learning that some pupils were not in school uniform because their families could not afford it:

Lisa: I just cried and cried and cried, and I just, I- like it just, it's just, I like as much as it was upsetting I think it was a really, really good like lesson for me? [*Émilie*: Yeah] Because like I, I was sat, I was sat there like just getting so upset thinking about what I'd spend £2 on - that's' not even a coffee (.) and yet there's a child that can't afford a school uniform because they, like they don't have £2 and it just, oh god it just hit me like I got the biggest reality check in the world at that point ... I know it sounds silly but when I look back on it now I actually like smile about it 'cause it's made me realize that like (.) stuff's not that important anymore. [*Émilie*: Yeah] It's like obviously it's not, you're not gonna change everything, it's just the lifestyle isn't it but [*Émilie*: Hmm] it like, even if you just think about it (Lisa 2, 16: 30).

What is telling about this passage is the satisfaction that Lisa is able to draw from a seemingly distressing episode during her stay in Kenya. She can look back on this upsetting time and 'smile' because of the redemptive 'appreciation' that it has instilled in her. This process, in which a negative experience leads to a positive lasting outcome, is reminiscent of the literature on trauma in psychology. Janoff-Bulman and Berger (2000) argue that people who undergo traumatic life events frequently experience positive outcomes, such as the development of greater appreciation for their lives and the reassessment of priorities. However, what makes Lisa's case different is the lesser degree of trauma, its anticipated nature and the cultural context that renders her encounter traumatic and implicates her identity in a problematic way. By examining how Lisa's narrative allows her to continue with her lifestyle after Kenya, we can see that 'appreciation' carries strategic and defensive significance rather than just being a natural post-trauma response.

In the final part of Lisa's account we can see the inertia and continuity of lifestyle that 'appreciation' permits; Lisa accepts that her materialistic lifestyle is unlikely to 'change' drastically as a result of her experience, but insists that it is enough to simply have a changed state of mind and be able to 'just think about it'. Thus, 'appreciation' defends the Self against anxiety induced by what is now a neutralized object and allows volunteer tourists to maintain a Western lifestyle in a guilt-free way. This is similar to the ideological function Cremin (2007) sees the gap year as providing, in which subjects are returned to 'the same' after a successful period of travel. Not only is poverty neutralized in this process, but because a positive change is brought about in the Self poverty actually becomes transformed from a threatening, anxiety-inducing object into one associated with moral redemption – delivering Western subjects from a state of ignorance and ingratitude. What makes this particularly interesting from a geographical perspective is that moral redemption is performed by volunteer tourists as a spatial practice, involving travel to spaces charged with enough potency, in terms of extremes of poverty, to bring about the transition to an 'appreciative' state of mind.

This spatial practice of defence is problematic for volunteer tourism, not only in the sense that it effectively helps to legitimize and perpetuate apathy and global disparities in wealth, but also because it modulates the encounter between hosts and guests. As the quest for 'appreciation' begins long before departure, encounters with the Other and with poverty are stripped of their radical, transformational potential and can instead only be apprehended through premeditated defensive mechanisms. Although, as we have seen, poverty retains its potential to shock and distress volunteer tourists, the outcome of such experiences becomes largely a foregone conclusion.

Problematic Seductions

Volunteer tourism promises to take the traveller beyond the realms of normal tourist experience; from gazing at a landscape to interacting with its people, from consuming a place to helping to construct it, and from purchasing staged tourist displays to witnessing the 'reality' of a place. Yet, these distinctions are not clear-cut and, for some, conventional tourist conduct may be so ingrained that it becomes difficult to snap out of this mode of practice, even when shifting to a volunteer tourist role. In this section I will show how poverty can become embedded in a seductive landscape of Otherness, authenticity and the exotic, and thus a problematic object of volunteer tourists' desire. I will draw particular attention to how consumption of people, places and poverty through photography and other instantiations of the 'tourist gaze' (Urry 1990) stands in stark and potentially damaging opposition to the ethical, reciprocal and de-commodified ideals of volunteer tourism (Wearing & Wearing 1999; Wearing 2001).

During the first wave of interviews, most of my participants did not have many preconceptions about what Kenya would be like, with the most consistent description referring to a place that would be hot, dry, dusty and dilapidated. However, after we had arrived in Africa, it became apparent that there were feelings of deep ambivalence arising in relation to the landscape with which we were confronted. This appeared to be because the volunteer tourists found themselves admiring features of a landscape that represented simultaneously authenticity and poverty. The following passage encapsulates this sentiment well:

> Ash: °Mud huts° I- I didn't know whether that'd be a myth or there would be actually be mud huts, you know kinda thing. I-, but it is [Émilie: Yeah, yeah] you know it is, they're living in houses of mud and stick. (laughs) You know just like ah no, no they'll have brick. [Émilie: Yeah] (coughs) (.) That was good though. Real, not good for them I suppose but I suppose they're pro- probably not bothered (laughs) but you know, [Émilie: Hmm] °authentic° (Ash 2, 24: 13).

I had asked Ash to tell me whether Kenya was as he had expected it to be and he expresses his surprise at the presence of 'mud huts', a stereotypical image of rural Africa that he takes as a marker of what is 'real' and 'authentic'. However, Ash seems aware that he is celebrating a feature of poverty when he assesses the huts as 'good' but then acknowledges that this form of housing may not be 'good' for those having to dwell in them. In a similar passage, Sarah also demonstrates an ambivalent relationship towards the African landscape:

> *Émilie*: What did you make of the landscape and everything?
> *Sarah*: Um it's c- it was crazy. When we were landing in the plane and you can see like all the huts at the side and you're like oh my god it <u>actually</u> looks like that. [*Émilie*: Yeah] And then when you're driving through and it's like (.) and like one of the first people I saw was like a woman with a vase on her head carrying [*Émilie*: Yeah] something. Like, it is cool (.) and everything's, it's like really sad that there's poverty and that everything's like that (.) but.
> *Émilie*: Yeah (.) w- why is it sad?
> *Sarah*: 'Cause it's so different. 'Cause everything's all run down and they haven't got like (.) you just take what you've got at home for granted, don't you? [*Émilie*: Hmm] And then you see the people like (.) living with <u>barely</u> anything and walking around like (.) in like a dishevelled town [*Émilie*: Hmm] and it's like, it's like one of the <u>main</u> cities, yet it's like (.) falling apart. [*Émilie*: Hmm] It's yeah (.) I like it but it is sad if you [*Émilie*: Yeah] think about it (Sarah 2, 03: 03).

Here, we can see the recurrence of stereotypical features of the exotic African landscape – mud huts and a woman carrying a pot on her head – and the excitement and delight in Sarah's voice when she was telling me this was tangible. Yet Sarah too feels the need to qualify and restrain her enthusiasm by acknowledging that the landscape she admires is also one that afflicts those who live in it. Sarah's final statement, 'I like it but it is sad', demonstrates her inability to resolve this tension.

In addition to these accounts of experiencing the African landscape, I found it fascinating to observe the very conventional touristic conduct that took place during the month that I spent with my participants. The volunteer tourists took their cameras with them everywhere we went, including to the sites of projects where we would be doing dirty, manual work; there was a preoccupation with capturing in images everything that we saw or did. Thus, in addition to photographing landscapes and one another, it became the norm to photograph people's homes and local people themselves. I witnessed the tourists pointing their cameras at small children that they had not yet spoken to and was horrified when we visited a class at one of the local schools only for the majority of the group to start photographing the students as the teacher was trying to introduce us. There was also an 'incident' of pictures being taken of a woman in traditional dress, standing with her children who, as it later transpired when somebody asked her permission, did not want to be photographed.

These observations seemed to reveal how not only were traditional 'mud huts' and other features of the built environment becoming subsumed into the seductive African landscape, but so too were the people. Local people, many of whom were extremely poor, were themselves becoming markers of an exotic, authentic Otherness that could be celebrated, objectified and ultimately consumed through practices of the tourist gaze. The marketing of Third World countries as authentic, unspoiled and primitive – a discourse which implicates indigenous people as much as features of the landscape – is well documented (Silver 1993). In a study based in Eastern Indonesia, Cole (2007) shows how tourists preferred visiting villages which appeared poorer, thereby reproducing this connection between poverty and perceived authenticity through touristic practice. However, the present research complements this existing literature by showing how tourists actively negotiate place meanings, often dilemmatically, rather than passively reproducing the images fed to them as consumers.

Psychosocially, we can understand what is happening here as the harnessing of volunteer tourists' desire by seductive landscapes that have in part been forged by the Western cultural imagination (Terkenli 2002; Cartier 2005). Africa becomes seductive because its Otherness is cast in fantasy as exotic, providing exciting, colourful and disorderly contrasts to the mundane, and as authentic, presenting a vision of society untainted by the disorientating simulacra, pluralism of social formations and erasure of traditions symptomatic of post-modernity (Munt 1994). Poverty is easily absorbed as a feature of this seductive landscape and thus also becomes subject to tourists' desires. I would argue that this also provides a defensive function, as the conversion of poverty into just another consumable object in the landscape neutralizes the threatening properties otherwise associated with it. In this context, the ambivalence observed in the volunteer tourists' responses to the Kenyan landscape can be interpreted as a conflict arising from the conscious recognition of poverty as a negative feature of the landscape and the unconscious enjoyment of poverty-as-Otherness that stems from a participation in Western cultural fantasy.

These findings show the difficulty of matching the practice of volunteer tourism to its ambitious ideals. With conventional touristic behaviour so pervasive, the objectification of people and places in Third World countries still occurs and the cavalier use of photography is likely to produce a barrier to the engagement and intimacy with local people that volunteer tourism endorses, as well as enacting damaging power relations. Additionally, there is a risk that the identified practices of experiencing poverty as part of a consumable landscape makes it decipherable for volunteer tourists as part of an aesthetic and cultural framework rather than an economic and social one, with a potential result of masking, romanticizing and trivializing poverty.

Contented Communities

Lisa: they literally have nothing and they're so happy. They're just happy playing. You see them in their like raggedy, torn clothes and they're not bothered (Lisa 2, 19: 24).

Some of the volunteer tourists had heard stories from others who had gone before them about how contented and happy people were, despite the poverty, in Africa. Others reacted with surprise at the swathes of smiling, waving children found in every village that we arrived at. In this section I want to examine how the picture painted by Lisa above of the poor but happy children became extended by the volunteer tourists I spoke with to characterize all of the local people. I will show how volunteer tourists are simultaneously invested in host communities being poor and also happy, and how these investments must be negotiated. Before departing, many of the volunteer tourists told me about wanting to help poor communities:

> *Sarah*: I like the thought of helping people and everything like that, helping them get along. And it's, it's not a nice thought is it to think of them like (.) not being very happy (*laughs*). So it's nice to go out there and actually do something rather than sit here and do nothing about it (Sarah 1, 03: 08).

Here, poor people are depicted as unhappy. Volunteer tourists are, in a way, invested in such bleak images of poor communities because it creates a sense of urgency and need that allows the volunteer tourist to positively assume the role of 'helper' in a way that affirms their sense of agency. The opposition drawn in Sarah's account between going 'out there' to 'do something' rather than sitting 'here' and doing 'nothing' also emphasizes the spatial dynamics of helping, in which it is assumed that action cannot be taken remotely. Instead, the problem of poverty is located in anOther place and an assumption is made that it can be ameliorated only by journeying to that place; thus, philanthropy is sought through travel.

Sarah was surprised and possibly disappointed to find that the people she had travelled all this way to help were not as unhappy as she had expected them to be. Instead the volunteer tourists encountered poverty with a smiling face – communities that they came to understand as 'poor-but-happy' (Simpson 2004). Below, Kate reflects on this conundrum, which leads her to compare her home society with the one that she has travelled to:

> *Kate*: You know, back home there's, kids are always, the babies, the toddlers that are, they're always crying, always screaming, you can hear them on the bus and the, it's just not like that here? I'm not quite sure why that is ... I dunno whether it's 'cause you have little you appreciate more and (.) whether it's more about like family and love and friends and that kind of thing rather than material possessions that our Western world's become (Kate 2, 10: 13).

Here we find the ideal of 'appreciation' imprinted on to the host communities and contrasts are drawn between the 'screaming' children 'back home' and the con-tented children 'here'. Far from appearing desperate and in need of development and assistance from Westerners, such as the volunteer tourists, the Kenyans arise as an embodied critique of Western society and materialism, for despite their socio-economic deprivation they are the happiest of the two societies because of the wealth they draw from alternative sources such as 'family and love and friends'. Simpson's (2004) research on the gap year also found accounts that constructed local people as 'poor-but-happy', with young people claiming that the locals did not mind being materially poor, thereby romanticizing and trivializing poverty. As an extension of the defences against poverty as a source of anxiety outlined in the first analytical section, these stereotypical portrayals of poor communities as contented and happy neutralizes their disturbing potential. In this way, extending the very noticeable exuberance of the local children to characterize the whole society created a comforting illusion for the volunteer tourists.

However, what seemed to arise for many volunteer tourists was a sense of contradiction between the cultural stereotype of contented Third World societies and their own distress at sights of poverty, and between their desire for local people to be suffering so that they could then be helped and for them to be happy so as to not be troubled by this suffering. The following excerpt, in which Tess is telling me about being upset by an encounter with a sick boy from the local village who was unable to play with the other children, exemplifies these tensions:

> *Tess*: I didn't want to cry, I <u>hate</u> crying near them 'cause they like just must think like, I don't know, I don't want to look like they're a sob story, d'you know what I mean? [*Émilie*: Yeah] I don't want them to think like, it's fine, they're happy, 'cause they <u>are</u>, most like the majority of people are <u>so</u> happy here like I'm sure they didn't (.) ask for mo-, some ask for more but [*Émilie*: Hmm] you know they all seem quite happy but I really just had to walk away and just kind of collect myself but that's the only thing that really got to me 'cause it just, they're so <u>young</u> I suppose and like (.) don't know, they deserve more I suppose (Tess 2, 13: 54).

What is immediately striking about Tess's account is her concern about how her behaviour might be interpreted by the locals as judgmental and disparaging. And yet the strength of feeling roused in her by the sight of the little boy is such that she struggles not to cry despite her worries about making the local people feel like a 'sob story'. Tess stresses over and over that the people here are 'happy', almost in an attempt to reassure herself rather than me, but finishes by reflecting that the children – simultaneously the bearers of the broadest smiles and those who bear the effects of poverty the most – 'deserve more'.

For volunteer tourism, these constructions and negotiations of host communities present various challenges. Competing investments in cultural stereotypes, be it of the 'poor and destitute' or 'poor but happy' variety, provide lenses through which communities can be seen and experienced, potentially changing volunteer tourism from an arena for authentic and mutual cultural exchange to one that reinforces cultural preconceptions through desirous and defensive 'appropriation' (Hollway 2004).

Conclusions

In this article I have tried to make the case for studying volunteer tourists' encounters with poverty, given the increasingly interrelated nature of these two social phenomena, and for studying tourist subjectivity psychosocially. I have shown how responses to poverty in tourism are shaped in part by defence mechanisms operating to protect the Self against threatening objects and by investments in particular portrayals of host communities. By deploying psychosocial concepts, it has been possible to go beyond simply describing these responses and instead to explain why, through the operation of particular mechanisms, volunteer tourists respond in the ways that they do. We can see from these explorations how poverty's capacity to shock, move and leave potentially life-changing impressions on people is dampened because it is perceived through the lens of cultural stereotypes and fantasies, imprinting images of the 'exotic', 'authentic' and of 'happy' communities upon 'voluntoured' destinations, and because it must be constantly negotiated by volunteer tourists who are simultaneously invested in poverty and threatened by it.

In evaluating the ethics of volunteer tourism and other forms of tourism that bring people into contact with poverty, it is necessary to consider tourist subjectivities as a factor of as much relevance as material outcomes for host communities. These subjectivities form the basis for beneficial contact and engagement as well as for potentially nefarious objectification and stereotyping, ultimately shaping what all parties involved take from their encounters with the other. I have attempted to show how, as well as modulating perceptions of poverty, psychosocial processes may constitute barriers blocking the engagement and intimacy with local people that sits at the core of the volunteer tourism ethos. Volunteer tourism providers should be aware of the ways in which tourists potentially stereotype host communities or romanticize poverty, and must also be mindful of their own role in propagating such representations. In light of these findings, we should heed Simpson's (2004) suggestion that the industry should advocate a 'pedagogy of social justice' to enable volunteer tourists to develop more complex and politicized understandings of their hosts in the Third World. However, such a pedagogy should be mindful of the difficult emotional responses involved in volunteer tourism and would, therefore, have to go beyond simply the dissemination of information.

The psychosocial exploration undertaken in this article may provide a method-ological opening for other tourism geographers to explore, as it provides a model of tourist subjectivity with psychological depth and, therefore, greater explanatory power, whilst resisting individualization and psychological reductionism. One po-tentially productive application of the methodology would be in the field of tourism emotions, as an increasing number of researchers are beginning to assess difficult feelings in tourist encounters for their political, moral and transformative potentialities (Zahra & McIntosh 2007; Tucker 2009; Crossley 2012). The psychosocial approach has the potential to complement this existing work by providing theoretical resources which deal explicitly with difficult emotions and defences against them. Furthermore, future research will be able to build on the current work by continuing to explore tourists' encounters with poverty, whether in a volunteer tourism context or not, and by using theorizations that allow us to comprehend the complex negotiations that tourists experience through these encounters.

Appendix: Transcription Notation

(.) Short, untimed pause in the flow of speech
text Emphasized word(s)
(*text*) Non-speech sounds, such as laughter
°text° Word(s) spoken quietly
text? A question or raised intonation at the end of a phrase
te- Preceding sound is cut off

Acknowledgements

The research for this article was supported financially by the UK Economic and Social Research Council. I also wish to thank my supervisors, Prof Valerie Walkerdine and Dr Gabrielle Ivinson, the participants who gave up their time to speak to me, and the anonymous reviewers for their insightful comments on earlier drafts.

References

Bærenholdt, J. O., Haldrup, M., Larsen, J. & Urry, J. (2004) *Performing Tourist Places* (Aldershot, UK: Ashgate).

Birkeland, I. J. (2005) *Making Place, Making Self: Travel, Subjectivity, and Sexual Difference* (Farnham, UK: Ashgate).

Britton, S. (1991) Tourism, capital, and place: Towards a critical geography of tourism, *Environment and Planning D: Society and Space*, 9(4), pp. 451–478.

Broad, S. (2003) Living the Thai life – A case study of volunteer tourism at the Gibbon Rehabilitation Project, Thailand, *Tourism Recreation Research*, 28(3), pp. 63–72.

Cartier, C. (2005) Introduction: Touristed landscapes/seductions of place, in C. Cartier & A. A. Lew (Eds) *Seductions of Place: Geographical Perspectives on Globalization and Touristed Landscapes*, pp. 1–20 (Abingdon: Routledge).

Cartwright, D. (2004) The psychoanalytic research interview: Preliminary suggestions, *Journal of the American Psychoanalytic Association*, 52(1), pp. 209–242.

Cole, S. (2007) Beyond authenticity and commodification, *Annals of Tourism Research*, 34(4), pp. 943–960.

Cremin, C. (2007) Living and really living: the gap year and the commodification of the contingent, *Ephemera*, 7(4), pp. 526–542.

Cromby, J. (2005) Theorising embodied subjectivity, *International Journal of Critical Psychology*, 15, pp. 133–150.

Crossley, É. (2012) Affect and moral transformations in young volunteer tourists, in D. Picard & M. Robinson (Eds) *Emotion in Motion: The Passions of Tourism and Travel*, (Farnham, UK: Ashgate).

Dann, G. M. S. (Ed.) (2002) *The Tourist as a Metaphor of the Social World* (Wallingford, UK: Cabi).

Desforges, L. (2000) Travelling the world: Identity and travel biography, *Annals of Tourism Research*, 27(4), pp. 926–945.

Dixon, J. & Durrheim, K. (2000) Displacing place-identity: A discursive approach to locating self and other, *British Journal of Social Psychology*, 39, pp. 27–44.

Edley, N. (2006) Never the twain shall meet: A critical appraisal of the combination of discourse and psychoanalytic theory in studies of men and masculinity, *Sex Roles*, 55, pp. 601–608.

Franklin, A. & Crang, M. (2001) The trouble with tourism and travel theory? *Tourism Studies*, 1(1), pp. 5–22.

Freire-Medeiros, B. (2011) *Touring Poverty* (Abingdon: Routledge).

Frosh, S. (2003) Psychosocial studies and psychology: Is a critical approach emerging? *Human Relations*, 56, pp. 1547–1567.

Frosh, S. & Baraitser, L. (2008) Psychoanalysis and psychosocial studies, *Psychoanalysis, Culture & Society*, 13(4), pp. 346–365.

Frosh, S. & Saville Young, L. (2008) Psychoanalytic approaches to qualitative psychology, in: C. Willig & W. Stainton-Rogers (Eds) *The Sage Handbook of Qualitative Research in Psychology*, pp. 109–126 (London: Sage).

Frosh, S., Phoenix, A. & Pattman, R. (2003) Taking a stand: Using psychoanalysis to explore the positioning of subjects in discourse, *British Journal of Social Psychology*, 42(1), pp. 39–53.

Gray, N. J. & Campbell, L. M. (2007) A decommodified experience? Exploring aesthetic, economic and ethical values for volunteer ecotourism in Costa Rica, *Journal of Sustainable Tourism*, 15(5), pp. 463–482.

Hall, C. M. (2007) *Pro-Poor Tourism: Who Benefits? Perspectives on Tourism and Poverty Reduction* (Clevedon, UK: Channel View).

Hall, C. M. & Tucker, H. (Eds) (2004) *Tourism and Postcolonialism: Contested Discourses, Identities and Representations* (Abingdon: Routledge).

Henriques, J., Hollway, W., Urwin, C., Venn, C. & Walkerdine, V. (1984) *Changing the Subject: Psychology, Social Regulation and Subjectivity* (London: Routledge).

Hollway, W. (1989) *Subjectivity and Method in Psychology* (London: Sage).

Hollway, W. (2004) Editorial, *International Journal of Critical Psychology*, 10, pp. 5–12.

Hollway, W. & Jefferson, T. (2000) *Doing Qualitative Research Differently: Free Association, Narrative and the Interview Method* (London: Sage).

Janoff-Bulman, R. & Berger, A. R. (2000) The other side of trauma: Towards a psychology of appreciation, in: J. Harvey & E. D. Miller (Eds) *Loss and Trauma Handbook*, pp. 29–44 (Abingdon: Routledge).

Kingsbury, P. (2005) Jamaican tourism and the politics of enjoyment, *Geoforum*, 36, pp. 113–132.

Lyons, K. D. & Wearing, S. (2008) Volunteer tourism as alternative tourism: Journeys beyond Otherness, in: K. D. Lyons & S. Wearing (Eds) *Journeys of Discovery in Volunteer Tourism: International Case Study Perspectives*, pp. 3–11 (Wallingford, UK: Cabi).

MacCannell, D. (1976) *The Tourist: A New Theory of the Leisure Class* (New York: Shocken).

McCabe, S. (2005) 'Who is a tourist?': A critical review, *Tourist Studies*, 5(1), pp. 85–106.

McCabe, S. & Stokoe, E. H. (2004) Place and identity in tourists' accounts, *Annals of Tourism Research*, 31(3), pp. 601–622.

McGehee, N. G. & Santos, C. A. (2005) Social change, discourse and volunteer tourism, *Annals of Tourism Research*, 32(3), pp. 760–779.

McIntosh, A. J. & Zahra, A. (2007) A cultural encounter through volunteer tourism: Towards the ideals of sustainable tourism?, *Journal of Sustainable Tourism*, 15(5), pp. 541–556.

Mowforth, M. & Munt, I. (1998) *Tourism and Sustainability: New Tourism in the Third World* (London: Routledge).

Munt, I. (1994) The 'Other' postmodern tourism: Culture, travel and the new middle classes, *Theory, Culture and Society*, 11, pp. 101–123.

Neumann, M. (1992) The trail through experience: Finding self in the recollection of travel, in: C. Ellis & M. G. Flaherty (Eds) *Investigating Subjectivity: Research on Lived Experience*, pp. 176–201 (London: Sage).

Noy, C. (2004) This trip really changed me: Backpackers' narratives of self-change, *Annals of Tourism Research*, 31(1), pp. 78–102.

Pearce, D. G. (1992) Alternative tourism: Concepts, classifications, and questions, in: V. L. Smith & W. R. Eadington (Eds) *Tourism Alternatives: Potentials and Problems in the Development of Tourism*, pp. 15–30 (Philadelphia: University of Pennsylvannia Press).

Silver, I. (1993) Marketing authenticity in Third World countries, *Annals of Tourism Research*, 20, pp. 302–318.

Simpson, K. (2004) 'Doing development': The gap year, volunteer-tourists and a popular practice of development, *Journal of International Development*, 16, pp. 681–692.

Terkenli, T. S. (2002) Landscapes of tourism: Towards a global cultural economy of space?, *Tourism Geographies*, 4(3), pp. 227–254.

Tucker, H. (2009) Recognizing emotion and its postcolonial potentialities: Discomfort and shame in a tourism encounter in Turkey, *Tourism Geographies*, 11(4), pp. 444–461.

Urry, J. (1990) *The Tourist Gaze: Leisure and Travel in Contemporary Society* (London: Sage).

Wearing, S. L. (2001) *Volunteer Tourism: Experiences that Make a Difference* (London: Cabi).

Wearing, S. L. & Wearing, M. (1999) Decommodifying ecotourism: Rethinking global–local interactions with host communities, *Society and Leisure*, 22, pp. 39–70.

Wearing, S. L. & Wearing, M. (2006) 'Rereading the subjugating tourist' in neoliberalism: Postcolonial otherness and the tourist experience, *Tourism Analysis*, 11(2), pp. 145–162.

Wetherell, M. (1998) Positioning and interpretative repertoires: Conversation analysis and post-structuralism in dialogue, *Discourse and Society*, 9(3), pp. 387–413.

Wetherell, M. & Edley, N. (1999) Negotiating hegemonic masculinity: Imaginary positions and psycho-discursive practices, *Feminism & Psychology*, 9(3), pp. 335–356.

Young, M. (1999) The social construction of tourist places, *Australian Geographer*, 30(3), pp. 373–389.

Zahra, A. (2011) Volunteer tourism as a life-changing experience, in: A. M. Benson (Ed.) *Volunteer Tourism: Theory Framework to Practical Applications*, pp. 90–101 (Abingdon: Routledge).

Zahra, A. & McIntosh, A. J. (2007) Volunteer tourism: Evidence of cathartic tourist experiences, *Tourism Recreation Research*, 32(1), pp. 115–119.

Notes on Contributor

Émilie Crossley is a doctoral candidate in the School of Social Sciences at Cardiff University, UK. Her research interests include psychosocial studies and the relationships between volunteer tourism, poverty and youth travel.

Slum Tourism: Representing and Interpreting 'Reality' in Dharavi, Mumbai

PETER DYSON

Department of Geography, Emmanuel College, University of Cambridge, UK

ABSTRACT *This article examines how Dharavi is represented to, and interpreted by, tourists participating in walking tours around Mumbai's largest slum. Across the world 'the slum' is positioned as space more authentic and realistic than the artifice of the concrete cityscape, as demonstrated by the recent fascination surrounding 'Slumdog Millionaire'. By first exploring the complex geography and history of Dharavi, this article lays the foundation for arguing that any representation of this place can only ever be subjective, conditional and uncertain. Through interviews and surveys with tour guides, tour-goers and slum dwellers this article evaluates how Dharavi is represented by 'Reality Tours and Travel', and how its message is interpreted by their tour-goers. It becomes clear these tours do have a capacity to change negative perceptions about slums, albeit in a highly individualized context. The article concludes that the tour partially achieves its transformative aims, although its ability to alter any negative images of slums remains restricted by the very techniques it uses to position Dharavi as a place of archetypal 'reality'.*

Introduction

Human kind cannot bear very much reality (Eliot, T.S. 1945)

The emergence of 'slum tours' over the past two decades appears to contradict T. S. Eliot's statement; tourists are not only 'bearing' reality but they are actively pursuing it. Getting a 'taste of real life' by exploring the people and landscapes that sit off the standard tourist itinerary is fast becoming a priority for many tourists across the world. If the earliest forms of tourism were founded upon the principles of exploration and discovery then it appears that the emergence of alternative travel illustrates a return to these values. For many, holidays are not solely a time for 'relaxation and recuperation' but also a time for immersion into foreign landscapes and cultures. Slum tours appear to present the perfect opportunity to experience otherwise inaccessible landscapes, see how people 'really' live and learn about the day-to-day challenges that face millions of people across the world. Tour-goers' motivations are diverse, but working from the premise that 'moving across the world is also a movement within ourselves' Hutnyk, J. (1996: 7), these tours are as much about discovering new forms of 'the self' as they are about discovering new places.

Slums feature heavily in recent academic work (most notably Davis 2006), but have recently come to the forefront in popular books, film and television, and these mainstream presentations have arguably been most influential in shaping potential tourists' perception of slums. The Oscar-winning film 'Slumdog Millionaire' encapsulates the Western curiosity and fascination with 'the slum'. This 'rags-to-riches' tale of romance triumphing over adversity may have achieved box-office success and critical acclaim, but it also revealed the controversial and fractured discourse of the politics of representing the urban poor. The polarized reaction to the film is symptomatic of the controversy that surrounds the ethics of 'poverty tourism'. For many people, the film resonated with a fascination to see the lives of the urban poor celebrated in a sanitized form, leading the *New York Post* to review it as 'Slumderful!' (Lumenick 2008). For others, it epitomized Hollywood's insatiable desire to glamorize and romanticize the poor, causing the *The Times* to dub it 'poverty porn' (Miles 2009). Like slum tourism, it is evident that these presentations create problems for determining who is trusted to represent the lives of the urban poor and how that presentation of poverty is invariably moralized.

Recent Western media attention on slum tourism has been extensive, although reports tend to present a very certain (but arguably naive) judgement of the debate that surrounds its ethics. As is so often the case, geopolitical and social context gives way to superficial and anecdotal narratives. Whilst each journalist quite legitimately conveys a personal position, reports are invariably constructed around the dualism of slum tourism being either voyeuristic or non-voyeuristic. The space for nuances appears slim. Weiner's (2008) *New York Times* article, 'Slum Visits: Tourism or Voyeurism' is typical in this regard, illustrating the tendency to homogenize and present either a force for good or evil. In many ways, the contemporary media discourse reflects the early tourism scholarship of the 1970s, a period where 'ambivalence, sweeping generalizations, and stereotypes abound' (Crick 1989: 4) and mass tourism was treated as a powerful new phenomenon painted in black and white. Indeed, Ramchander's (2007) article 'Township Tourism: Blessing or Blight?' is evidently inheriting the dualism adopted in Young's (1973) book, 'Tourism: Blessing or Blight?'. I argue that such a binary construction neglects the nuances existing between the many different slum tours across the world, whilst simultaneously conflating the many different views of all stakeholders involved in creating these 'experiences'. Consequently, this research deconstructs the dualistic analysis of slum tourism and, instead, argues we must look towards the different perspectives found in the middle ground in order to genuinely advance the debate.

Selinger and Outterson (2009: 2) argue that this current debate surrounding slum tourism 'perpetuates one-sided polemics and consequently requires reorientation in order to become a topic of mature deliberation'. Until very recently, the few empirical studies of the slum tourism phenomenon that exist are markedly restricted to two areas: the favelas of Rio de Janerio (Dwek 2004; Freire-Medeiros 2008; 2009; Williams 2008) and the townships of South Africa (Butler 2003; Nemasetoni & Rogerson 2007; Rolfes *et al.* 2009). These analyses are unified by their ability to evaluate tourists' motivations and the economic, social and cultural impact of tours, but are divided on whether power lies in the hand of the tour guides, the tour-goers, or both.

This research aims to reinforce existing literature, but also widen its geographical breadth and explore an under-researched case study using unexplored questions, for instance, evaluating techniques slum tours use to represent their message and the extent to which this social phenomenon might be transforming how 'the slum' and its people are understood. Centrally, we are concerned about the politics of representation and interpretation.

When examining how 'reality' is represented, three primary questions are crucial. What do these tours show and what message do they construct? What techniques allow them to convey this representation? To what extent can the 'reality' they present be deconstructed? When, secondly, evaluating the politics of interpretation, three further questions are crucial. What does Dharavi *mean* to tour-goers? Does the tour transform perceptions? To what extent do tour-goers question the tour's representation of Dharavi?

To appreciate the interplay between representation and interpretation two funda-mental ideas will be drawn upon; 'the gaze' and the 'quest for authenticity'.

The tourist gaze, proposed by Urry (1990), forms the basis of how a tourist's subjective experience can be understood. To be a tourist is to gaze upon sites of difference and, accordingly, 'tourism results from a basic binary division between the ordinary/everyday and the extraordinary' (Urry 1990: 11) that generates a form of 'Othering'. Crucially, the tourist gaze is, therefore, the filter that acts between what is being represented and what is being interpreted. Consequently, for Urry (1990) the study of the gaze is the study of the filters through which tourists see the people, places and landscapes they encounter. However, many researchers have found Urry's (1990) gaze to be too deterministic and conceptually limiting (Bruner 2001; MacCannell 2001; Gillespie 2006). Bruner (2001) justifiably accuses it of being 'too empiricist, too monolithic, too lacking in agency, and too visual to encompass such varied tourist reactions' (Bruner 2001: 902). In many ways, the singular tourist gaze simply cannot capture the complexity and diversity of the slum tourism experience, a more multi-sensory and holistic perspective is more powerful (Dann 2002). I suggest we must, therefore, expand the concept of the gaze to include the 'questioning gaze' (Bruner 2001) and the 'reverse gaze' (Gillespie 2006). The former recognizes that tourists have agency, they do not merely accept but interpret, and frequently question, the producers' messages. The latter recognizes that local people also have a gaze focused on their tourist visitors and this reciprocity 'engages tourists in self-reflection' (Gillespie 2006: 358), compelling the tour-goer to become conscious of their identity as a tourist/observer.

MacCannell (1973: 597) was highly influential in arguing that 'touristic conscious-ness is motivated by the desire for authentic experience'. If we work from the premise that tours exist because they facilitate access to spaces perceived to be inaccessible to outsiders, whilst also aiming to unveil the inner workings of these spaces, then au-thenticity and realism of the experience for the tour-goer is fundamental (MacCannell 1973). Following Cohen (1988), the term 'authenticity' needs to be deconstructed in order to shift the discussion away from a structural dichotomy between 'fake' and 'real' and move it towards a nuanced appreciation of multiple 'realities'. Framed in these terms, whether a slum tour actually represents an accurate image of the place is not as important as *how* and why a tour-goer might perceive such a representation to be authentic. Tourists interpret authenticity through their own experiences, as shown by Conran (2006) for backpackers in Thailand. The tourists' search for authenticity, therefore, makes the slum an ideal canvass on which the image of the 'backstage' (following Goffman 1959) of the city can be painted – an image that is positioned as more truthful and realistic than the artifice of the hotel, beach or other tourist sites (Jaguaribe & Hetherington 2004). However, MacCannell (1973) and Cohen (1989) showed that 'staging' can mask subjective images of a place and its people, and communicate them as objective 'reality'.

Dharavi, Mumbai

Dharavi holds the dubious honour of being crowned 'the largest slum in Asia'. Located in the centre of the city, it is confined by two converging train lines on the east and west, and Mahim creek to the north. At 551 acres (approximately 2.5 km^2) in size, Dharavi's distinct shape and significance has given it the name, 'the heart of Mumbai'. Estimates of the population vary considerably; a 1986 survey counted 530,225 people living in 80,518 structures, a more recent Harvard Business School review revised this to 700,000 people (Iyer *et al.* 2009), although media reports frequently state an excess of 1,000,000 million people (see Blakely 2009; Richardson 2009). Most strikingly, these estimates mean that Dharavi's population density exceeds 400,000 people per km^2, nearly ten times the density of daytime Manhattan (Sharma 2000). To understand Dharavi's touristic appeal we need to examine the city in which it sits. Mumbai has both the highest absolute number and the highest proportion of slum dwellers of any city in the world (Iyer *et al.* 2009), with an estimated 5 million people (40% of total population) spread across two thousand slums (World Bank 2006). Such statistics have caused the leading activist Sheela Patel to subversively rename the city 'Slumbai' in reflection of the slums' dominance on the landscape. Crucially, the urban poor are highly visible to even the most blinkered visitor to the city; 5–10 percent of the population are pavement dwellers (Appadurai 2000) and there are approximately 250,000 street children (Nijman 2009). Consequently, 'poor spaces'

Table 1. Is Dharavi a slum?

UN Habitat (2003) definition		How Dharavi relates
I	Inadequate access to safe water	Water runs for only three hours per day, and waterborne diseases are common
II	Inadequate access to sanitation and other infrastructures	Estimated that on average there is one toilet per 1,440 people (Kumar Karn & Harada 2002)
III	Poor structural quality of housing	Majority of homes are semi-permanent structures with corrugated plastic or AC (asbestos cement) sheet roof (Sharma 2000)
IV	Over-crowding and insecure residential status	Average household of 5–6 people occupying a single-room dwelling (Sharma 2000)

are thoroughly integrated into the city's landscape and, in this sense, a visitor to the city would need to take only one step out of their hotel to be immersed in Mumbai's stark economic inequalities. Yet slum tours remain an increasingly popular attraction.

Is Dharavi a Slum?

For Gilbert (2007) the term 'slum' is pejorative and imprecise, and yet it is used almost automatically and without question. How we define 'poor spaces' mediates how they are represented and understood by society. The answer to the question, 'is Dharavi a slum?' is not as straightforward as it may first appear. On the one hand, the Indian government places Dharavi under the jurisdiction of the Slum Rehabilitation Authority, and Dharavi certainly conforms to the UN Habitat (2003) definition of a slum shown in Table 1.

On the other hand, by other measures its slum status is contested and Dharavi is not a 'conventional' slum. Judged purely on economic terms it is undoubtedly exceptional. Annual turnover is estimated at US$665 million (Patel & Jockin 2007), which is generated by around 10,000 small and large manufacturing units, with 80 percent of Dharavi's residents employed in industries within the slum (Engqvist & Lantz 2008: 49). This sits in sharp contrast to Mumbai's other slums, where Sharma (2000) estimates less than 10–15 percent of residents are employed within in the slum itself.

Such exceptional characteristics have led to the creation of several monikers for Dharavi. It is known as 'the city within a city' and the 'heart of Mumbai'. One reporter concluded that 'Dharavi is not just a slum, it is also a node on the global economy' (Lancaster 2007: 3). Sharma (2000) argues it is better characterized as 'an amazing mosaic of villages and townships from all over India'. Chatterjee (2008, quoted in Iyer *et al.* 2009: 9) prefers it to be known as 'an industrial township rather than just

Table 2. Reality Tours fact file

Established	2006
Category	The company defines itself as an 'ethical travel company'
Founded by	Chris Way (English) and Krishna Poojari (Indian)
Size	Five local guides paid on a salary basis
Number of tourists	Averaging 30 tourists per day in peak season (December 2009).A total of 10,000 tour-goers from 2006–09
Tour price	Dharavi walking tour: Rs400 (£6)
Marketing	Featured in Lonely Planet and Rough Guides, with a strong online presence (http://www.realitytoursandtravel.com/)
Tourist demography	Predominantly European and American, white, middle class, 20–50 years old. Roughly 5–10% are Indians/Mumbaikars
History	Inspired by the Favela Tours in Rio de Janeiro. Formerly linked with the MESCO Trust.
Organization	80% of tour profits (after tax) are donated to the sister company, 'Reality Gives' which operates a kindergarten and a community centre in Dharavi.
Tour conduct	Maximum group size – six people. Strict no camera policy. Encouragement to donate/engage with Dharavi's social projects

a residential area'. Apte (2009) calls it 'a self-sustaining "village" community' and Prince Charles (who visited Dharavi in 2003; quoted in Booth 2009) was struck by its 'underlying intuitive grammar of design'.

Such a diverse selection of representations of Dharavi demonstrates that there is no *one* way of understanding this place. In this sense, Bruner's (2004) postmodern perspective is most appropriate as it emphasizes there are not necessarily 'true' or 'false' representations, but merely different understandings of Dharavi.

Reality Tours and Travel

Unlike the highly competitive and commercialized slum tour industries of Rio de Janeiro and Cape Town (where dozens of tour operators exist in each city), there is just one tour company dominating the market in Mumbai. Attendance on the tours by Reality Tours and Travel has more than doubled year on year since 2006; Table 2 expands on the details of the company's history. With such an unchallenged position in the tourist market, the significance of how these tours represent Dharavi can hardly be overstated. The fervent media attention surrounding the company is testament to this importance; numerous major British and US newspapers have reported on the tours and Channel 4's 'Indian Winter Season 2010' commissioned a documentary on Dharavi (Slumdog Secret Millionaire) in which the tours were featured. However, most significant was a thirty-minute 'Times Now' national Indian television debate

Table 3. Summary of the multi-method approach

Data	Participant		Date
Participant observation	Tour-goers, tour guides and local people (how they interact)		3–13 July
Semi-structured interviews	Tour company owners	Krishna Poojari	15 July
		Chris Way	25 July
	Tour guides	Ganesh	11 July
		Suneil (tour guide as translator)	9 July
	16 slum residents		14 and 23 July
Questionnaire	150 tour-goers (filled out at the end of their tour)[a]		Questionnaire run from 22 July–20 August

[a]Estimated response rate: 70–80 percent.

in which tourists were accused of 'treating humans like animals' and the tour owners were charged with 'cashing in on the "poor India" image' (Times Now 2006). A government official on the panel called the tour operators 'parasites [who] need to be investigated and put behind bars' and a state lawmaker threatened to shut them down.

Whilst admirable, the company's philanthropic aspirations (Table 2: organization) do create a dilemma. Although not driven to maximize profits, they have created a moral obligation to feed tour revenues into charitable work and, whilst it is not within the scope of this investigation to evaluate whether their 'pro-poor' tourism model is effective at alleviating poverty, it must be remembered that their business model demands they sell tours. This company's tours are clearly inscribed with significance that extends far beyond that of the conventional tourist attraction. This research aims to maintain an underlying appreciation of these tours' symbolism of not only Dharavi but also Mumbai's urban poor, India's international image and developing world slums more generally.

The research was conducted over four weeks in July 2009 and required an inductive and deductive approach; hypotheses will be created and then tested. Table 3 is a summary of this method.

This research cannot be understood without some awareness of the ethical considerations involved. If these tours *are* an exercise in voyeurism then my status as a 'researcher' can hardly be used to exclude me from being involved in exploiting Western images of Dharavi and its people. Although this work intends to contribute to the wider literature and suggest recommendations for improving slum tourism, it can offer few tangible benefits to the people of Mumbai. Whether my possession of a notebook and dictaphone afforded me a status above the common tour-goer is very debatable, an avenue worthy of further consideration (see, most recently, Fennell 2011).

Representing 'Reality'

From its name 'reality tours' and its slogan "see the 'real' India", it is clear that this tour positions itself as representing an accurate, candid and truthful account of Dharavi. However, given that contemporary tourism theory now recognizes that there is no 'one reality', but rather multiple and often conflicting 'realities' (Bruner 2004), the central question becomes: what reality is the tour representing?

What's the Message?

Beyond just *showing* tour-goers the landscape and people of Dharavi, the tour presents a definable *message* about the place. This message can be separated into three sub-sections.

Transforming the 'false' Western image of slums. Before entering the slum, guides provide a 'pre-tour briefing' where they state, 'in this tour we hope to dispel the negative image that a lot of people have about Dharavi, and slums in general – that it's just dangerous, dirty, with people sitting around doing nothing'. As Figure 1 demonstrates, reconfiguring the negative image of Dharavi is their highest priority. The co-owner, Chris Way, maintains that 'we do the tour to show the positive side of the people and the enterprise, despite the negative circumstances in which they live'. The crux of the message is that despite contrasting lifestyles, the tour-goers should feel an affinity with the people of Dharavi, who are framed as 'normal people, with normal problems just like anyone else, they love their kids, they love their family, and they're looking to have their own dreams and better their lives'. Consequently, the tour first constructs a 'typical Western' image of slums as an unduly negative and false representation of the place, from which it then positions its contrary perspective – a positive and 'realistic' image. Accordingly, the tour is intended to be transformative, or as the other co-owner, Krishna Poojari, puts it, 'the central message is to change the mindset of the people'.

I.	Break down the negative image of Dharavi (and India's slums) and its residents
II.	Highlight the small-scale industries in the area
III.	Use tour funds to develop our Community and Education Centre
IV.	Give 80% of tour profits after tax to NGOs helping in Mumbai's poorer communities

Figure 1. Reality Tours and Travel: tours main objectives (from the company's promotional leaflet, see appendix).

Dharavi as the key to understanding wider society.   The second aspect of the message is to position Dharavi as the archetypal 'poor space' of Mumbai, which represents the lives of the urban poor that are so crucial to the city's condition. Chris Way argues that 'in Mumbai, rightly or wrongly, 55 percent of its population live in slums – so if you want to understand Mumbai you need to visit the slum, and understand the slum'. In this sense the urban poor are framed as an unrecognized and undervalued group who live a life 'more real' than can be observed in the 'rich spaces' of the city. Indeed, the company's promotional leaflet markets the tours as a chance to 'glimpse into the reality of everyday life in Mumbai and India', with the tagline, 'See the "real" India'. Dharavi is used to represent Indian society more generally because of two distinct traits. First its diverse ethnic composition; communities and cultures are drawn from all corners of the country, leading Sharma (2000) to describe it as an 'amazing mosaic of villages from all over India'. Second, the spirit of enterprise, determination and entrepreneurship that Dharavi's economic activity embodies (a trait Indian society is so frequently cited to hold as well). Crucially, the tour inscribes slum spaces with a symbolic value that renders any understanding of Mumbai and India incomplete without an appreciation of Dharavi and its people. However, the tour does not make it clear whether this symbolism should be extended to the rest of the world, and Dharavi is not related to slums in other parts of the world.

Poverty is problematic.   The issues that face Dharavi's materially deprived people are not simple and neither are the solutions straightforward. Krishna Poojari argues, 'we want to show Dharavi with a question mark . . . we want people to think about the conditions, to think "what can be done about this?"'. This aspect of the tour's message dovetails with its transformative intentions as it strives to challenge and question the tour-goer's assumptions about 'solutions' to the 'problems' found in slums. Centrally, definitions of poverty must extend beyond purely economic measures. The Kumbharwada area is used to epitomize the strong social and cultural capital that connects the people of Dharavi, and gives them a 'powerful community spirit' (Krishna). Consequently, the tour disputes the Western lens through which 'poor spaces' are viewed and encourages tour-goers to see beyond Dharavi's material deprivation.

Techniques of Representation: How is the Message Articulated?

The tour's message is conveyed by the tour guides using four dominant techniques.

The visual.   Sight is emphasized as the primary sense through which Dharavi should be experienced. Krishna Poorjari contends that 'people can see there are very poor conditions – they can see the open drains, the hanging wires, and can see children playing at the garbage site', supported by Chris Way's point that 'the reality is there for the tour-goers to see'. Underlining sight as the dominant sense conforms to the 'tourist gaze', which MacCannell (2001) argues hinges on the transparency of visual meaning; 'what you see is what you get'. Framed in these terms, 'sight' is privileged as an uncritical lens through which the slum can be experienced. However (as the 'Interpreting Reality' section will demonstrate), tour-goer's are often conscious of the visual's partiality and also draw upon sound and smell to compose a more multisensory and immersive impression of Dharavi.

The inquisitive gaze. The tour encourages tour-goers to constantly question their observations. I suggest that they are advocating a new form of observation I call the 'inquisitive gaze'. Throughout the tour, guides invite questions and tour-goers frequently take the opportunity to raise new issues that are important to them. Unlike Bruner's (2001) 'questioning gaze', the inquisitive gaze is not an attempt to challenge or contest the producer's representations, but rather an effort from the consumer to shape the content according to their individual interests. Chris Way recognizes that 'we can't push people to form an opinion' but, by encouraging an inquisitive attitude, they are more likely to engage tour-goers with the issues raised on the tour whilst providing room to question their own assumptions and expectations about Dharavi.

Symbolism: the recycling industry. The recycling industry located in '13th Compound' is used to symbolize the tour's wider message. In much the same way as the Zabaleen people of Cairo, or the Olususun dump workers of Lagos, the recycling workers of Dharavi are positioned as symbols of entrepreneurship and the unrecognized value of slums as productive urban spaces. Krishna Poojari describes the recycling industry as the part of Dharavi he is most proud of, 'what they do there is they turn dirt into gold'. Crucially, '13th Compound' is used to connect Dharavi to the rest of Mumbai, as the tour guides maintain that '80 percent of all Mumbai's plastic waste is recycled here'. Such symbolism allows the tour to emphasize that an understanding of Mumbai is incomplete without an appreciation of how slums are integrated into the city's globalized functions.

The slum dwellers' perspective. This tour has chosen the slum dwellers' point of view, as Chris Way maintains the central message is 'very much from the people living there's perspective'. This is achieved by using local guides, some of whom live in Dharavi themselves, who construct a narrative that places the people of the slum at its centre. This narrative is reinforced by interaction with the local people who will occasionally engage the tour-goers in a spontaneous dialogue (with the tour guide acting as a translator). Such a technique evidently generates empathy among tour-goers, probably drawing on the idea that 'the experience of being embedded in the midst of poverty can differ significantly from being exposed to poverty through media representations' (Engstrom & Selinger 2009: 17). This, therefore, connects directly back to the tour's primary aim of addressing the negative image of slums it feels the Western media wrongly perpetuates.

Deconstructing 'Reality'

Representing the reality of Dharavi is clearly central to the design of the tour, but what does the tour company mean by 'reality'? How do such representations connect with 'authenticity'? If we accept there are 'multiple realities', then as Chambers (1997) asks, whose 'reality counts'?

The evidence of the interviews and leaflet analysis illustrate the tour position's 'reality' in opposition to a 'fake'/'fictional' negative image of Western representations. If the tour's prerogative is to 'unmask'/'unveil' the correct and truthful way of seeing Dharavi and Mumbai, then the notion of 'authenticity' becomes critical. MacCannell (1973: 592, 593) argued that tourists are primarily 'motivated by the desire to see life as it is really lived', driven by what he calls the 'quest for authentic experiences'. Because tours, by their nature, open up the spaces that are otherwise inaccessible to tourists, they are invariably constructed as an excursion into the 'backstage' (following Goffman's (1959) terminology). I argue the Dharavi tours consciously construct the entire slum as a 'backstage' landscape in relation to the 'frontstage' of Mumbai's official tourist sites, like the Gateway of India, Malabar Hill or the Hanging Gardens. As Krishna Poorjari puts is, 'Bombay is not all about the main sites, there is also another side ... the people want to see the reality, which is behind the scenes'. Such a strategy enhances the perceived realism of the tours, or to put it another way; to experience Dharavi is to experience the inner workings of the city, where the 'real' work goes on and the touristic performance is dissolved.

This frontstage/backstage dichotomy is simultaneously applied to the slum space as well. Within Dharavi itself there remains a frontstage (the main road, the market and shops) and a backstage (the industries, the schools and the residential homes). The message of the tour is evidently constructed through the representation of the latter, and the marketing of the tour plays off this point; 'the beauty of Dharavi lies not on the main roads but in the small gullys and alleys where the place comes to life'.

MacCannell's (1973) highly influential work on 'staged authenticity' argues that tourist spaces can be made to look like the 'backstage' when, in fact, they are just as 'dressed up' and 'artificial' as the frontstage. It is implied that 'contrived tourist spaces' (MacCannell 1973: 599) undergo a substantive transformation and are physically manipulated to appear more authentic than they really are. Research by Rolfes *et al.* (2009) and Camm (2009) on Cape Town's township tours depicts elements of performance used to actively enhance 'realism'. However, whilst this investigation has found little evidence of this, it has exposed a rather different form of staging that has been neglected by other slum tourism studies. In Dharavi, the tours use 'communicative staging' (Cohen 1989) to make the landscape appear unquestionably 'real' and 'authentic', despite the message being just one of many possible representations. The transformative message can be enhanced by communicating an idealized reality to the tour-goer. The tour communicates *its* reality as the most convincing reality. I argue that because Reality Tours and Travel have no competitors and non-commercial interests there may have been no reason to resort to substantively staging the slum to gain more tourists, as has been the case in Cape Town and Rio. This staging undoubtedly targets their intended consumer (someone looking for an 'alternative' and 'genuine' tour) whilst bolstering the credibility of the company (who frequently face intense media criticism).

Finally, whilst representing Dharavi through 'reality' can be interpreted as an 'accurate portrayal' of the place', there is a second possible meaning, the notion that 'poverty and hardship is more 'real' and 'true' than contemporary urban middle class culture' (Engqvist & Lantz 2008). 'Western lifestyles can be denigrated as empty, culturally unfulfilling, materialistic, meaningless, while, on the contrary, Third World cultures are bestowed with meaning, richness, simplicity and, of course, authenticity' (Mowforth & Munt 2008: 77). In this sense, to tour the slum is to see a romanticized landscape 'more real' than the artifice of the tour-goer's Western life. Whether tour-goers interpret 'reality' to conform to this secondary meaning will be a subject to debate in the following section.

Interpreting 'Reality'

The previous sections highlight that the tour is designed to be dramatically transformative. However, tour-goers interpret these representations through a number of filters, and cannot all be expected to absorb the message in the same way or to the same extent. This section approaches the tour-goers' interpretations in four parts:

1. Tourist reflections: relating Dharavi to expectations;
2. The transformative aspects: accepting 'reality';
3. The non-transformative aspects: questioning 'reality';
4. The power of reflection.

Tourist Reflections: Relating Dharavi to Expectations

Tour-goers are a diverse group whose experiences are conditioned by very different frames of reference. This international tourist group contains young 'gap year' backpackers, professionals (teachers, doctors, lawyers), academics, families (including local Mumbaikars and Indians) and business people (the company has run educational 'corporate group tours' for UBS and Deutsche Bank). Whilst the tour is delivered identically to all, we must recognize that each tour-goer has different preconceptions

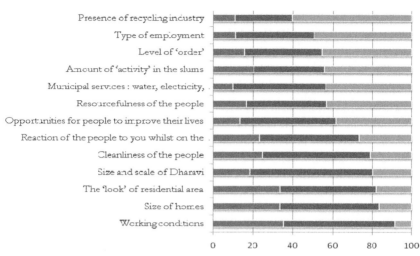

Presence of recycling industry
Type of employment
Level of 'order'
Amount of 'activity' in the slums
Municipal services : water, electricity, .
Resourcefulness of the people
Opportunities for people to improve their lives
Reaction of the people to you whilst on the .
Cleanliness of the people
Size and scale of Dharavi
The 'look' of residential area
Size of homes
Working conditions

0   20   40   60   80   100

○ - 'totally unexpected'
● - 'as expected'
● - 'sort of as expected'

Figure 2. Graph to show certain aspects of how Dharavi related to tourist expectations.

about the slums, different expectations about Dharavi and probably holds different hopes for what they might gain from the experience.

Figure 2 uses survey data to illustrate how thirteen different aspects of Dharavi related to expectations. Although generalizations must be used with caution, the key conclusion is that aesthetic qualities of Dharavi (for example, the 'look' and the size of homes) conform closely with tour-goers expectations, whereas humanistic qualities (for example, employment and perceived activity/resourcefulness) are the most unexpected elements.

In this sense, the tour conforms to visual preconceptions of Dharavi but presents an unanticipated image of the people that live there. This appears to support the tour company's argument that the Western image of slums is not negative because it visually misrepresents the slum, but because it centres on characterizing its people as 'lazy', 'dangerous' and 'uneducated'. Film, television and news media are often cited by tour-goers as key to shaping their prior understanding of Dharavi and the visual emphasis of these media may explain why the tour is so powerful in 'peopling' the otherwise dehumanized slum landscape. Gilbert (2007: 710) astutely argues that 'the very word "slum" confuses the physical problem of poor quality housing with the characteristics of the people living there'. I argue that for the tour-goer, the apparently simple act of seeing people at work (rather than begging on the streets) may be both unexpected and transformative.

The Transformative Aspects: Accepting 'Reality'

Reality Tours and Travel measure their success not based on revenue or profit, but on the extent to which they are able to 'correct' the negative image of slums. Therefore, it is necessary to ask are these tours actually transformative? Are they able to reconfigure tour-goers' images of Dharavi, Mumbai's slums and poverty more generally? If so, what aspects are they most successful in transforming?

The responses to the question 'if you would recommend this tour to others, why?' reveal many tour-goers not only endorse the tour but also consider it to be transformative. Three dominant narratives emerge.

1. 'Eye opening' – symptomatic of the importance given to the visual, there is an explicit awareness of the tour's power to challenge assumptions; 'it's enlightening and makes you think beyond your preconceptions', 'opens the mind and expands the vision' and 'you have to see it to really understand it'.
2. 'Corrects misconceptions' – a new and truer understanding has been gained, which is positioned as an improvement on the 'old' and 'less real' understanding; 'now you have a better point of view', 'it enriches my perspective' and 'it gives a correct impression of slums'.
3. 'Reconfigures poverty' – the conception of how poverty and slums interact is reconfigured; 'I see slums not as places of "the poor" but as places of "life"', 'slums are not just for the poorest people' and 'forces one to re-evaluate the notions of child labour, poverty and education'.

These narratives reveal that some tour-goers certainly do absorb the tour's message. I have argued that no unitary 'true' reality exists; after all, representation is always political. However, some tour-goers interpret their experience more structurally and are keen to stress their 'new' understanding as a better and more informed one.

Tour-goers were asked to choose three adjectives that best describe Dharavi; Figure 3 illustrates their responses. A semantic analysis shows the dominance of positive adjectives and the tour-goers' decision to choose synonyms such as 'resourceful', 'industrious' and 'energetic' indicates the value they ascribe to the intangible personal qualities of Dharavi's people. Arguably more striking is the fact that out of the 400 adjectives collected there are only five counts of the word 'poor', with just 15 percent of adjectives containing any negative connotation. The popularity of 'dirty' (total of 26 counts) is confusing, given its distance in meaning from the other common adjectives. 'Dirty' is primarily visual and tangible, it dehumanizes the landscape and conforms directly with the supposed negative stereotype of slums. Although not in the scope of this article, the discussion surrounding the politics of dirt offers fascinating

Figure 3. Responses to the question: 'Choose three adjectives that best describe Dharavi'. Presented in a 'word cloud' where the size of the word is proportional to the frequency of the response (created using www.wordle.net).

insights (see Koven 2004; Heap 2009). It may be the case that the tour can transform perceptions of people, but cannot transform perceptions of the built environment.

The qualities of the *people* of Dharavi are cited as the most unexpected, the most challenging, and the most important part of Dharavi's landscape. However, there is no evidence to suggest the tour transforms the visual stereotype of slums and, to some extent, it actually appears to reinforce them as 'dirty spaces'. I argue that communicative staging has been effective in presenting the positive attitude of the people of Dharavi, but the lack of 'substantive staging' has meant that the 'dirt' of the built environment remains highly visible. But perhaps this constitutes a success for the tours? They are transforming tourists' perceptions of the people, whilst enhancing awareness of the objectively poor infrastructure, homes and living conditions.

Bruner's (1991) examination of New Guinea's 'Cannibal Tours' argued that 'tourists are not radically challenged on tour, since what is presented to them tends to confirm their expectations' (*ibid*: 242). I contend that in Dharavi the opposite is true; the tour goer's experience radically challenges their expectations and, for some, they feel their understanding of Dharavi and its people has been transformed. Perhaps the Dharavi tour goers enter with a more open mind, or perhaps representations in New Guinea's tours were designed to confirm and consequently did conform to tourist expectations.

The Non-transformative Aspects: Questioning 'Reality'

Tourists are not a 'passive' group capable only of either absorbing or repelling the message presented to them. Because the tourist gaze filters representations through individual understanding tour-goers are liable to accept or refute certain points, contest and question others and remain conscious of their own partiality as observers.

We must, therefore, consider the counter-argument that illustrates the limitations of the tour's transformative power.

Misunderstanding and confusion. Some tour-goers feel their preconceptions are challenged but are unsure how they can rationalize their experience. Confusion arises from how to relate Dharavi to other slums. When asked, 'how has this tour changed your impression of other slums?', responses were very mixed: 'left wondering what people do in other slums', 'I guess Dharavi might be better than slums across the world?' and 'not sure as have not seen other slums'. Such indecision is a symptom of the tour's content lacking comparative references to slums beyond Mumbai and because of the tour's emphasis on experiencing a slum 'firsthand' as the essential way of perceiving 'reality', making tour-goers reticent to pass judgement on slums they have not physically been to. I argue that 'communicative staging' has unintentionally undermined the wider transformative message of the tour, resulting in tour-goers feeling confused about whether or not Dharavi is representative of Mumbai's slums and how they might relate this to urban poverty around the world.

Contesting the message. Bruner's (2001) 'questioning gaze' recognizes that tourists have agency; they frequently question the producers' representations and may refuse to accept them at face value. Whilst the tour is designed to encourage an 'inquisitive gaze', it appears that some tour-goers go further to dispute the wider message: 'the recycling industry should not be celebrated, the working conditions are far below acceptable standards'; another tour-goer argues 'Dharavi is so much richer than other slums in Mumbai, they are much poorer there'. The first comment clearly contests the tour's use of the recycling industry as the epitome of resourcefulness and ingenuity, and the second contests the use of Dharavi as representative of the city's urban poor more generally.

During the participant observation stage of the research I encountered a young backpacker from the UK who was very cynical about the tour's transformative capacity. She derided the tour's transformative agenda, maintaining that many people had so little pre-existing knowledge about Dharavi that they would gain little from the tour experience, 'most people only even know this place exists because of Slumdog'. She insisted that her reading of the novel *Shantaram* (Roberts 2003) was much more significant in transforming her understanding of Mumbai's slums and the plight of the poor than the tour could ever be. It is interesting that such vociferous criticisms are not demonstrated in the questionnaire data, this may be because such impressions are very rare or it may indicate a systematic failing of the technique, neither can be certain.

Tourist consciousness. Tour-goers' interpretations are best explained by applying Urry's (1990) tourist gaze. Unlike previously mechanistic theories, this will recognize that tourists have agency and free will. It is evident that not all tour-goers accept representations at face value. Instead, they can be conscious that their knowledge is partial, their preconceptions are biased and their touristic identity is subjective. As one Dharavi tour-goer writes, 'I've not been to any other slums, I can only compare to what's seen in the media, although of course this can be distorted'; another writes 'I've only seen Dharavi on Slumdog, but that's a Hollywood movie'. I argue that such self-reflexivity conforms to Urry's (1990) notion of the 'post-tourist', the type of tour-goer conscious of the tour's partiality and aware that their preconceptions are a product of a biased media discourse on slums and, in this sense, these tours conform closely to the recent 'Long Tail' trend that has fragmented the tourist industry (Lew 2008).

The Power of Reflection

Thus far the research has attended to the reciprocity between tour company representations and tour-goer interpretations. We must now connect the gaze of Dharavi's residents to this relationship, recognizing that they powerfully influence how tour-goers understand the place. The preceding findings have illustrated that observations of Dharavi's residents as 'resourceful', 'industrious' and 'energetic' have been the most transformative elements of the tour. The tourist gaze undoubtedly passes judgement on the residents. When asked, 'what do you think the residents of Dharavi think of the tourists?', the responses were scattered across a wide spectrum. Doxy's (1975) 'level of host irritation index' (Doxy's Irridex) model provides a broad framework from which tour-goers' perceptions of locals can be understood. They sit in three categories:

1. euphoria/friendliness: open pleasure with tourist presence: 'they're so curious and welcoming';
2. apathy/indifference: unresponsive reaction to tourists : 'they're too busy to pay attention to us';
3. annoyance/frustration: openly negative reaction to tourist presence: 'I think we got in their way, they weren't happy'.

Out of 150 responses the majority fell into categories one and two, but some tourists were concerned that their presence was unwelcomed. One tour-goer was very concerned that residents may not be aware of his benign intentions, 'I hope they don't see us as onlookers to poverty'.

Gillespie (2006) terms this phenomenon the 'reverse gaze'. It must be acknowledged that this form of tourist perception is not based on what the residents themselves *actually* think, but on what tour-goers think the residents think. Consequently, I argue that some tour-goers may enter the 'slum space' presupposing that they are unwelcome intruders and this conditions how they interpret the people they encounter. In an account of his experience (written on Reality Tour's online discussion forum), one tour-goer writes, 'I found myself walking slowly, in a bubble almost, my gaze covering everything but lingering nowhere where people were'. This tour-goer was evidently mindful of accusations of voyeurism and actively distances himself from the reverse gaze.

Conclusions

This research has shown that slum tourism in Dharavi is not the insidious and tactless venture that many media reports have derided it as, but equally, neither does it offer a benign and impartial representation of the place. By engaging with the politics of presenting 'the slums', these tours have crossed the boundary of conventional tourism; they bring the contrasts between the First and Third World, the rich and poor and the 'haves and have not's' into sharp relief. Likewise, tourists are stepping outside the borders of conventional travel by touring Dharavi; whilst these are now sites of touristic experiences, they are also the homes and workplaces of many hundreds of thousands of people. Whether they like it or not both parties are engaged with the deeply contentious issues that arise when tourism and poverty collide so explicitly.

Dharavi's complex geography and history prove that it eludes definitive representation. By deconstructing the message of Reality Tours and Travel this research has questioned how and why 'reality' is presented to the tour-goers. The findings demonstrate that the line between fact and fiction, staged and authentic, is subjective. What each tour-goer derives from their experience is equally individualized, confirming the importance within tourism research of avoiding generalizations centred on the 'model tourist'. Importantly, this research has taken the premise of work undertaken in Rio and Cape Town and applied it to Mumbai, in doing so discovering new techniques of representation. Although superficially appearing substantively non-staged, the Dharavi tour actually conveys its message by communicating an idealized 'reality'. The result is that the tour's message is veiled as *the* true and correct representation of Dharavi when, in fact, it is merely one of many possible images of the slum, Mumbai's urban poor and poverty more generally.

I conclude that whilst the tour certainly has been successful in partially transforming the negative image of slums, it could be more effective. Presently, Dharavi is represented in isolation; as a unique space of ingenuity and determination. The upshot is that tour-goers are left confused about whether what they have just seen symbolizes urban poverty in Mumbai or whether it is a unique example of an exceptionally prosperous slum. In order to be truly transformative I believe the tour must engage with the wider issues of global poverty in order to show that the day-to-day issues faced by Dharavi's residents are not abstracted from those of the one billion other slum dwellers across the world. Further research would have to test the extent to which tour-goers take their experience 'back home' with them; whether the positive image of slums still resonates as time passes, and whether they pursue their interest in slums elsewhere. I have presented my recommendations to Reality Tours and Travel and I hope that it will motivate them to consider adapting their tour accordingly.

Finally, although this research has been critical of Reality Tours and Travel's use of 'reality' to communicate their message, there is no doubt that this company could act as a positive/useful model for other slum tourism enterprises across the world. Tour profits are channelled directly into Dharavi's community projects, residents generally welcome the tour's positive message about their slum and the aspirations of the company to transform warped stereotypes of the urban poor are laudable.

The phrase 'we should never forget' is often thought to capture the abhorrence felt towards *past* acts of immorality. I suggest that in the context of slum tourism the phrase 'we should not avoid' best captures the importance of understanding *present* disparities of wealth and opportunity that exist in society. These tours play a crucial role in raising questions about the current world order, regardless of the diversity of conclusions which they engender. The deliberations of the journalist John Lancaster after the Dharavi tour are particularly poignant: 'Were the people I saw in Dharavi the victims of globalization, or its beneficiaries? I still don't know. But at least the question had been raised in my mind' (Lancaster 2007: 3).

References

Appadurai, A. (2000) Spectral housing and urban cleansing: Notes on Millennial Mumbai, *Public Culture*, 12(3), pp. 627–651.

Apte, P. (2009) Dharavi: India's Model Slum, *Planetizen: Urban Planning, Design and Development Network*. Available at http://www.planetizen.com/node/35269 (accessed January 2011).

Blakely, R. (2009) Slum tours get Slumdog Millionaire boost. *The Times*, January 21. Available at http://www.timesonline.co.uk/tol/news/world/asia/article5555635.ece (accessed January 2011).

Booth, R. (2009) Charles declares Mumbai shanty town model for the world, *The Guardian*, February 6. Available at www.guardian.co.uk/artanddesign/2009/feb/06/prince-charles-slum-comments (accessed January 2011).

Bruner, E. (1991) Transformation of the self in tourism, *Annals of Tourism Research*, 18, pp. 238–250.

Bruner, E. (2001) The Maasai and the Lion King: Authenticity, nationalism, and globalization in African tourism, *American Ethnologist*, 28(4), pp. 881–908.

Bruner, E. (2004) *Culture on Tour: Ethnographies of Travel* (Chicago: University of Chicago Press).

Butler, S. (2003) The Museum, the Tour, the Senses. Paper presented at the CONSERT Meeting, November 13. Available at www.david-howes.com/WebButlerMuseum-Tour-Senses.doc (accessed January 2011).

Camm, R. (2009) Performance within the Townships: An investigation into township tourism in Cape Town, South Africa. BA Hons dissertation, Department of Geography, University of Cambridge.

Chambers, R. (1997) *Whose Reality Counts?* (London: ITDG).

Cohen, E. (1988) Authenticity and commoditization in tourism, *Annals of Tourism Research*, 15, pp. 371–386.

Cohen, E. (1989) Primitive and remote hill tribe trekking in Thailand, *Annals of Tourism Research*, 16, pp. 30–61.

Conran, M. (2006) Beyond authenticity: Exploring intimacy in the touristic encounter in Thailand, *Tourism Geographies*, 8(3), pp. 274–285.

Crick, M. (1989) Representations of international tourism in the social sciences: sun, sex, sights, savings and servility, *Annual Review of Anthropology*, 18, pp. 307–344.

Dann, G. (2002) *The Tourist as a Metaphor of the Social World* (London: CABI Publishing).

Davis, M. (2006) *Planet of Slums* (London: Verso).

Doxy, G. (1975) A causation theory of visitor-resident irritants: methodology and research inferences, in: M. Mowforth & I. Munt (Eds) *(2008) Tourism and Sustainability: Development, Globalisation and New Tourism in the Third World*, pp. 265–267 (London: Routledge).

Dwek, D. (2004) Favela Tourism: innocent fascination or inevitable exploitation?, MA Dissertation, King's College London.

Elliot, T. S. (1945) *Four Quartets* (London: Mariner Books).

Engqvist, J. & Lantz, M. (2008) *Dharavi: Documenting Informalities* (Sweden: Fälth & Hässler, Värnamo).

Engstrom, T. & Selinger, E. (2009) *Rethinking Theories and Practices of Imaging* (London: Palgrave Macmillan).

Fennell, D. (2011) Ethics: We're stuck with it (in tourism) … whether we like it or not!, *Journal of Tourism Geographies*. Plenary session transcript available at http://www.tandfonline.com/sda/1256/audioclip-transcript-rtxg.pdf (accessed January 2011).

Freire-Medeiros, B. (2008) Selling the favela: thoughts and polemics about a tourist destination, *Revista Brasileira de Ciências Sociais*, 4, pp. 1–26.

Freire-Medeiros, B. (2009) The favela and its touristic transits, *Geoforum*, 40, pp. 580–588.

Gilbert, A. (2007) The return of the slum: does language matter?, *International Journal of Urban and Regional Research*, 31(4), pp. 697–713.

Gillespie, A. (2006) Tourist photography and the reverse gaze, *American Anthropological Association, Ethos*, 34(3), pp. 343–366.

Goffman, E. (1959) *The Presentation of Self in Everyday Life* (New York: Anchor Books).

Heap, C. (2009) *Slumming: Sexual and Racial Encounters in American Nightlife, 1885–1940* (Chicago: University of Chicago Press).

Hutnyk, J. (1996) *The Rumour of Calcutta: Tourism, Charity and the Poverty of Representation* (London: Zed Books).

Iyer, L., Macomber, J. & Namrata, A. (2009) Dharavi: Developing Asia Largest Slum (Harvard Business School: India Research Centre). Available at http://hbswk.hbs.edu/item/6399.html (accessed January 2011).

Jaguaribe, B. & Hetherington, K. (2004) Favela tours: indistinct and maples representations of the real in Rio de Janeiro, in: M. Sheller & J. Urry (Eds) *Tourism Mobilities: Places to Play, Places in Play*, pp. 155–165 (New York: Routledge).

Koven, S. (2004) *Slumming: Sexual and Social Politics in Victorian London* (Princeton: Princeton University Press).

Kumar Karn, S. & Harada, H. (2002) Field survey on water supply, sanitation and associated health impacts in urban poor communities – a case from Mumbai City, India, *Water Science and Technology*, 46(11), pp. 269–275.

Lancaster, J. (2007) Next stop, squalor, *Smithsonian Magazine*, March. Available at http://www.smithsonianmag.com/people-places/squalor.html (accessed January 2011).

Lew, A. (2008) Long tail tourism: new geographies for marketing niche tourism products, *Journal of Travel & Tourism Marketing*, 25, pp. 409–419.

Lumenick, L. (2008) Slumderful, *The New York Post*, November 14. Available at http://www.nypost.com/p/entertainment/movies/item_m6hZxlflQZ9pCLxqta5a1J;jsessionid=FDEF6073A569D66045463398020F1930 (accessed January 2011).

MacCannell, D. (1973) Staged authenticity: Arrangements of social space in tourist settings, *American Journal of Sociology*, 79(3), pp. 589–603.

MacCannell, D. (2001) Tourist agency, *Tourist Studies*, 1(1), pp. 23–37.

Miles, A. (2009) Shocked by Slumdog's poverty porn, *The Times*, January 14. Available at http://www.timesonline.co.uk/tol/comment/columnists/guest_contributors/article5511650.ece (accessed January 2011).

Mowforth, M. & Munt, I. (2008) *Tourism and Sustainability: Development, Globalisation and New Tourism in the Third World* (London: Routledge).

Nemasetoni, I. & Rogerson, C. (2007) Township tourism in Africa: Emerging tour operators in Gauteng, South Africa, in: C. Rogerson & G. Visser (Eds) *Urban Tourism in the Developing world: the South African Experience*, pp. 205–222 (New Jersey: Transaction).

Nijman, J. (2009) A study of space in Mumbai's slums, *Tijdschrift voor economische en sociale geografie*, 101(1), pp. 4–17.

Patel, S. & Jockin, A. (2007) An offer of partnership or a promise of conflict in Dharavi, Mumbai?, *Environment and Urbanization*, 19, pp. 501–510.

Ramchander, P. (2007) Township tourism: blessing or blight? The case of Soweto in South Africa. In G. Richards (ed.) *Cultural Tourism: Global and Local Perspectives*, pp. 39–67. New York: Haworth Press.

Richardson, N. (2009) Slumdog Millionaire: on the trail of Mumbai's slumdogs, *The Telegraph*, January 22.

Roberts, G. (2003) *Shantaram* (Australia: Picador).

Rolfes, M., Steinbrink, M. & Uhl, C. (2009) *Townships as Attraction: An Empirical Study of Township Tourism in Cape Town* (Potsdam: University of Potsdam).

Selinger, E. & Outterson, K. (2009) *The Ethics of Poverty Tourism*, Boston University School of Law Working Paper, No. 09-29. Available at http://ssrn.com/abstract=1413149 (accessed January 2011).

Sharma, K. (2000) *Rediscovering Dharavi: Stories from Asia's Largest Slum* (New Delhi: Penguin).

Times Now. (2006) Slum Tourism: Selling Poverty. *Times Now*, August 26.

UN Habitat (2003) *The Challenge of Slums: Global Report on Human Settlements* (Sterling, VA: Earthscan).

Urry, J. (1990) *The Tourist Gaze: Leisure and Travel in Contemporary Societies* (London: Sage).

Weiner, E. (2008) Slum Visits: Tourism or Voyeurism? *New York Times*, March. Available at http://travel.nytimes.com/2008/03/09/travel/09heads.html?pagewanted=all (accessed January 2011).

Williams, C. (2008) Ghettourism and voyeurism, or challenging stereotypes and raising consciousness? Literary and non-literary forays into the favelas of Rio de Janeiro, *Bulletin of Latin American Research*, 27(4), pp. 483–500.

World Bank and Sanitation Program (2006) The Mumbai Slum Sanitation Program: Partnering with slum communities for sustainable sanitation in a Megalopolis. Available at http://www.archidev.org/article.php3?id_article=392 (accessed January 2011).

Young, Sir G. (1973) *Tourism: Blessing or Blight?* (Harmondsworth: Penguin).

Informal Urbanism and the Taste for Slums

KIM DOVEY & ROSS KING
Department of Architecture, Building & Planning, University of Melbourne, Parkville, Australia

ABSTRACT *This paper explores the aesthetics and politics of slum tourism – what are the attractions and what are the dangers of aestheticizing poverty? We first present eleven images of slums and informal urbanism in south and Southeast Asia and suggest a complex mix of attractions for Western tourists. On the one hand informal urbanism can be picturesque with elements of nostalgia and a quest for authenticity; on the other is the shock of the real, the spectacle of intensive labyrinthine urbanity and an uneasy voyeurism. We suggest the attraction is more the anxious and awe-filled pleasure of the sublime than any formal beauty. The paper then changes scale to connect such imagery to the political economy and geography of the city where the visibility of slums and urban informality is linked to state and market ideologies. Informal settlements generally have negative symbolic and political capital; the developing state paradoxically needs tourists yet seeks to control the urban image for purposes of branding and to signify law and order. The slum is often hidden from the public gaze in a manner that is complicit with the reproduction of poverty. While the voyeuristic gaze of the Western tourist produces an aestheticization of poverty this does not depoliticize so much as it opens up new connections and potential transformations.*

Introduction

When Walter Benjamin and Asja Lacis toured the slums of Naples in 1924 and wrote their famous essay, they portrayed the slum as a place of great ambiguity – a place of shock where 'the travelling citizen ... loses his nerve' (Benjamin & Lacis 1978: 164); at once the dystopia of poverty yet teeming with intensity, vitality and ambiguous attraction. The theatre critic and the director described the scene in terms of a theatre where backstage and frontstage interpenetrate:

> ... the house is far less the refuge into which people retreat than the inexhaustible reservoir from which they flood out. Life bursts not only from doors,

not only into front yards ... From the balconies, housekeeping utensils hang like potted plants ... Just as the living room appears on the street, with chairs, hearth and altar, so – only much more loudly – the street migrates into the living room ... Poverty has brought about a stretching of frontiers that mirrors the most radiant freedom of thought. There is no hour, often no place, for sleeping and eating ... How could anyone sleep in such rooms? To be sure there are beds – as many as the room will hold. But even if there are six or seven, there are often more than twice as many occupants ... (Benjamin & Lacis 1978: 171–2).

The tenements of Naples and elsewhere have long been supplemented in the collective imagination by the proliferation of squatter and informal settlements of developing cities. The terms 'slum', 'squatter' and 'informal' are not synonymous, of course – in general terms a slum is defined in terms of poor sanitation and shelter; squatting in terms of legality of tenure; and informality in terms of practices that fall outside state control (Roy & Alsayyad 2004; UN-Habitat 2006). These are contested terms that identify stereotypes and mask more ambiguous realities. Informality emerged initially from critiques of the informal economy and now applies also to people (floating populations) and places (informal settlements). Informality is a framework for understanding the encroachment of informal activities and settlements within formally planned cities (Roy & Alsayyad 2004). There are, however, many kinds of informal settlement (Dovey & King 2011) and many degrees and kinds of formality within them (Freire-Medieros 2009). While informality becomes identified with its settled outcomes it is fundamentally a process rather than a form; there can be no easy division between the formal and informal city. There can be high levels of morphological informality without slums; the medieval remnants of many European cities (now global tourist sites) are amongst the oldest of informal settlements.

The slippage between our uses of the terms 'informal' and 'slum' reflects the ambiguities as we shy away from 'slum' and 'squatter' as terms of denigration towards 'informal' with its respect for the complexity, ingenuity and creativity of everyday adaptations. While there is no such thing as a pure slum, the rhizomic incremental housing of informal settlements often comes to signify slum conditions and the informality is part of the attraction of slum tourism. The more recent revival in the use of the term 'slum' in turn reflects an imperative to not shy away from poverty, indeed to look harder at urban informality and the representations of 'slums', even their attractions.

In 'Slumming it', the 2010 British television documentary, some aspects of this ambiguity find a popular audience. In an echo of the British tradition of the Grand Tour, Kevin McCloud (host of the popular TV series 'Grand Designs') is to spend two weeks living in Dharavi, Mumbai, and he has a particular set of questions before he goes:

Dharavi looks like a hellhole, disease is rife, water's contaminated and sanitation is rudimentary. But it's also claimed that this slum has got a strong sense of community, high employment and little crime. Architects, planners and even Prince Charles are convinced that Dharavi has got what we lack ... When I think about a slum what I think about is misery in a way yet these people are saying they're not miserable, they're intensely happy. I don't buy that; I'm going to see for myself if this place can in any way be the answer to anyone's problems (Channel 4, 2010).

Before he enters Dharavi the audience are shown dwellings on a rubbish heap, children defecating on the pavement, mountains of rubbish and putrid drains with 'toxic sludge'. He enters the dense labyrinth with a guide and the initial shock is soon mixed with a sense of amazement at the sheer density of it all and the severe disorientation – he would have no idea how to get out of this 'mind boggling maze of lanes' without a guide. The narrative begins as largely negative – in a fire they would be trapped, the food is prepared on the floor, twenty people live in one tiny house where he cannot sleep for the rats. Over time more positive responses begin: there is a safe, welcoming and all-embracing sociality; the women are beautifully dressed in colourful saris; the children go to school; everyone seems productive and happy. The excitement on McCloud's face is evident: 'if there is one word for all this it is "intensity"'. As he explores the settlement he finds aspects that are purely horrifying (the working conditions), yet also places where he suggests they place heritage controls. There is a sense of this being a hidden world that looks negative from the outside and turns out both worse and better than it appears. Towards the end of the documentary a small group of young Westerners files past the camera and into Dharavi with a comment from McCloud 'there goes a tour'. This documentary will inevitably promote further tourism in Dharavi and it raises issues about the aesthetic attraction of the slum, the public visibility of slums and questions of political and economic context to which we will return.

Images of Informality

We begin this paper with a series of speculative accounts of how and why such dystopic places become attractive, with examples drawn from our encounters in Southeast and South Asia. In doing this it may prove useful to extend our necks a little while acknowledging that this encounter always says more about the tourist or the researcher than the slum. The following images have been selected because we regard them in some way as compelling and because we either know or sense that they attract tourists to take photographs. Our goal in what follows is to read our own unease in confronting and photographing these places as much as to describe the content and interpret the attraction.

The Chao Phraya river in Bangkok is a major public transport route and its public boats are popular with tourists photographing the public monuments of palace, temples and forts (Figure 1 (upper)). Yet their cameras also seek out the passing panorama of riverside communities with informal housing offering fleeting glimpses of exotic lives. The informal housing is framed by a screen of flags and images proclaiming nation, king and religion (King 2011).

Figure 1. Bangkok (photos: upper by Ross King; lower by Kim Dovey).

Visitors to Thailand are also likely to join the tourist boats that trawl the smaller *khlongs* (canals) lined with informal housing extending over the water with a visible social life on the water's edge (Figure 1 (lower)). Such waterfront communities are seen as remnants of a traditional Thai authenticity that is no longer found in the streets; one can hear the tourist's say: 'this is the real Bangkok'. The 'authentic' Thai lifestyle is consumed from the safe distance of the boat as locals bathe and hang out in the traditional open pavilions (*sala*) over the water and floating shops ply their trade. While dilapidation is often evident and even severe, the crowding and the real slum remains hidden.

Until the 1980s Gondolyu was a very makeshift settlement clinging to a steep riverbank in Yogyakarta where it was highly visible to passing traffic and threatened with demolition due, in large part, to this visibility. It has since been upgraded in a manner that deploys traditional Javanese roof types and wall paintings in a dense but informal manner reminiscent of a traditional village (Khudori 1987). The new buildings and wall paintings were, in part, a show of community identity and pride that has led to a much higher level of tenure security. The visibility of the riverbank also means that the image of the settlement is juxtaposed with advertising signs that cut across any fantasy of authenticity and construct an incongruity of rival yet mutually dependent economies (Figure 2 (upper)).

Figure 2. Left: Yogyakarta (photo by Wiryono Raharjo). Right: Manila (photo by Kim Dovey).

From the rooftops of a sea of slums in Manila rises a single-room tower three storeys taller than the surroundings, all on one footprint and clad in scavenged corrugated iron sheets (Figure 2 (lower)). The rooms have been built in stages with differently coloured cladding – surrounded by a landscape littered with rocks, plastic, boards and domestic items. The tower has an aesthetic quality linked to collage or bricolage; to the consistency of corrugated iron; to the typology of single-room extrusions; and to the sense of order that is introduced in contrast to the surrounding chaos. The visibility is produced by a relatively new pedestrian walkway connecting two railways stations – looking down and across the slums becomes a substitute for negotiating the city at street level.

In East Bandra, Mumbai, is another view produced by the desire to lift the middle classes off the street (Figure 3 (upper)). This conglomeration of houses up to five storeys high is constructed mostly of plywood sheets, interspersed with tarpaulin and steel sheeting. None of the floors or walls appear to line up, there are no signs of internal circulation and it is often impossible to tell where one room or house begins. From a small window a young boy looks out and above him a large television aerial extends from the roof. This image raises some problematic questions – why was it taken, how was it cropped and what are the political implications of such an aestheticization of poverty?

On a canal in Manila is a three-storey assemblage, most of it in some state of collapse. The supporting poles rise from a soup of garbage; looming above is the empty frame for a billboard suggesting failure at both ends of the economy (Figure 3 (centre)). This is a shocking scene that evokes horror and pity but also a certain awe at the necessity for life under such conditions. In these encounters one hesitates to go any further as if on the edge of an abyss – to enter is to lose the distance necessary for photography.

The most visible of such settlements line the railways of Mumbai with more than a million passing commuters every day (Figure 3 (lower)). These are fleeting glimpses of everyday lives, children playing, a sequence of apparent communities. Yet these real lives and real people are gone in an instant unless the camera snaps an image we can reflect on. Façades are strung with washing and lined with potted plants; the windows are small and shuttered. One of the buildings is a shop with signs and a phone booth outside. If it were not for the railway within two metres of the front doors this could be a village. These momentary flashes of other lives can be mere spectacle or profoundly disturbing; as can the act of photographing and publishing such an image. To what degree is this an exercise in self-gratification, the self-indulgence of living our own lives vicariously through others? Are the residents of this settlement better off if we avert the camera and the gaze? What are the politics of turning away?

Along the river in Surabaya, Indonesia, a string of row houses are propped above the water, clad in rusted corrugated iron sheets with few windows or balconies and no access to the water (Figure 4 (upper)). At the end of the row some of the houses are slowly collapsing. Behind this row of rust and dereliction is a brightly

Figure 3. Upper and lower: Mumbai; centre: Manila (photos by Kim Dovey).

Figure 4. Upper: Surabaya; lower: Bangkok (photos by Ross King).

coloured commercial complex with a large billboard demonstrating how it will soon be extended. This is the elite model of a water-front city which the waterfront communities have resisted (Dovey 2010). The juxtaposition between formal and informal in this image reflects a real politics of resistance and part of this resistance involves a determination to exclude the tourist. Yet this is an ambivalent position: residents might seek exposure for a specific political purpose, yet pride coupled with resentment will cut in and privacy will be insisted upon.

In Bangkok an informal settlement lines the edge of a canal that has also been used for an elevated freeway (Figure 4 (lower)). The uppermost house with open verandah and gabled roof could present an almost bucolic image if it were not for the fact that it is located immediately on top of a number of other houses (some in advanced states of collapse) and immediately beneath the freeway. Here the juxtaposition of fundamentally different urban processes, forms and lifestyles becomes part of the attraction.

Kampung Bahru in Kuala Lumpur is scarcely an attraction in itself, yet tourists will visit for the Sunday Market. They may then find it a good location from which to photograph the Petronas Towers – emblematic of the city and the nation – juxtaposed against the informality (Figure 5 (upper)). A similarly juxtaposed image appeared in the 1998 movie 'Entrapment', but Kampung Bahru was considered insufficiently sordid and an image from a more archetypical slum was spliced in (Bunnell 2004). The scene caused political outrage; not only was it inauthentic and violated the preferred national image, but it also opened some sensitive political issues since Kampung Bahru is regarded as a hotbed of Islamic and political radicalism (King 2008).

Pavement squatters in Mumbai live in a two-storey row backed against the blank wall of an industrial building (Figure 5 (lower)). The makeshift buildings are covered on the street facades by domestic paraphernalia, the entire pavement is consumed by domestic space and all pedestrian traffic is forced into the street. This is a voyeuristic photograph that raises questions about the ethics of slum tourism and photography under conditions where the public gaze necessarily and constantly penetrates deeply into domestic space. But again where is the morality in aversion?

Aesthetics of Informality

We will now explore some of the issues identified above through a series of more general themes. We begin from the view that the tourist encounter with poverty and urban informality is at once a moral, aesthetic and epistemological encounter – these three realms of critique that Kant would keep separate are here inextricably intertwined. While we intend to focus on the aesthetic, this is not to presume any priority so much as to explore this dimension and its connections. In the eighteenth century Burke (1958) drew a sharp distinction between the beautiful and the sublime: the beautiful brings us delight and submits to our gaze while the sublime is a pleasure

Figure 5. Upper: Kuala Lumpur (photo by Ross King); lower: Mumbai (photo by Kim Dovey).

born of fear in the face of the unknown and the overwhelming. While we want to identity the pleasures of slum tourism primarily with the sublime, it is clear that there are also elements of delight. We begin with the experience of nostalgia, the quest for authenticity and the pleasures of the exotic and picturesque; moving towards the shock of the real, the potency of dialectic juxtapositions and the lure of labyrinthine intensity.

Beauty

Nostalgia is the sentimental affection for a real or imagined past; it can be evoked when the informal settlement becomes reminiscent of a traditional village through its vernacular architecture, spatial structure or social life (Figures 2 (upper) and 3 (lower)). Such sentiment can be linked to a quest for authenticity (Conran 2007). For MacCannell (1989: 41) this quest is based in a perceived lack in modern life where the city has become contrived spectacle: 'Modern man has been condemned to look elsewhere, everywhere, for his authenticity, to see if he can catch a glimpse of it reflected in the simplicity, poverty, chastity or purity of others'. Slums can also embody the attractions of the exotic – not so much other times as other lives, beliefs and customs. The exotic is a spectacle to be photographed while maintaining a distance (Figure 1), an identity we borrow to augment the one we retain. Informal urbanism is often picturesque – what is seen can be reduced to a picture. The aesthetic idea of the picturesque was, from its eighteenth century beginnings, linked to the practice of tourism and the Grand Tour (Gilpin 1782). While Burke had tried to draw a mutually exclusive line between the beautiful and the sublime, here was a movement to render the sublime beautiful, to reduce it to a picture (Figures 2, 3 (upper) & 5 (upper)). From its beginnings, the picturesque also incorporated elements of poverty, including imagery of worker-hovels (MacArthur 2007).

The aesthetic delights and pleasures of informal settlements have often been noticed by those who study them. Peattie (1992) suggests that such a discourse is inherently political and draws attention to the way Perlman (1976) used the dramatic imagery of *favelas* to promote a positive image of stigmatized communities in her seminal book *The Myth of Marginality*. Such positive interest in the aesthetic of urban informality is not easily reduced to sentimental nostalgia; the *favelas* have been the subject of aesthetic interest since the early twentieth century (Freire-Madieros 2009). There is also a broader interest in the aesthetics of vernacular architecture that burgeoned in the wake of Rudofsky's (1964) highly influential book *Architecture Without Architects*. This was a photographic essay in traditional vernacular architecture – exotic, picturesque and highly potent images with poverty erased. Some of the attractions of more recent informal settlements can be seen to have a similar source in the ways an informal urban morphology is produced through a repetition of simple building types and materials yet where every house and lane is different. The informal process produces a certain order of repetition but variegated by an incremental adaptive process (Figures 2, 3). While this is a social process, it produces a variegated landscape that can be seen at a distance as 'organic' in the sense of parts fitting together into a whole – an urban morphology produced by informal adaptations within an ecology of scarcity. As Perlman (2010: xviii) puts it:

> From the beginning, I found the *favelas* visually more interesting and humanly more welcoming than the upper-middle-class neighbourhoods ... with their high-density low-rise architecture, featuring facades variously angled to catch a breeze or a view, and shade trees and shutters to keep them cool ... they followed the organic curves of the hillsides rather than a rigid grid pattern.

The typology of single-room increments sets up a rhythm, both vertically and horizontally. The adaptive process often produces an inventive architecture of one-off solutions. Where informal settlements cling to steep escarpments they often produce a spectacular urban profile that follows the topographic contours – a landscape thickly coated with houses with both a consistency and a myriad of variations in form and materials. The materiality of informal urbanism (steel, plastic, concrete) is largely modern rather than traditional and the typology of single-room accretions is global rather than local even while the emergent visual effects differ markedly with topography and climate. What renders such an urban landscape picturesque is visibility at a distance – it relies on a particular conjunction of topology and morphology.

The Sublime

All of the themes discussed thus far – the experience of nostalgia, the quest for authenticity, the idea of the exotic, the picturesque and vernacular – can be loosely seen within the framework of an aesthetic of beauty. Yet, while slums have their delights, this is never pure delight but often mixed with horror – here we turn to an understanding of the sublime. The aesthetic of the sublime, as originally conceived by Burke in 1757, involves the encounter with overwhelming scale or force, particularly related to overwhelming forces of nature (Burke 1958). The aesthetic passion stems from fear, horror or terror that becomes an awe-filled pleasure as we realize our own safety from it. While beauty involves the love of what submits to us, the sublime involves submission to a larger force that threatens to overwhelm us (Eagleton 1990). The sublime is the combination of anxiety and pleasure we experience when we encounter a potentially overwhelming threat under conditions of safety. For Kant (1974), our inability to understand and to grasp the enormity of the sublime involves a loss of the sense of the rational moral self. Yet the key to the pleasure is that the danger is not real – the pleasure depends on being safe in this encounter with the overwhelming. Such pleasure, for Kant, comes from a reassertion of a transcendent moral and rational order – we surrender to the thrill of danger in the knowledge that we are safe and can rise above it. More recently Lyotard (1994) suggests that the power of the sublime is to expose the limits of human reason and the conceits of the enlightenment project with its master narratives of truth, progress, justice and development. He identifies the sublime with the foundational move of avant-garde modern art. The avant-garde offered the shock of such realization in the safety of the gallery. Within this framework of the sublime we suggest that a key attraction of slum tourism is that it offers safe passage through a potentially overwhelming poverty (Figures 2 (lower), 3).

Any quest for the 'real' or 'authentic' city in the slums soon yields to the 'shock of the real' – the terrible realization of the world as given, against Utopian dreams of what should be. Photographs or television reports on slums might lead to reactions of outrage, philanthropy or activism, but an actual visit can evoke a further set of reactions: not only fear but shame, guilt, pity and embarrassment at the thought of intrusion. Any aesthetic response is always already entangled with a failure of reason and moral outrage. There is an inevitable tension between our own moral discomfort and a real concern for the state of humanity (Figures 3, 5 (lower)). The tourist's horror in confronting the slum and its denizens is always tinged by the dread of a loss of morality and a loss of self – the preservation of the moral subject is at stake. Turning away (with or without the photograph) is one response to this dilemma; commitment to action is another.

The informal settlement is often labyrinthine in that it is visually and function- ally impenetrable; its spatial structure is informal, its laneways narrow and irregular. Whatever one sees from the formal public space is but an entrance that suggests the first of many layers that disappear into the depths (Figures 2, 3). The labyrinth offers the mix of dread/pleasure suggested by the sublime. The threat here is largely episte- mological, a threat to the rational subject – the terror of the unknown. The labyrinth is unreadable and infinitely disorientating. The maze of lanes and openings threatens, should we enter, a loss of the knowing subject, of who we are and where we are. For Deleuze (1993: 3–6) the labyrinth is a multiplicity of slippages or 'folds' where one place or identity folds into another with every turn – a place of 'becoming' (Dovey 2010). The labyrinth threatens a loss of orientation, an unravelling of self-identity; but it also promises new understanding. A 'maze' implies spatial complexity – it is a puzzle and a challenge to reason. To become 'amazed' is a term that suggests awakening or understanding as one becomes lost in another world. The labyrinth is at once threatening yet enticing.

Benjamin saw modern society of mass culture as a dream world – at once a kind of false consciousness but also a form of collective imagination with potential for collective awakening, for seeing the dream as a dream (Buck-Morss 1989: 261–3). Part of the potency of the image of the slum is that of a dystopic counter image that cuts through the dream of modernity. For Benjamin the city generally produces deceptive visions of our history and future where the seemingly permanent is really transient (Gilloch 1996). In the encounter with slums the supposedly transient appears as permanent – an awakening from the dream of a modern world of enlightenment and abundance. Slums can be seen as an insurgent urbanism where the shock of the real cuts through ideology.

While informal settlements may become a spectacle in themselves, their spatial position as urban interstices means they are often juxtaposed with counter images to form a dialectic image where it is the incongruity of the image that carries the effect – one element of an image deconstructs another and both are called into question. Dialectical images compel discourse. Benjamin was interested in the ways the juxtapositions of difference in urban life could reveal something of a larger truth – spatial logic could reveal what a linear logic could not through a 'dialectic of awakening' (Buck-Morss 1989: 262). The MacDonalds sign, the Petronas Towers and the freeway (Figures 2 (upper), 4 (lower), 5 (upper)) each counters any fantasy of the authentic traditional village, *khlong* or *kampung*, as it hits the observer with the obscenity of inequality. Such images of traditional/modern, local/global, informal/formal, poor/rich, village/nation open a space for re-thinking such relations and mythologies. Advertising images may be juxtaposed in a manner where Utopian wish images contrast with a dystopic landscape – billboards become windows on to a world of plenty that is the diametric opposite of poverty. At a smaller scale and close-up, the dialectic image may be created by the way images of beauty can cut through the dereliction, poverty and chaos with small-scale practices of pride – tiny gardens, flowers, shrines, birds, artworks. The dialectic image may reveal social differences where formal and informal morphologies, rich and poor, are co-located. One finds the infrastructure of the formal city (pedestrian overpasses, elevated expressways, residential and commercial towers, shopping malls) in a cheek-by-jowl juxtaposition with urban slums (Figure 4 (upper)). At times the landscape exposes the sharp geographical divisions between rich and poor, and there are locations where the picturesque beauty of the informal city from a distance can make the formal look dull by contrast.

The shock value of the slum is linked to the density and intensity of both built form and urban life – densities that are often more than 100 times that of the suburban homes of the tourists. This shock can be linked to what Deleuze (originally Spinoza) calls 'affect' – not a feeling or emotion but a pre-conscious bodily response to intensity; not what an image or event *means* but what it *does* (Deleuze & Guattari 1994; Colebrook 2002: xix–xx). While this response may or may not be positive, it has an aesthetic dimension of a similar kind to our bodily response to intense music. Intensity has to do with excess. Here scale is important, where a little bit of dilapidation looks tawdry, an overwhelming disorder becomes interesting. Detached buildings in disrepair do not have the same impact as a four-storey assemblage of contiguous dwellings in the same condition (Figure 3 (upper)). A few power cables strung along a street can interfere with the urban spectacle, yet when they approach saturation of the spatial field they become the spectacle. Intensity is linked to multifunctionality and multiple use of space; informal settlements fill interstices with an intensive aesthetic of efficiency – every scrap of sunlight is used for drying clothes or food; every scrap of material finds a use; every scrap of space is used for many things (Figure 5 (lower)).

The intensity of the informal settlement is linked to the quality that Benjamin & Lacis (1978) identified as 'porosity' – the degree to which the spatial and social segmentarity of the city dissolves under conditions of high density and poverty. In particular there is a dissolution of boundaries between private and public as domestic life spills into public space and the public gaze penetrates into the private realm:

> Building and action interpenetrate in the courtyards, arcades and stairways. In everything they preserve the scope to become a theatre of new, unforeseen constellations. The stamp of the definitive is avoided. No situation appears intended forever, no figure asserts its 'thus and not otherwise'. This is how architecture, the most binding part of the communal rhythm, comes into being here ... One can scarcely discern where building is still in progress and where dilapidation has already set in. For nothing is concluded. Porosity results ... above all from the passion for improvisation, which demands that space and opportunity be preserved at any price. Buildings are used as a popular stage. They are all divided into innumerable simultaneously animated theatres. Balcony, courtyard, window, gateway, staircase, roof are at the same time stage and boxes (Benjamin & Lacis 1978: 166–8).

One can read in this passage nearly all of the attractions we have introduced above, the experience of nostalgia, the picturesque and labyrinthine intensity. The slum is seen as an unfinished constellation of people and buildings in a dynamic state of both creativity and dilapidation. The attraction in part is that 'nothing is concluded' in this everyday festival, this theatre of the unforeseen. While the informal settlements of the developing world are not the slums of early twentieth-century Naples, there are significant parallels in this exposure of domesticity that makes the private public. There is also an element of making the public private – informal settlements often protect their privacy to some degree by remaining hidden to the gaze from the formal city. While there may be little privacy within such settlements, many are invisible and largely impenetrable from the formal public spaces of the city. Even when visible from a distance informal settlements are often enclaves, as impenetrable to outsiders from a different social class as gated communities – they may, indeed, be informally gated and guarded; their streets and lanes do not appear on street maps. Here we return to the quest for authenticity – slum tourism as the only way to see the 'back-stage' (MacCannell 1989).

The issue of visibility and, therefore, the prospect of slum tourism, is strongly mediated by both topography of the landscape and the morphology of urban development. We have argued elsewhere that the morphology of informal settlements can be viewed as a loose constellation of types: escarpments, waterfronts, districts, easements and pavements (Dovey & King 2011). The visibility and imagery of informal settlements plays an important role in the politics of eviction and displacement as well as the quest for tenure security.

Political Economy of the Sublime

We conclude this paper by opening up some questions about the politics and ethics of slum tourism. These are not easy questions and we can take no more than a few short steps here. If we are vaguely correct in identifying some of the aesthetic attractions of the slum, then one of the dangers is that we engage in an aestheticization of poverty, producing a depoliticized image that becomes attractive for capitalist exploitation. As Roy (2004: 302) puts it: '... the aestheticization of poverty is the establishment of an aesthetic and aestheticized (rather than political) relationship between viewer and viewed, between professional and city, between First and Third Worlds. It is an ideology of space'.

For Roy (2004: 298–303), the aesthetic gaze largely reduces the slum to a kind of 'primitive organicism' – aesthetic discourse directs attention and resources to design outcomes and away from the deeper political issues of global poverty. While we acknowledge that such can well be the case, how separate are the aesthetic and the political?

Perhaps the most potent critique of the relationship of politics to aesthetics comes from the work of Bourdieu (1984), for whom judgements that appear to draw aesthetic distinctions between things also work to draw social distinctions between people. He makes the observation that to take and frame a photograph of rubbish as a work of art is to distinguish a particular social class – working classes do not photograph rubbish (or slums?). For Bourdieu, aesthetic judgements operate within a field of power wherein what is at stake is 'symbolic capital': one of a range of forms of capital – symbolic, social, cultural, economic, political – that circulate through fields of power and are convertible to each other in different ways. One way of understanding the informal settlement within the urban field of the developing city is as a place with negative symbolic capital. For local middle classes these are places to avoid or to avert one's eyes; the informal city becomes the 'other' of the formal city and hence essential to its identity. This helps to explain why informality continues to signify the 'slum' even after slum conditions and tenure are upgraded:

> Perhaps the single persistent distinction between *favelas* and the rest of the city is the deeply rooted stigma that adheres to them and to those who reside in them ... Even after the extensive ... upgrading programs ... there is little doubt as to where the *asfalto* (pavement) ends ... The visual markers of each are unmistakable, whether viewed from above or on street level (Perlman 2010: 30).

Informal settlements largely occupy the interstices of cities that compete in the larger field of the global market wherein place marketing or urban branding are seen as crucial for attracting investment (Kearns & Philo 1993; Klingman 2007). In this larger field the image of urban informality cuts across the brand image. Furthermore, images of slums embody negative political capital since governments are embarrassed by signification of failure and a lack of law and order. In response to both negative symbolic and political capital, informal settlements are sometimes upgraded or demolished because they are visible. Slum tourism provides an interesting twist in that in some cities it turns the slum into part of the brand – the image of Rio incorporates the *favelas*. The place branding schemes of many developing cities – importing Western models of waterfront development and dressing up local places according to global formulae – can ironically render them placeless from a global viewpoint. In this context the slum adds value as an authentic urbanism cutting through the spectacle of globalization, modernity and placelessness, an insurgent urbanism that resists global capitalism and authoritarian politics. If the slum adds tourist value then the paradox is that the developing state needs the flows of tourists yet seeks to control the urban image for purposes of branding and to signify law and order. While this could ultimately be seen as some kind of protection against demolition it will not necessarily encourage upgrading – self-help and sanitation programmes are not particularly photogenic.

Bourdieu has little place in his scheme for the sublime, but Lyotard's (1994) identification of the sublime with the shock of the avant-garde in modern art provides a connection. For Bourdieu the avant-garde works through an overturning of codes; to see a blank canvas or an off-the-shelf urinal as fine art is to overturn the dominant code of aesthetic taste. While this overturning appears to be revolutionary, the autonomy granted to the avant-garde is conditional on the reinvigoration and, therefore, the reproduction of the field. For Bourdieu, the primary role of the avant-garde is to inject the field with new strains of symbolic capital, to reinvigorate the art market with novel forms of expression (Bourdieu 1984: 254). What appears to be an autonomous aesthetic field is integrated with cycles of symbolic capital. While Bourdieu's insights are crucial they can be seen as overly reductionist; there is a chorus of social theory (Foucault on Delacroix, Deleuze on Bacon, Leotard on Duchamp) that suggests in different ways that avant-garde art is fundamentally political in that it can open doors into new ways of seeing and thinking. So what has all this to do with slum tourism? We suggest that slum tourism can be construed as a parallel to the idea of the avant-garde: explorations of an urban frontier that feed a market for the new and different. It gains potency from the shock; it relies on a certain safety and distance for contemplation; it is inducted from its inception into tourist markets and capital flows and it may be complicit with forms of social reproduction. It can also open windows on to new ways of seeing and thinking.

While the consumption of slums may be critiqued in aesthetic terms, such practices are thoroughly implicated in epistemological and ethical issues. Slums offer a challenge to our sense of reason and morality as well as our sense of beauty or place – the separation of these three zones of critique (as in the Kantian philosophical paradigm) cannot be sustained. It follows that to exclude aesthetic critique on the basis that it becomes complicit with an aestheticization of poverty is no way to address the issue. The invisibility of slums is part of a closed cycle of socio-economic reproduction; the voyeuristic gaze of the tourist opens this up to potential transformation. There is no simple answer to the question of whether photographing slums is legitimate; in our case we leave the reader to decide. Yet, to avert our gaze from the image in favour of politics or social practice is to ignore the political and social potency of the image. Whether it produces shock, horror, delight or political activism, slum tourism is unlikely to abate and seems destined to open these settlements to Western eyes. The question of how much it may open Western eyes (and pockets) to the enduring problems of poverty is more complex, but the prospect is enticing.

References

Benjamin, W. & Lacis, A. (1978) Naples, in: W. Benjamin *Reflections*, pp. 163–173 (New York: Harcourt, Brace & Jovanovich).

Bourdieu, P. (1984) *Distinction: A Social Critique of the Judgement of Taste* (London: Routledge).

Buck-Morss, S. (1989) *The Dialectics of Seeing* (Cambridge, MA: MIT Press).

Bunnell, T. (2004) Reviewing the Entrapment controversy, *Geojournal*, 59(4), pp. 297–305.

Burke, E. (1958 [1756]) *A Philosophical Enquiry into the Origin of Our Ideas of the Sublime and Beautiful* (London: Routledge & Kegan Paul).

Channel 4 (2010) Kevin McCleod-Slumming it, 2 Part TV series (London). Available at: www.channel4. com/programmes/kevin-mccloud-slumming-it/4od (accessed 20 January 2011).

Colebrook, C. (2002) *Understanding Deleuze* (Sydney: Allen & Unwin).

Conran, M. (2007) Beyond authenticity: Exploring intimacy in the touristic encounter in Thailand, *Tourism Geographies*, 8(3), pp. 274–285.

Deleuze, G. (1993) *The Fold* (Minneapolis: University of Minnesota Press).

Deleuze, G. & Guattari, F. (1994) *What Is Philosophy?* (London: Verso).

Dovey, K. (2010) *Becoming Places* (London: Routledge).

Dovey, K. & King, R. (2011) Forms of informality: Morphology and visibility of informal settlements, *Built Environment*, 37(1), pp. 11–29.

Eagleton, T. (1990) *The Ideology of the Aesthetic* (Oxford: Blackwell).

Freire-Medieros, B. (2009) The *favela* and its touristic transits, *Geoforum*, 40, pp. 580–588.

Gilloch, G. (1996) *Myth and Metropolis* (Cambridge: Polity).

Gilpin, W. (1782). *Observations on the River Wye, and Several Parts of South Wales, etc. Relative Chiefly to Picturesque Beauty* (London: R. Blamire).

Kant, I. (1974) *The Critique of Judgement* (trans. J. Bernard) (New York: Hafner).

Kearns, G. & Philo, C. (Eds) (1993) *Selling Places* (Oxford: Pergamon).

Khudori, D. (1987) *Towards a Community of Liberation*, Research paper, Rotterdam: Institute of Housing Studies.

King, R. J. (2008) *KL and Putrajaya: Negotiating Urban Space in Malaysia* (Singapore: NUS Press).

King, R. J. (2011) *Reading Bangkok* (Singapore: NUS Press).

King, R. J. & Idawati, D. (2010) Surabaya *kampung* and distorted communication, *SOJOURN: Journal of Social Issues in Southeast Asia*, 25(3), pp. 00–01.

Klingmann, A. (2007) *Brandscapes* (Cambridge, MA: MIT Press).

Lyotard, J-F. (1994) *Lessons on the Analytic of the Sublime* (trans. E. Rottenberg) (Palo Alto: Stanford University Press).

MacArthur, J. (2007) *The Picturesque* (London: Routledge).

MacCannell, D. (1987) *The Tourist: A New Theory of the Leisure Class* (New York: Schocken).

Peattie, L. (1992) Aesthetic politics, *Traditional Dwellings and Settlements Review*, 3(2) pp. 23–32.

Perlman, J. (1976) *The Myth of Marginality* (Berkeley: University of California Press).

Perlman, J. (2010) *Favela* (Oxford: Oxford University Press).

Roy, A. (2004) Transnational trespassings, in: A. Roy & N. Alsayyad (Eds) *Urban Informality*, pp. 289–318 (New York: Lexington).

Roy, A. & Alsayyad, N. (Eds) (2004) *Urban Informality* (New York: Lexington).

Rudofsky, B. (1964) *Architecture Without Architects* (New York: Doubleday).

UN-Habitat (2006) *The State of The World's Cities* (London: Earthscan).

Notes on Contributors

Kim Dovey is Professor of Architecture and Urban Design in the Faculty of Architecture, Building and Planning, the University of Melbourne, Australia.

Ross King is Professorial Fellow in the Faculty of Architecture, Building and Planning, the University of Melbourne, Australia.

Mobile Imaginaries, Portable Signs: Global Consumption and Representations of Slum Life

ULI LINKE

Rochester Institute of Technology, Sociology and Anthropology, Rochester, USA

ABSTRACT *This essay explores how iconic representations of slum life are produced for transnational consumption in Europe. The focus is on the manner in which the logics of spectacle and entertainment have come to organize images of urban poverty. The use of slums as global entertainment spectacle requires that core images be detached from social life to produce a repertoire of free-floating emblems and signs that can be variously deployed, assembled, appropriated and discarded, depending on shifting cultural desires in a capitalist commodity market. The research suggests that a limited register of signs is recycled by artists, photographers, urban critics and private entrepreneurs, some of whom have built faux-shantytowns as theme parks in global cities such as Zurich, London and Berlin. The 'bare life' of these informal cities is branded for consumer publics that can afford to refashion their social identities by physical or symbolic contact with the portable icons of poverty.*

Introduction

A globalized world, marked by reform and openness, unsettles old identities and unlocks new imaginaries (Terkenli 2002). From such a perspective, the global human condition comes into view through the possibilities and signs of motion: mobile populations, permeable borders, transnational flows of capital and the traffic of culture across space and time (Appadurai 2001). Advanced communication technologies have encouraged consumers to become travellers and venture across national borders and distant continents to see something of desire and interest. Tourist destinations have, in turn, relied on image-making industries (photography, film, media and the internet) to promote curiosity about faraway lands and to incite longing for long-distance travel. In the contemporary era, under conditions of 'escalated globalization', tourist imaginaries are amplified by digital and electronic communication practices that rely on 'a globally linked network through which images, media, forms, cultural products and texts circulate throughout the world' (Sturken & Cartwright 2009: 390). In this context, visual information about distant events, social life and places is disseminated with increasing speed along tourist routes and across dispersed consumer markets. As John Urry (2002: 156) phrased it most succinctly: 'Not only do tourists travel but so too do objects, cultures, and images'. The manner whereby these mobile imaginaries are manufactured for transnational consumption is the subject of my investigation. Yet rather than scrutinizing cultural encounters at specific tourist destinations, I examine how distant places are visualized and inserted into global circuits of commodity capitalism. This approach is not entirely new. The availability of portable images and objects, as Dean MacCannell (1976: 13, 91–108) suggested many years ago, can promote tourist consumption by 'bringing the exotic' back home. In the twenty-first century, these mobile imaginaries have been stocked with representations of urban poverty and deprivation. Such visual artefacts are retrieved from across the globe as portable icons of difference.

My research on iconic representations of slum life builds on the burgeoning literature of 'slum tourism', a term that refers to organized, commercial sightseeing tours and venture capitalism in areas of urban poverty (Holloway 2009). The genre belongs to a broader pattern of commodity consumption that scholars have variously described as 'reality tourism' (Freire-Medeiros 2007), 'dark tourism' (Lennon & Foley 2000), 'disaster tourism' (Gotham 2007a: 93–95, 2007b: 838) and 'poverty tourism' (Rolfes 2010; Freire-Medeiros 2011; Meschkank 2011). Such tourist practices are focused on sites of human tragedy or deprivation that can be branded, showcased and meaningfully re-imagined by consumer-travellers. While promising to deliver memorable experiences, such tourist destinations also appeal to the growing desire to retrieve a humanizing dimension from a world that is perceived as inhumane, objectifying, catastrophic and uncaring. This motivation clearly emerges from in-depth studies of slum life and poverty tourism in Brazil (Perlman 2010; Freire-Medeiros 2011). It is also evident in attempts to reframe 'toxic tourism' (organized, non-commercial sightseeing tours to places and communities affected by chemical pollution) in terms of justice and agency (Pezzullo 2007). These humanizing endeavours, as Kevin F. Gotham (2007b: 843–844) suggests, rely on 'a process that involves the deployment of symbols and imagery to neutralize negative publicity, counter stigma, and project globally a coherent and transparent image of urban rebirth and vitality'. The expansive industry of slum tourism is thereby necessarily engaged in a broader enterprise of image-making. Distinguished as a form of 'semiotic warfare' (Gibson 2006: 84), such representational practices are propelled by efforts to forge alternative imaginaries and competing representations of disfranchised urban life.

While navigating competing fields of vision, national and transglobal tourist fantasies of place-specific worlds of poverty are shaped by a 'new politics of visibility' (Freire-Medeiros 2009a: 580). Slums are promoted as destination sites by visual exposure. The tourist gaze is enticed by signs, symbols and images that aim to inspire investment and secure commitments to travel and sightseeing. 'Images of a place that circulate through news agencies, films, ... photographs, magazines, travel guides, and advertising campaigns,' as Bianca Freire-Medeiros (2009a: 589) suggested, 'help build expectations and desirabilities that are an intrinsic part of the so called travel culture'. My essay examines the production and circulation of such representations of place-embedded sights of poverty. Building on the notion of the 'travelling city' (Freire-Medeiros 2002), I explore one trajectory of the global images industry. My aim is to scrutinize how 'slums' are visually appropriated, represented, trafficked, exhibited and consumed along global media circuits to become pictorial objects, imaginative cultural forms, virtual artefacts, material icons and signifying practices in a global tourist panopticon.

Drawing on existing scholarly insights, I inquire how iconic representations of slum life are produced for transnational consumption in Europe. Propelled by variable capitalist interests, the iconicity of the 'shantytown' or 'ghetto' is circulated as a popular commodity form throughout Europe's metropolitan centres. My research suggests that a limited register of signs is recycled by European artists, photographers, urban critics and private entrepreneurs, who ventured to build faux-shantytowns as theme parks in global cities such as Zurich, London and Berlin. Such a production of slum-images as entertainment spectacle simulates a commitment to multi-ethnic cityscapes in a united Europe, where citizenship rights, religious freedoms and articulations of ethnic diversity have been increasingly restricted by recourse to border protection, anti-immigrant sentiments and the 'whitening' of urban space in the interest of 'national security' (Linke 2010; 2011). By tracing the manner whereby the logics of spectacle and entertainment have come to organize slum-images in Europe, my research shows how signifiers of nature, race, art and space are variously produced and encoded in the iconicities of urban inequality.

Slum Geographies in the Transglobal Imaginary

My discussion begins with an overview of distinctive slum geographies by inquiring how representations of place, space and poverty are encoded in urban iconicities. While the world system of growing inequalities may be accurately described in terms of a 'planet of slums', as Davis (2007) provocatively suggests, the majority of slum-communities are located in cities. Although linked to the expansive growth of mega-cities and global cities (as 'basing points' and symbols of economic globalization), a closer reading of these sites of urban deprivation reveals that slums are not confined to the great metropolises of the global South (e.g. Sassen 2002; Friedmann 2006; King 2006). Urban poverty is globally dispersed across all continents, from the geopolitical peripheries to the economic centres – from the Third World to the First World.

The spatial concentrations of urban poverty across the globe reveal a specific pattern, whereby the topography of slum areas may be identified in different parts of the world. In North American cities, the 'inner-city ghetto' has become an ideogram of salient non-white others: black, disfranchised 'poor people concentrated in derelict cores and inner suburbs' (Davis 2007: 31). Constructed as a carceral space, the ghetto is conceived as a proxy-prison or poverty warehouse in the urban centre, which is imagined as a template of violence and illegality (Mendieta 2007). Confined to 'the 'racialized core of the US metropolis,' the 'ghetto' becomes a 'negative' social space that breeds and reproduces criminality (Wacquant 2008: 2). In continental Europe, by contrast, the existence of the 'ghetto' is denied. In the aftermath of National Socialism, the Holocaust and World War II, the politically sanctioned concentration of select population groups has become a contentious issue. The image of the 'ghetto' as a carceral space and a 'political machine of "exclusionary enclosure"' (Mendieta 2007: 384) evokes memories of trauma and state violence: the *Warsaw Ghetto*, concentration camps and genocide. In Europe, the regime of the ghetto signifies an unspeakable reality (Goldberg 2006). Excised from public discourse, confined to an imaginary exile (in time and space), spatial agglomerations of the deprived have been rendered unseen. In European cities, the urban poor have been pushed out of the urban centres, out of public sight, into the metropolitan peripheries, 'with immigrant and unemployed populations marooned in highrise housing on the urban outskirts' (Davis 2007: 31). Such a spatial marginalization of the poor or disfranchised is not confined to Europe. The displacement of select population groups to the outer edge of metropolitan centres appears to be a world-wide phenomenon.

Even though poverty may occupy a variety of urban orbits, as scholars have suggested, 'the majority of the world's urban poor no longer live in inner cities' (Davis 2007: 37). People without means are forced to inhabit shelters or build houses on the outer margins of world cities. In the US, 'trailer parks' and 'tent cities' are extensions of this neo-liberal pattern of urban exclusion, which relocates the disfranchised in natural settings: parks, forests, fields. Pirate urbanization and squatter settlements in other parts of the world lay claim to land outside of cities in 'a hazardous, health-threatening location' (Davis 2007: 121). Such emergent urban landscapes, composed on shanty settlements, consist of large numbers of self-built housing, often with few infrastructural provisions. In contrast to the North American inner-city ghetto, which is spatially confined to an urban core, shantytowns tend to expand horizontally. Such 'disparate sociospatial formations' (Wacquant 2008: 3) have become templates in a global imaginary of portable signs, which position squatter cities and the ghetto in antithetical terms. As I show in the following, each template carries distinctly different possibilities for consumer fantasies and, as such, tourism.

The Ghetto-look: Signs of the 'Strange', 'Monstrous' and 'Intimate'

The camp, the ghetto and the prison are global icons of interconnected spaces of biopolitical control and intervention (Agamben 1998). Human beings who find them-selves entrapped within the confines of these carceral spaces are imagined as part of a 'multitude' of undesirable others, signs of a 'dangerous' teaming humanity that needs to be contained and controlled (Mbembe 2003). Framed by these imaginaries, 'inner-city' residents are treated as societal waste products: valueless, useless and disposable (Giroux 2007). It is revealing that these meanings of disposability and confinement have been encoded in the very lexicon 'ghetto': the term has been traced to the fourteenth-century Venetian phrase 'campo gheto', which referred to the designated site used by iron foundries when cooling and storing slag (the waste produced by smelting ore). This location simultaneously served as a judicial/political space of social confinement and exclusion – the very place where Jews were compelled to live ('Venetian ghetto'). Propelled into the present, the construct of the 'ghetto' thus fuses two political moments of late capitalism: a regime of warehousing poverty (by dehumanization) and controlling non-productive labour (by criminalization). As such, following Loïc Wacquant (2008: 2), the US ghetto must be understood as a 'nexus of racial domination, class inequality, and state (in)action' whose effects are 'materialized in the geography of the city'. The socio-spatial formation of the 'ghetto' carries the distinctive imprints of power.

In contrast to shantytowns, depictions of the North American 'ghetto' as a penal containment-space are founded on fantasies less inclined to promote global romance or desire. In the US, according to Stephen Steinberg (2010: 217), 'we speak euphemistically of "the urban jungle", and social scientists, who portray the inner city as a haven of pathology, disorder, and immorality, are only a word away from declaring its inhabitants "uncivilized"'. The euphemism of the inner city ghetto as a 'jungle' implies wilderness, a dangerous place, the habitat of untamed nature, 'where the wild things are' (Mexal 2004: 238): the primal, violent and sexually unrestrained urban 'savages'.

> The urban wild [is] a fraught, dangerous space … a symbolic space charged with racial and economic tensions, a space outside space. As such, the ideology of wilderness dictates that it be fenced off, that it be restrained as a site of geographic and political domination (Mexal 2004: 238).

Representations of the 'ghetto', in turn, mobilize signs that confirm the presumed subhumanity of those imagined to inhabit the inner city: the figure of the 'black' other, whose existence is defined by the spatial and temporal coordinates of the 'urban jungle', which is a construct inflected by the racial logic of the white gaze and the controlling exercise of state power (Wacquant 2008). Confined within this metaphorical field, as Allen Feldman (1994: 409) suggests, the body of the black other is marked by 'the stigma of animality', a 'beastial imagery' that simultaneously prescribes police responses of 'taming and caging'. Such racial archetypes are sustained by additional frames. The 'urban jungle' metaphor, I argue, can be linked to an *Africanization* of the ghetto. The discourse of Africa, as theorized by Achille Mbembe (2001: 1), operates as a template for the iconicity of the American inner-city 'ghetto':

The African human experience constantly appears in the discourse of our times as an experience that can only be understood through a *negative interpretation*. Africa is never seen as possessing things and attributes properly part of 'human nature' ... At another level, discourse on Africa is almost always deployed in the framework (or on the fringes) of a meta-text about the *animal* – to be exact, about the *beast*: its experience, its world, and its spectacle.

Following this meta-frame, the imagined life of the 'ghetto' unfolds under several related signs: 'the strange and monstrous' and the intimate, specifically the 'intimacy' of primal bodies (Mbembe 2001: 1–3). Such notions are encoded in signifiers of the ghetto-look, whereby the animalistic and presocial disposition of the salient 'ghetto' other is reified and recycled in transglobal (white) consumer fantasies. In other words, visual markers of the abject body are made available as cultural commodities. Fashion accessories for purchase, which include 'ghetto fab nails' (designed to mimic claws or talons), 'ghetto fab wigs' and 'afro visor hats' (made with hair), and baggy or loosely fitting, sagging pants, are mass-produced and branded as 'ghetto chic', thereby transforming dominant notions of a contested black civility into white fashion statements. 'Ghetto chic' or 'slum fashion' is embedded in a discourse of mimesis and performance that transforms the 'bare life' (Agamben 1998) of poverty into domesticated, aestheticized objects – free-floating signifiers for forging identities that are performed on bodies uncoupled from the symbolic space of the black ghetto. Commoditization unlinks and uncouples signs by metonymic fragmentation and dissection – procedures that are frequently cited in feminist literature as 'demeaning', 'objectifying' and 'fetishistic' (e.g. Bartky 1990; MacKinnon 1992; Kilbourne 1999). Global appropriations and enactments of the ghetto-look may be experienced as libratory by mainstream consumers of American popular culture. While symbolically charged, when commodified as fashion, the ghetto-look provides a safe entry into a rebellious stance on consumer culture while promoting participation in its identity conferring promises. Thereby notions of the inner city ghetto as a negative space and depictions of its inhabitants as 'primitive', 'uncivilized' and 'premodern' are continuously recycled in material form. Transported as commodity fetishes, images of the failed city and the abject body are offered up for purchase to global consumers and translocal tourists as popular identity accessories.

Imagining Shantytowns: Representations of Urban Poverty on a Global Stage

How do these machinations of the 'inner city' poor in North America compare to views of urban deprivation in the global South? What kinds of tourist fantasies are propagated by images of those informal mega-settlements called 'shantytowns'? While the portable signs of the 'black ghetto' are encoded by racial histories and assertions of a failed modernity, shantytowns are seen as part of 'a new urban world'

(Neuwirth 2006). In contrast to the racially homogenized life-world of the 'black ghetto', shantytown builders are typified as utterly diverse populations, composed of international refugees, victims of civil war, desperate peasants, labour migrants, returning combat veterans, unemployed workers, poor families and low-income professionals (Neuwirth 2007: 74; Bauchner 2009; Perlman 2010). Although the social diversity and transnationality of squatters may be experienced as threatening by global city elites and middle class urbanites, who see flux, mobility and difference as signs of a destabilizing national and global economic order (Guano 2004), the global tourist-consumer gaze paints a different picture. Shantytowns are imagined as a new urban frontier, situated on the edge of wilderness, where makeshift houses are built in undesirable locations. Squatters are described as 'pioneer settlers' who transform uninhabitable spaces: 'swamps, floodplains, volcano slopes, unstable hillsides, rubbish mountains, chemical dumps' (Davis 2007: 121). Urban squatters are, in turn, regarded as positive agents, who labour to produce value and transform environments while patiently enduring the repressive apparatus of state and municipal governments. The figure of the squatter is correspondingly idealized as 'spirited, intelligent, and hard-working', with 'family values', who 'builds and rebuilds' and 'invests in community' (Neuwirth 2007: 71, 73). Such notions 'tend to romanticize squatters', who are envisioned as an emergent form of humanity, forged by economic globalization (Davis 2007: 42). Described as energetic, creative and vibrant, 'with the motivation and willingness to work' (Perlman 2010: xiii), squatters are imagined as urban pioneers, as builders of houses, families and communities, who strive to overcome conditions of displacement, impermanence and poverty.

The visual codes whereby shantytowns enter into global commodity culture are centred on images of architectural styles: the homes and living spaces built by squatters. Following Janice Perlman (2010: xiii), who draws on her long-time research in Rio de Janeiro, Brazil, shantytowns or *favelas*

> could be seen as the precursors to the 'new urbanism' with their high-density, low-rise architecture, featuring facades variously angled to catch a breeze or a view, and shade trees and shutters to keep them cool. The building-materials were construction-site discards and scraps that would now be called 'recycled materials'. They were owner-designed, owner-built, and owner-occupied. And they followed the organic curves of the hillsides rather than a rigid grid pattern.

In contrast to machinations of the 'black ghetto', which spectacularize the abject body to reify race, place and difference, shantytowns are typified by pictorial representations of the built environment. Since neo-liberal capitalism valorizes the products of work and labour, visual attention correspondingly shifts from the commoditization of bodily signs to signifiers of material culture, specifically architectural icons. The incidental use of rudimentary materials in building shelter housing is taken as a sign of creative ingenuity, as suggested by the following pastiche of commentaries:

[The inhabitants] try to make something beautiful out of whatever little they have (Nandy 2010). These are creative people who ... find ways to design ANYTHING to be desirable [by using the] 'styling' elements of poverty (Karsten 2007). Slum-Looks presents you [with] the need-based protection ... from the immutable forces of nature. The rawness and nakedness of plain materials, colors, and shades bring up the crudeness against which fashion receives its true beauty (Slum-Looks 2010).

The imagined life of squatters, in opposition to the imagined world of the ghetto, unfolds under the signs of naturalism, realism, labour and beauty. Global imaginaries and European representations of shantytowns accentuate urban poverty as a creative challenge, as I discuss in the following. My presentation of distinct case studies reveals the complexities of image-production and brings into focus the signifying strategies for the practice of global slum tourism.

Auto-iconic Architecture: Shantytowns as Works of Art

The works of European artists and photographers disclose a preoccupation with slums as material forms. This focus is apparent in depictions of shantytown architecture as works of art, a representational practice that identifies shanty-house builders as creative agents. Following Barbara Kirshenblatt-Gimblett (1998: 25, 242–243), the transformation of ethnographic artefacts into art not only refashions such objects in terms of a 'universalizing rhetoric' but grants those material edifices civilizational status: 'art transcends' conventional designations of difference which, she argued, are encoded in labels such as 'ethnic, folk, or primitive', by drawing on a 'humanizing' language of 'legitimation' and 'inclusiveness'. In other words, 'art' objects defy classification; they are, by definition, perceived as unique. Whereas the bodies and practices of ghetto inhabitants are imagined and commodified as 'quintessential attributes' or racialized traits of a rejected type of humanity (cf. Kirshenblatt-Gimblett 1998: 12), representations of shantytown architecture incite tourist desire and viewer attention by a turn to artistic appreciation. Through the universalizing code of art, western tourists can project a common understanding and transcend difference in the practice of looking without having to abandon an elite subject position. This is suggested by the following photographic example.

In an exhibit, titled *Case Study Homes*, German photographer Peter Bialobrzeski shows a series of snapshots of make-shift buildings from Baseco, a squatter settlement at the edge of Manila, which is home to approximately 70,000 people, mostly labour migrants from the Philippine countryside (Bialobrzeski 2010). The shanty houses are concentrated near the port of Manila, along the banks of the Pasig River Bay, which is a hazardous landscape that stretches across the grounds of a former garbage and chemical dumpsite. The case study photographs reveal provisional structures, small dwellings made from drift wood, bits and pieces of cardboard, corrugated metal and

Figure 1. *Case Study Homes*: Baseco, Manila, 2008. Photo by and copyright Peter Bialo-brzeski. Courtesy L.A. Galerie – Lothar Albrecht, Frankfurt, Germany.

other cast-off materials (Figure 1). As revealed by the photographer's portrait shots of single houses, each unit is uniquely fashioned. Assembled from scavenged materials, composed as a distinct architectural montage, 'these buildings bear an anarchical, piratic, improvised appearance' (Schmitt 2009). When Bialobrzeski prepared his photographs for an exhibit in Frankurt in 2008, the stock market collapsed and the media declared a global economic crisis. These events seemed to lend resonance to the artist's photographic collection. The images capture the material conditions of poverty and displacement by showing an urban landscape composed of homes with tattered walls and stick-branched roofs, makeshift constructs, which are hesitantly anchored to the ground by uneven wooden poles.

The photographs not only make visible the material conditions of poverty in Manila's urban periphery but also attest to the inhabitants' resourcefulness in making a living. But in addition to revealing the labour migrants' home-building efforts, the transglobal and European appeal of the photos is further enhanced by their presentation as art forms. The crafting of a visual aesthetic of shantytown houses is consequently of central importance. This is clearly articulated by one exhibit review:

The pictures of this photographic investigation follow a strict composition. The self-made shacks [built from] old slats and posts, covers, roofing cardboard, corrugated metal, and all kinds of cloth fill out each picture in its entirety, like in a portrait. In many cases the photographer chose a slanted front view, displaying both the front and side wall of the house. Pure front perspectives are rare, as are two or more buildings in one picture. The soft natural light of the clouded sky makes for even lighting, without stark light and shadow contrasts. Pictures showing people beside the buildings are the exception (Schmitt 2009: 1).

The images magnify architectural eccentricities in a naturalized urban landscape. Public space is shown devoid of people, history and culture. Signs of social life are missing. Poverty artefacts are shown as auto-iconic art objects. The photos 'provide no commentary; the scenes are marked by both an exaggerated lack of identity and a paradoxical self-referentiality' (Glasmeier 2008). The shacks are displayed as curiosities, strange but fascinating pebbles on a beach. Nearly all traces of the inhabitants have been removed. Even the sandy-ground bears no evidence of human presence: artefacts of domestic activity, including scraps of building material or scatters of garbage have been expunged from the visual field. Glimpses of freshly washed clothing hanging to dry in the wind allude to the occupants' presence. The photographs show shanty houses as edifices of architectural distinction and conjure attention by vibrant colours: 'Peter Bialobrzeski here as in all of his previous series uses color photography. From a Westerner's perspective, the makeshift dwellings with their colorful tarpaulins and converted advertising billboards turn into works of art: they are collages of color and diversity' (Schmitt 2009: 2). The Baseco settlement is not only beautified but staged as a world of wondrous and exotic houses, an urban dreamscape, in which the allure of colour functions as 'the vehicle of spectacle' and as 'the language of consumption' (Lutz & Collins 1993: 94).

Rendered visually devoid of contextualizing signifiers, viewers can conjure variable interpretations about the identities of the home builders and their life circumstances, as articulated by the following commentary by an exhibit spectator: 'The developing world clutter of shantytowns [is] the new global grassroots of style. They inspire aesthetically, displaying amazing inventiveness and endless formal variation. Shantytowns are exemplary recyclers and have extremely modest environmental footprints' (Imomus 2009). As suggested here, urban poverty is deemed a positive 'practice' that promotes creative survival skills and enhances environmental sustainability. Sociologist Janice Perlman (2010: 334) calls into question such a 'glorification' of shanty residents 'as models of utopian sustainability' whereby the living conditions of the poor (whether in the Philippines or Brazil) are depoliticized by a global imaginary that romanticizes poverty 'as the solution to environmental problems, overpopulation, and housing shortages'. In the photos by Bialobrzeski, the alter-realities of global capitalism, the conditions of displacement and the impact of poverty on families or communities are expunged from the visual field by transforming poverty artefacts into aestheticized art objects: clean, colourful and uniquely spectacular. In an emancipatory move that simultaneously obscures the human faces of the inhabitants, the photographer's works 'let "art" speak for itself' (Kirshenblatt-Gimblett 1998: 245). The exotic foreignness of the objects is subdued by the spectators' familiarity with the artistic frame and, therefore, inspires touristic attention throughout Europe.

Estranged Typifications: (Re)Imagining Shantytowns for a Global Market

Other representational works are preoccupied with tactics of estrangement. Rather than featuring magnified portrait shots of single slum dwellings, which are displayed as works of art, this technique records the architectural panorama of entire shanty-towns. In every case, however, shantytown architecture is not only typified as colossal, but as a monumental construct whose meaning on the ground is inaccessible or unin-telligible to the Western observer. The photographic images are, in turn, modified and altered to inscribe a modernist coherence, a normative logical order. In the process, slum architecture is visually estranged, a process of intervention that is restaged as an artistic performance. Techniques of estrangement and defamiliarization provide an optical screen that translates the found object into a comprehensible composite (cf. Kirshenblatt-Gimblett 1998: 203, 235). New iconicities of shantytowns are thereby brought into existence, which incite both spectator and tourist curiosity by calling attention to the grotesque or uncanny.

Such a representational strategy is evident in the works of the Spanish photographer and video artist Dionisio González, who has become known in Europe for his startling depictions of shantytowns in Sao Paulo and Rio de Janeiro, Brazil. The artist's focus is on the 'geometric disarray' of these communal architectures. Whereas in the previous example, the photos idealized a unique, non-standard architectural design as a form of art, González attempts to visually redesign a form of urban architecture that he perceives to be 'unplanned', 'disorderly' and disturbingly 'chaotic'. According to a statement by his agency, '[t]he labyrinthine and improvised structures of the favelas are in a constant state of flux; they continually grow and change, completely untouched by the logical order of a planned city. Dionisio González attempts to capture this flux in his photographic works' (FTC 2006). But, in addition to his camera work, González relies on computer-assisted imaging techniques to superpose modernist structures and geometric forms on his photographic images, thereby fabricating a new architectural aesthetic. In an attempt to intervene in 'the architectural disarrangement of shantytowns in Sao Paulo, Brazil', the artist recombines 'the clean and modern with the grungy and scattered' (Spear 2006). While each of the works emphasizes different motifs, the artist pursues a modernist alteration of the shanty houses, which are reshaped by the visual insertion of objects, patterns and appendages to accentuate an orderly synchronicity of form. The result is a surreal urban landscape, in which

Figure 2. *An Assembled City*: Nova Heliopolis II, 2008. Photo by and copyright Dionisio González.

the colours and exterior shapes of squatter houses are blended and fused to create startling but impossible, non-functional designs (Figure 2).

The artist's *favela* images are always lifeless: streets and sidewalks are swept clean of garbage; cars, tyre tracks, windows, illusive entryways and sometimes laundry hanging from a clothes-line are the sole indexes and reference points for a human presence. In focusing attention on 'these massive, unregulated settlements', González not only attempts 'a partial intervention of these "chaotic spaces"' but 'proposes a radical restructuring' of shantytown architecture by 'improving the precarious conditions of habitability' (Maxestrella 2007). Although these representational works acknowledge the agency of shanty-inhabitants, the product of their labour is perceived as deficient, requiring intervention. Techniques of estrangement become a photographic or artistic tool for the visual erasure of poverty, as if *seeing* and *looking at* shantytowns must be facilitated by the transformation of social and architectural realities for a global consumer public. The manufactured images not only impose a modernist logic but also present visual realities emptied of people and social worlds. Through these tactics of estrangement, shantytown architecture is no longer envisioned as 'home', 'house' or 'dwelling' inhabited by real people. The artist's modernist critique of informal urban settlements is apparent in images of ruinous landscapes, dead zones and bizarre architectural forms, which are exhibited as 'exquisite cadavers' (see FTC 2006). The ideological turn against shantytowns is imprinted in the modus of representation.

Iconicities of Disempowerment: Politicized Representations of Shantytowns

The ideological moment is not absent from other artistic exhibits. But, in some instances, artists inscribe their work with a critique of the global dynamics of power, a perspective that is intentionally concealed in the previous examples. How can relations of urban global inequality be imaginatively staged as an artistic performance for tourists? In such works, the artists' political commitments are encoded by a shift in focus, perspective and means of representation. In one example, as I discuss in the following, the 'shantytown' or 'slum' is staged in the form of a miniature model. In the tourist encounter, miniaturization serves a strategic political statement of the squatters' disempowerment in a global terrain of exclusion, invisibility and domination. Such a shantytown-installation appeared at the 2010 Art Biennale in Sydney, Australia, an international exposition titled 'The Beauty of Distance: Songs of Survival in a Precarious Age'. In addition to other displays by prominent figures, the event featured the work of the French-Algerian artist Kader Attia, a vision of a shantytown called *Kasbah* (Figure 3). Although designed as a reflection on the living conditions of the urban poor world-wide, the artist reimagines slum architecture by use of a single icon: a series of metal roofs, assembled from corrugated steel slabs, constructed at different heights and installed at different angles. Stretched across the ground of an entire exhibit hall, the installation is a monumental patchwork of metallic silver, rust and colour, a construct replete with satellite dishes, doors, assorted tyres and other materials.

Figure 3. *Kasbah*: Shantytown installation by Kader Attia, Sydney Art Biennale 2010. Photo by and copyright Alison Young.

The installation emerged from a montage of memories and images that Kader Attia assembled by drawing on his own life experiences. The artist, whose family immigrated to France from Algeria, grew up in a *banlieue* of Paris, a North African immigrant community on the urban periphery, a site of poverty and discrimination. In addition to studying in Paris and Barcelona, Attia spent three years in Brazzaville and Kinshasa (Democratic Republic of Congo), where he acquired insights about urban disfranchisement that undoubtedly shaped his artistic visions and representational choices. Although his work consists of a bricolage of translocal images, Attia envisioned his installation in terms of the historical reality of a *Kasbah*, a North African *Medina* or Islamic city marked by a fortress or citadel built on the edge of town. By using the architectural trope of a North African frontier fortress, Attia reimagines shantytowns as defensive or protective constructs. In the exhibit, transported into the world of the present, this thematic is evident in the artist's use of silver-coloured sheet metal, a possible signifier of the slum occupants' protective armour. The installation is forged from corrugated metal slabs that are variously arranged across a horizontal ground or positioned in diagonal alignment to form visible roof coverings. The image of a shantytown as a protective enclosure is implied, simulated by an artistic construct that invites visitors to look at, walk across and step on the metal house-components to re-enact the tactics of power – visually and physically.

The socio-spatial formations of disadvantage, dispossession and disempowerment have been encoded into the exhibit. Positioned on the ground, at the spectators' feet, the shanty rooftops come into view as isometric miniatures, creating an illusion of spatial and social distance. The objects on display are apprehended from a bird's-eye perspective, which is a performative imprint of the 'tourist gaze' (Urry 2002): exhibit visitors, like slum tourists, appropriate the sight of power by 'gazing at the poor' from a safe distance, from an aerial view and from an elevated position (Freire-Medeiros 2009a; 2010), which are vantage points of privilege. In a further attempt to stage relations of inequality in performative terms, exhibit visitors were invited to walk across the installation's metal components. According to the artist,

> The difficulty of taking each cautious step over this uneven, variegated surface provokes a consideration of the successes and failures of the globalised economy and of the human ability to wrest a livable existence from nothing. Thus by walking tentatively over the work [across the metal roofs or the metal slabs], visitors were not only to become part of the project but also implicitly part of the economic and power matrix that created these shantytowns (Chung 2010).

The interactive experiment is further described by one observer:

> It was interesting to observe the reactions and behaviors of different people (children and adults). Some people just tromped and plodded along as if it was just another floor to walk on and others, mainly children, seemed to tread carefully and cautiously with a sense of contemplation (Temby 2010).

Kader Attia's work focuses attention on unequal power relations, striving to make visible acts of privilege through a performative endeavour. Whether practices of enactment can assist in dismantling tactics of domination and exploitation remains to be seen. In the exhibit, the primary signifiers of urban disfranchisement appear as material icons: shantytown architecture and shanty houses. In contrast to the centrality of the racialized human form, which is central for the imaginary of the North American 'ghetto', the slum inhabitants and city builders are rendered visually absent, as in the previous examples. But here 'human absence' signifies lack of power by those rendered unseen. Nevertheless, in the installation, the historical contexts and causal relations of urban poverty are discursively constructed rather than visually presented. In an act of 'topographical amnesia' (Verilio 1998), corrugated metal roofs become representational signs of shantytowns and their (dematerialized) inhabitants, which circulate as globally mobile signifiers that are consumed as art works by tourists.

Staged Authenticities: Miniaturized Shantytown as Portable Art Project

The miniature model of a slum does not necessarily convey an ideological critique of global power relations. A different intent and message is inscribed in the portable art project exemplified by the miniaturized *favela* known as 'Project *Morrinho*': a scale model of a Brazilian shantytown that has been displayed in various European cities. The project emerged in the late 1990s as a socially integrated practice, a children's game, based in the *Pereira da Silva favela* on the edge of Rio de Janeiro. Morrinho ('little hill' in Portuguese) came into being when local teenage boys began to build a model of their community on an abandoned hill by using scavenged bricks and other discarded materials. The brick city model-building was inspired by Nelcilan Souza de Oliveira, who 'arrived in Rio de Janeiro' in 1997 at the age of fourteen:

> Coming from a small city, Nelcilan went to Pereira to live with his parents. That was the first time he had seen or lived in a favela. He was so impressed by his new reality that he started to reproduce it in his backyard with bricks and paint, leftovers from his father's work in construction. [He invited his friends to participate in the construction of distinct neighborhoods.] Each boy became the 'owner' of one favela and was responsible for its maintenance, construction, and its inhabitants. These micro favelas represent real ones like Fogueteiro, Prazeres, Borel, Grota, Turano, Querosene, Fallete, and Encontro, among others. Morrinho became their daily game (Duarte 2010: 39–40).

The miniature model gradually expanded in size (covering over 350 m^2) as the boys began to use the mini-world project as a playground for enacting the social dramas of everyday life, using Lego block characters, toy cars and other props. In this miniature brick-city playground, the teenagers not only enacted gang wars, street violence and clashes with police but also forged dreams of a different life.

The creation of such safe play space proved to be important for several reasons. Based on her research and work in the favela, Rita Duarte (2010) offers several pertinent insights. Pereira da Silva is among the smallest *favela* communities in Rio de Janeiro. Until the twenty-first century, residents were intensely isolated from the outside world. Urban mobility, social activities and business enterprise were controlled by gangs, drug trafficking and violence. Street life was governed by fear. Following Duarte (2010: 36), this situation persisted until 1998, when the state government enforced rigorous security measures and implemented a new policy aimed at the societal integration of children and teenagers. Even though public violence has decreased, issues of safety remain tenuous (Rocha 2009). Government intervention fostered new endeavours, promoted contact with the outside world and initiated engagement with university researchers. A documentary film initiative titled *Projeto Morrinho* (by Fábio Gavião and Markão Oliveira) and subsequent media attention in 2001 attracted artists, tourists and journalists to the brick city playground. With the support teachers and university staff, the Morrinho project took shape as a non-governmental organization (NGO). Subsequent involvement with several external and international agencies promotes the expansion of the organization's various endeavours:

> As an NGO, Morrinho works in four different fields: TV Morrinho (production of audio visual material), Expo Morrinho (exhibition and reproduction of the scale model), Social Morrinho (providing courses for local kids in film production and foreign language), and Tourism Morrinho (tours to see the model and the NGO headquarter) (Duarte 2010: 40).

Encouraged by the public response to their work, the project's founding organizers began to craft small-scale replicas of the original playground model, which were displayed at international events, including the *Urban World Summit* in Barcelona (2004), *Point Ephémère* in Paris (2005), the *Venice Art Biennale* (2007), the *Brazilian Contemporary Art Festival* in Rotterdam (2008), and the *Festival Brazil* in London (2010). In this endeavour, art and capitalism have forged a productive alliance, attracting further interest by media representatives, prospective tourists and investors:

> Project Morrinho has increasingly garnered attention for its amazing aesthetics and the ingenuity of its child creators. We have been able to use that attention to evolve, not only as a work of art, but also into an organization with aspiration for social change (Morrinho 2010).

These are important points for consideration. While the production of works of art may be rewarding, even lucrative, the creation of *favela* models for a global consumer gaze has several consequences. The sculptures are crafted as visual representations of a Brazilian shantytown. Made for European tourists and consumer publics, the small-scale models foreground a stylized representation of an architectural template, which

Figure 4. The portable art project: The *Morrinho Project* at the Venice Art Biennale, June 2007. Photo by Paolo Tonon. Creative Commons license 2.0 generic; some rights reserved.

is in turn consumed as an iconic typification of a Rio de Janeiro slum by viewers (Figure 4). These replicas, commissioned to tour to European art exhibits and ethnic festivals, have been stripped of the dynamic signs of social life that once populated the original playground model. Transported to Europe, reduced to a physical form, transformed from an object of use-value (playground) to a commodity object (displayed model city), the exhibited artefact reifies *favela* architecture and signifies the vitality of a Rio de Janeiro *favela* by representational symbols, including vibrant colours. But a sculpture is, by definition, a fixed medium, a freeze-frame model, which cannot convey street life, activities and social dynamics through indexical signs. On display are the physical signifiers of city life: architecture, brick houses, streets and stairways, awash with colour, built on a hill, a simulation of public life, interspersed by a scatter of earth and sand, bushes and grass, signs of nature artificially implanted to create a sense of authenticity and realism. Abstracted as a work of art, the exhibited sculpture has been transformed into a consumable commodity for tourists.

My analysis is not intended to diminish the significance of the project or its relevance for the exhibitors. But the Morrinho project, like every artefact, has intrinsic signifying limitations. A miniature model, like a photograph, as I discussed earlier in this essay, inevitably renders hyper visible select moments of life while it excludes others. My aim is to render explicit the spectre of sight encoded in the Morrinho artefact as a physical model that is displayed as art (as a touristic commodity form) in Europe. And whether spectacularized as a work of art at the Venice Biennale in 2007 or the Festival Brazil in London in 2010, the exhibit shows a miniature *favela* as an ensemble of colourful 'houses on a hill', without visual attention to urban poverty or the dynamic life worlds of shantytown residents. The iconic emphasis is on slum architecture in an urban environment that is organically moulded to a natural landscape. The visual gaze is introverted, turned into itself: the model artefact focuses viewers' attention on the difficulties or hazards of physical mobility in an urban space designed along steep slopes, with narrow pathways and unfinished roads. While the immediacy of the natural environment is rendered visibly apparent, the *favela*'s proximity to wealthy neighbourhoods or the intrusive presence of the state apparatus is not included in the model's visual frame.

Nourishing a global consumer desire for realism and authenticity, the Morrinho models are presented as genuine artefacts, crafted by Rio de Janeiro's children. This image of a depoliticized carceral space, which is colourful, playful and vital, confirms such a message. The iconic typification of shantytowns as 'colourful' becomes a visual signifier for the diversity of *favela* inhabitants, who are not shown as ethnic or racial types. Rainbow colours, in Europe's consumer imaginaries, not only inspire visual interest but also evoke a sense of playful contentment: poor but 'happy', 'smiling natives', which are images that appeal to the echoes of the colonial imaginary (see Rolfes 2010). Such signifiers participate in the manufacture of consumable images for European tourists, a process Dean MacCannell (1976: 91–108) termed 'staged authenticities': objects or places are contrived to look as consumers or potential tourists expect them to look. The exhibit participates in such an endeavour by displaying a Brazilian shanty community as an exotic object for European consumption. An architectural artefact, like the Morrinho project, participates in the staging of authenticity by creating a freeze-frame picture, in which historical time stands still. As Barbara Kirschenblatt-Gimblett (1998: 8) suggests, in such cases the 'interface of a cultural encounter' between tourists and residents is hidden 'to foster the illusion of no mediation, to produce "tourist realism", which is itself a highly mediated effect'. My exploration of the symbolic messages of the Morrinho exhibit is thereby concerned with the process of cultural translation and the manner in which such understandings can become globally mobile imaginaries.

Attention to such representational strategies does not distract from questions of tourism. Visual artefacts that travel along international consumer routes undoubtedly influence the global perception of shantytowns as potential tourist destinations. But whether this travelling exhibit provides a successful strategy for urban economic development or social transformation in a Brazilian *favela* is difficult to assess and exceeds the scope of my essay. Scholarly research on the Pereira da Silva community is scarce. How do we assess the impact of the Morrinho exhibit on the revitalization of this *favela*? Based on an extensive study by Rita Duarte (2010), who not only carried out research in Pereira da Silva and Rocinha, but also worked as a long-term volunteer for the NGO Morrinho, we learn that in this small *favela* community, business enterprise is practically non-existent. Local entrepreneurship is based on individual initiatives, without collective community involvement and without collaboration between different initiatives; benefit sharing is absent and, according to Duarte (2010: 51), 'there are no efforts to move in that direction'. Financial returns for the Morrinho projects are limited and mainly derive from the NGO involvement in film production and the exhibitions (Duarte 2010: 47). Given the low profit margins, economic benefits for either project participants or community members are not apparent. Likewise low-frequency tourist travel to the community generates no significant business opportunities. Despite these findings, Rita Duarte (2010: 48) saw clear 'social benefits' from the NGO Morrinho, whose 'work seems to be appreciated by the residents and is a source of pride for the community'. As such, the transnational exhibit of the Morrinho project appears to be engaged in the role of a cultural ambassador – to forge an entry into the global imaginary and to thereby secure an identity-and-place-recognition for the *favela*.

Image Scavengers: Shantytowns as Icons of Political Protest in Europe

The mobile yet generic imaginings of shantytowns have found resonance among European urban rebels. In protests against the shiny global city, where corporate interests, tourist industries and private enterprise collude to produce urban space as marketable commodities and where, in turn, non-conformists, the homeless, the unemployed and members of alternative youth culture are increasingly marginalized, activists seek signs and icons to promote their attempts at resistance (cf. Mitchell 1995; Fenster 2005). Thus, in Zurich, Switzerland, youth groups and members of the alternative scene moved to take control of urban spaces adjacent to the city's financial centre and banking district. In the summer of 2005, protesters proceeded with plans to 'invade' and 'occupy' land by building makeshift shacks and huts along the city's river bank, drawing on free-floating images of a Third World shantytown (*Hüttensiedlung*) in order to reclaim a sense of political self-determination and cultural self-realization (Indymedia 2005). The protest was sparked by shrinking civil liberties and the intensifying police surveillance of urban public space in Zurich. The demonstration organizers also wanted to draw attention to rising costs of living in a global city that catered to the needs of upper class residents and big business while pushing the poor to the urban margins. As affordable apartments have been replaced by expensive condominiums and office spaces, working class residents are forced out of their homes in the city centre (Tagesschau SF 2005). The deployment of shantytown-imagery appeared to legitimate attempts to reclaim rights to the city by pirate urbanization and by the occupation of contested public space.

The imported image of a generic shantytown provided more than an empty ideational façade. In the context of political protest, a squatter settlement was designed and built in accordance with typified or generic assumptions about Third World slums. In addition to the provisional shantytown shacks, the squatter area was equipped 'with sleeping tents, an information center, an outlook tower, a prayer tent, a chicken coop, a town plaza, a wine bar, a whisky bar, two beer gardens, and a gay and lesbian center' (Whereisej 2005). As a realist moment, sanitary facilities were absent inside the squatter complex. During the protest, the squatter-inhabitants reclaimed public space as communal space. In the event, the global imaginary of the shantytown was strategically deployed as a system of signs that could be used to articulate local interests in opposition to the Swiss state and city government. The model of a typified shantytown was appropriated and socially performed in terms of a judicial discourse: the rights to urban space. Issues of poverty and the displacement of real-world shantytown residents were indirectly brought into focus by mimetically equating the plight of squatters in Third World cities with the disempowerment of global city residents in Europe. While this equation points to the structural approximations of urban inequality under global capitalism (see Sassen 2002), it also conceals the specific conditions of disempowerment and causes of marginalization in different parts of the world.

Johannesburg in Berlin: The 'Shantytown' as Corporate Amusement Park

The iconicity of shantytown architecture, as I have shown, has become a part of a mobile imaginary that can be appropriated for a range of tourist interests: art, politics, humanitarian endeavours, ideological struggle and entertainment. As a representational sign, which has retained its detachment from fixed human faces, unlike the mobile imaginary of the 'black ghetto', the construct of the shantytown can be installed for tourist viewing anywhere. I began the discussion of case studies with shanty houses as works of art. The final example provides a glimpse of the appropriation of the construct 'shantytown' as a profitable entertainment space in Germany. During the Johannesburg World Cup soccer games in summer 2010, private enterprise in Berlin sought to increase its profit margins by building a South African slum as an amusement park in the centre of the city (Figures 5 and 6). The idea was to bring Johannesburg to Berlin by building 'a slum-look-alike fun park' (Mösken 2010). The project of building a phantasmatic slum-city commenced. Urban junkyards were scavenged for the building materials: cardboard, rusty containers, old car tyres and corrugated metal were deposited on the Spree riverbank right next to *Bar 24*, a popular Berlin club. The materials were hammered together to create a rickety shantytown-style building complex, complete with a shaman-bar shack, paintings of stereotyped black people on the fence surrounding the fake squatter compound, and a gaming space with fake laundry hanging from clotheslines.

The club's shantytown amusement park included additional entertainment areas: 'The Johannesburg theme park contains a mini-stadium to watch the games on the big screen, a skateboard park, beach volleyball, a "Capetown" grill restaurant, and the

Figure 5. Johannesburg Shanty town as amusement park, Berlin 2010. Photo by and copyright Katharina Wagner.

Figure 6. Bar 25–Johannesburg in Berlin. Photo by and copyright Carolin Saage.

club itself has been enclosed in a fully decked out shantytown' (BPM Bella 2010). Berlin's residents were invited to sit in this simulated slum to watch live soccer games in the 'township' backyard, listen to techno back-beat music, drink champagne, eat the open-fire grilled steaks, and enjoy the realism of the experience with *Bar 25*'s signature confetti (see Mösken 2010).

> The concept of Bar 25 is a whole alternate universe where people can immerse themselves, not just in the parties for a few hours, but for days, and take up a session in the sauna, a dip in the pool and tan all day by the river to round off a good evening's dance-off (BPM Bella 2010).

The shantytown in Berlin 2010 was built as a total entertainment experience and eccentric lifestyle choice, a 'full immersion' fantasy-experience in a neo-liberal consumer paradise.

Concluding Reflections

The promise of globalization, conceived as a world without frontiers, is described as 'a world of flows' and 'liquid' social forms (Appadurai 1996; Bauman 2000). But in the new millennium, globalization has not produced a singular or unified world order. Neo-liberal capitalism does not operate as a single-space economy, 'as a non-contradictory, uncontested space' (Hall 2000: 32). In a global world, marked by flows, movements and mobilities, as Arjun Appadurai (2001: 5) observed, the structural order of things has been destabilized: 'objects, persons, images, and discourses are in relations of disjuncture'. Political forms, cultural imaginaries, social lives and economic interests engage global possibilities along different and sometimes contradictory trajectories. Capitalist imperatives and the manufacture of elusive authenticities may intersect to produce 'counterintuitive' results (Comaroff 2009: 1). Under globalization, ethnoracial or geospatial logics can be reclaimed for profit. Likewise, the imaginative geographies of privilege and disadvantage may be reconfigured: forged by recourse to space, signifiers of race and urban poverty, and by new consumer practices, including tourism.

From this perspective, we can further decipher the negation of the North American inner-city 'ghetto'. In the global imaginary, the 'ghetto' is identified as the antinomy of an open-ended future. Stigmatized by the machinations of neo-liberal capitalism, the urban-core inhabitants 'are vanishing into the sinkhole of poverty in desolate and abandoned enclaves of decaying cities' (Giroux 2007: 309). As such, the ghetto is presumed to hold no promise but presents the ruins of modernity, an archive of the failure of the industrial city, its crumbling infrastructure and its pathologized residents, who must be spatially contained or imaginatively harnessed – 'caught in a forever petrified freeze-frame' (Lafleur 2010: 208). These imagining are reified by popular culture industries, as I have shown, which have begun to mass produce racialized body-traits (nails, hair, garments) as commodities that can be marketed to white consumer-tourists as countercultural identity-enhancements. The manufacture of the oppositional status of the urban 'black ghetto' as a primitive, uncivilized and violent space is crucial for perpetuating consumer fantasies of difference and distance, which has most recently sparked a global demand for 'gangster tourism' in the US inner city (Smith 2010). The construct of the shantytown, by contrast, appears to engender a more optimistic interpretation. As a global artefact, it embodies the 'hope of history': each foot of non-arable urban frontier-land transformed by squatter settlers, each house built, however incomplete, is perceived as a 'relaunch of an ongoing promise, a "not yet", a "what is coming", which – always – separates hope from utopia' (Mbembe 2001: 206). While the end of modernity is conceived through temporal metaphors of urban ruination and traces of the abject body (the Africanized ghetto), the future of globalization itself remains yet undetermined. Located 'at the nexus of global forces of transnational flows and networks of activity' (Gotham 2007b: 827), urban squatters and their transformative labour are conceived as iconic manifestations of this (unconsummated) futuristic 'hope of history'. Shantytowns, identified as productive works of transglobal (postmodern) agents, engender tourist desire and embody Western longing, which can be manufactured and encoded in consumable signs.

Under global consumer capitalism, the relation of people to the city and urban space has come to be imagined and represented as a lifestyle. As I have argued, the Western signs of difference (poverty, race, place and housing) are visually appropriated, enacted, performed and consumed in European ontological space by placing emphasis 'on conjuring affect, itself ever more a commodity, by aesthetic means' (Comaroff 2009: 16). While culture can perform the work of difference and distinction, by drawing on variable aesthetic and affective repertoires, the emergent volatility of white (European) privilege in a global world order is stabilized by recourse to mobile imaginaries and portable signs of urban poverty, which simulate existential life worlds and transform attention, empathy or desire into generic discourses of artistic appreciation. In this context, slum tourism and the consumption of mimetic objects and exotic artefacts have become central practices. Most recently, the iconicity of the shantytown has been deployed to create new consumer experiences by total immersion, although this modus of adventure tourism, as I have shown, is staged at home, in Berlin or elsewhere in Europe, and is provided as a mere simulacrum, as a corporate intervention in facilitating amusement and entertainment.

References

Agamben, G. (1998) *Homo Sacer* (Stanford, CA: Stanford University Press).
Appadurai, A. (1996) *Modernity at Large* (Minneapolis, MN: University of Minnesota Press).
Appadurai, A. (2001) Grassroots globalization and the research imagination, in: A. Appadurai (Ed.) *Globalization*, pp. 1–20 (Durham, NC: Duke University Press).
Bartky, S. L. (1990) *Femininity and Domination* (New York: Routledge).

Bauchner, J. (2009) Caracas, the city that built itself, *Tripple Canopy*, May 7. Available at http://canopycanopycanopy.com/6/the_city_that_built_itself (accessed August 2010).

Bauman, Z. (2000) *Liquid Modernity* (Cambridge: Polity Press).

Bialobrzeski, P. (2010) *Case Study Homes* (Ostfildern: Hatje Cantz).

BPM Bella (2010) Berlin's infamous Bar 25 does world cup Joburg style, *BPM Life*, June 22. Available at http://bpmlife.co.za/?p=1725 (accessed October 2010).

Chung, F. (2010) Kader Attia: Kasbah installation, *Designboom*, May 23. Available at http://www.designboom.com/weblog/cat/10/view/10286/kader-attia-kasbah-installation.html (accessed 29 December 2010).

Comaroff, J. L. J. (2009) *Ethnicity, Inc.* (Chicago, IL: The University of Chicago Press).

Davis, M. (2007) *Planet of Slums* (London: Verso).

Duarte, R. (2010) Exploring the social impacts of favela tourism, Master's dissertation, Environmental Sciences, Wageningen UR, The Netherlands.

Feldman, A. (1994) On cultural anesthesia, *American Ethnologist*, 21(2), pp. 404–418.

Fenster, T. (2005) Identity issues and local governance, *Social Identities*, 11(1), pp. 21–36.

Freire-Medeiros, B. (2002) The travelling city, Doctoral dissertation, Binghamton University, State University of New York.

Freire-Medeiros, B. (2007) A favela que se vê e que se vende, *Revista Brasileira de Ciências Sociais*, 22(65), pp. 62–72.

Freire-Medeiros, B. (2009a) The favela and its touristic transits, *Geoforum*, 40(4), pp. 580–588.

Freire-Medeiros, B. (2009b) *Gringo na laje* [Gringos on the roof top] (Rio de Janeiro: Editoria FGV).

Freire-Medeiros, B. (2010) Gazing at the poor. Available at http://events.sas.ac.uk/fileadmin/documents/postgraduate/Papers_London_Debates_2010/Freire_Medeiros__Gazing_at_the_poor.pdf (accessed 25 March 2011).

Freire-Medeiros, B. (2011) *Touring Poverty* (London: Routledge).

Friedmann, J. (2006) The world city hypothesis, in: N. Brenner & R. Keil (Eds) *The Global Cities Reader*, pp. 67–71 (New York: Routledge).

FTC (2006) Dionizio González: an assembled city, *Galerie Fiedler Taubert Contemporary*, Press Release, April 3. Available at http://fiedler.null2.net/index.php?id=329&presse=1 (accessed 5 January 2011).

Gibson, T. A. (2006) City living, D.C. style, in: T. A. Gibson & M. D. Lowes (Eds) *Urban Communication*, pp. 83–110 (New York: Rowman and Littlefield).

Giroux, H. A. (2007) Violence, Katrina, and the biopolitics of disposability, *Theory, Culture, and Society*, 24(7–8), pp. 305–309.

Glasmeier, M. (2008) The presentness of the unpredetermined, *L.A. Galerie Lothar Albrecht*. Available at http://lagallery-frankfurt.de/PBTransitionUK.pdf (accessed October 2010).

Goldberg, D. T. (2006) Racial Europeanization, *Ethnic and Racial Studies*, 29(2), pp. 331–364.

Gotham, K. F. (2007a) Critical theory and Katrina, *City*, 11(1), pp. 81–99.

Gotham, K. F. (2007b) (Re)branding the Big Easy, *Urban Affairs Review*, 42(6), pp. 823–850.

Guano, E. (2004) The denial of citizenship, *City & Society* 16(1), pp. 69–97.

Hall, S. (2000) The local and the global, in: A. D. King (Ed.) *Culture, Globalization, and the World-System*, pp. 19–39 (Minneapolis, MN: University of Minneapolis Press).

Holloway, J. C. (2009) *The Business of Tourism*, 8th ed. (Harlow: Financial Times Prentice Hall).

Imomus (Nick Currie) (2009) Click opera–case study homes, *LiveJournal*, April 29. Available at http://imomus.livejournal.com/453897.html (accessed 10 October 2010).

Indymedia (2005) Zürich: shanty-town besetzt, *indymedia.org*, July 30. Available at http://de.indymedia.org/2005/07/123976.shtml (accessed 10 January 2011).

Karsten (PolluteLessDotCom) (2007) Any change is welcome, *Grist*, comments section, October 1. Available at http://www.grist.org/article/fashion-victim-of-climate-change#comments (accessed 29 December 2010).

Kilbourne, J. (1999) *Can't Buy my Love* (New York: Simon and Schuster).

King, A. D. (2006) World cities, in: N. Brenner & R. Keil (Eds) *The Global Cities Reader*, pp. 319–324 (New York: Routledge).

Kirschenblatt-Gimblett, B. (1998) *Destination Culture* (Berkeley: University of California Press).

Lafleur, M. (2010) Tracing the absent-present, *TOPIA: Canadian Journal of Cultural Studies*, 23–24, pp. 203–226.

Lennon, J. & Foley, M. (2000) *Dark Tourism* (London: Continuum).

Linke, U. (2010) Fortress Europe, *TOPIA: Canadian Journal of Cultural Studies*, 23/24, pp. 100–120.

Linke, U. (2011) Technologies of othering, in: M. Ribeiro Sanches (Ed.) *Europe in Black and White*, pp. 123–142 (London: Chicago University Press/Intellect Books).

Lutz, C. A. & Collins, J. L. (1993) *Reading the National Geographic* (Chicago, IL: University of Chicago Press).

MacCannell, D. (1976) *The Tourist* (Berkeley: University of California Press).

MacKinnon, C. (1992) *Only Words* (Cambridge: Harvard University Press).

Maxestrella (2007) Dionisio González: Cartografías para a remoçao, *Galeria Max Estrella*, January 25. Available at http://www.maxestrella.com/artistas/dionisio/expo%2007/prensa_eng.htm (accessed 5 January 2011).

Mbembe, A. (2001) *On the Postcolony* (Berkeley, CA: University of California Press).

Mbembe, A. (2003) Necropolitics, *Public Culture*, 15(1), pp. 11–40.

Mendieta, E. (2007) Penalized spaces, *City*, 11(3), pp. 384–390.

Meschkank, J. (2011) Investigations into slum tourism in Mumbai, *GeoJournal*, 76(1), pp. 47–62.

Mexal, S. J. (2004) Consuming the city, in: M. Allister (Ed.) *Eco-Man*, pp. 235–247 (Charlottesville, VA: University of Virginia Press).

Mitchell, D. (1995) The end of public space? *Annals of the Association of American Geographers*, 85(1), pp. 103–133.

Morrinho (2010) Project Morrinho – a small revolution, *Project Morrinho*. Available at http://www.morrinho.com/Morrinho/Projeto_Morrinho___Uma_Pequena_Revolucao.html (accessed 5 January 2010).

Mösken, A.-L. (2010) Johannesburg 24: corporate slumworld, *Exberliner*, June 30. Available at http://www.exberliner.com/reviews/johannesburg-24-corporate-slumworld (accessed July 2010).

Nandy, A. (2010) Planning cannot eliminate slums, *OneWorld South Asia*, opinion & comment, April 14. Available at http://southasia.oneworld.net/opinioncomment/planning-cannot-eliminate-slums (accessed August 2010).

Neuwirth, R. (2006) *Shadow Cities* (New York: Routledge).

Neuwirth, R. (2007) Squatters and cities of tomorrow, *City*, 11(1), pp. 71–80.

Perlman, J. (2010) *Favela, Four Decades of Living on the Edge in Rio de Janeiro* (New York: Oxford University Press).

Pezzullo, P. (2007) *Toxic Tourism* (Tuscaloosa: University of Alabama Press).

Rocha, L. D. M. (2009). *Uma favela "Diferente das outras?"* Research Academic Institute of Rio de Janeiro.

Rolfes, M. (2010) Poverty tourism, *GeoJournal*, 75(5), pp. 421–442.

Sassen, S. (2002) Locating cities on global circuits, *Environment and Urbanization*, 14(1), pp. 13–30.

Schmitt, B. (2009) Case Studies: Peter Bialobrzeski and Oliver Boberg (translation by Simone Schede), *L.A. Galerie Lothar Albrecht*, March 27, pp. 1–4. Available at http://www.lagalerie.de/CaseStudiesEN.pdf (accessed 29 December 2010).

Slum-Looks (2010) Forget Vogue. Available at http://www.facebook.com/pages/SLUM-LOOKS/110348722315870?v=info (accessed 29 December 2010).

Smith, D. T. (2010) Gangster tourism. Paper presented at *Destination Slum*, University of the West of England, Bristol, UK, December 9–11.

Steinberg, S. (2010) The myth of concentrated poverty, in: C. Hartman & G. D. Squires (Eds) *The Integration Debate: Competing Futures for American Cities*, pp. 213–227 (New York: Routledge).

Spear, J. (2006) Dionizio Gonzalez Photography, *JoshSpear.com*, December 11 (Monday). Available at http://joshspear.com/item/dionisio-gonzales-photography/ (accessed 5 January 2011).

Sturken, M. & Cartwright, L. (2009) *Practices of Looking* (New York: Oxford University Press).

Tagesschau SF (2005) Shantytown – Besetzung für Freiräume in Zürich, *Tagesschau SF DRS*, July 31. Available at http://www.youtube.com/watch?v=j9yud6tMfhE (accessed 11 January 2011).

Temby, C. (2010) 17th Biennale of Sydney – Cockatoo Island, *blogspot*, June 16. Available at http://caseydumdeedum.blogspot.com/2010/06/17th-biennale-of-sydney-cockatoo-island.html (accessed 30 December 2010).

Terkenli, T. S. (2002) Landscapes of tourism: Towards a global cultural economy of space?, *Tourism Geographies*, 4(3), pp. 227–254.

Urry, J. (2002) *The Tourist Gaze*, 2nd ed. (London: Sage).

Verilio, P. (1998) A topographical amnesia, in: N. Mirzoeff (Ed.) *The Visual Culture Reader*, pp. 108–122 (London: Routledge).

Wacquant, L. (2008) *Urban Outcasts* (Cambridge: Polity Press).

Whereisej (2005) 22 Zurich – shantytown map, *TravelPod*, August 3. Available at http://www.travelpod.ca/travel-photo/whereisej/whereisej/1123057680/s3000076.jpg/tpod.html (accessed 14 January 2011).

Notes on Contributor

Uli Linke is professor of cultural anthropology at Rochester Institute of Technology. Her research and writing are focused on issues of global social justice, gender, race and space. Her publications explore the interface of visual culture and terror, the political anthropology of the body, trauma and genocide, and the cultural politics of memory in post-colonial Europe.

Glimpses of Another World:
The *Favela* as a Tourist Attraction

THOMAS FRISCH
Independent scholar

ABSTRACT *The paper explores how the* favela *turned from a social problem into a touristic attraction by analysing the favela on three spatial levels. The first level deals with its consolidation as a social and geographical space and its manifestation as an international sociological category. On a second level the representations of the* favela *in public discourse are condensed into two main positions – the problem-centred representation (*favela*) and the idealized representation (*comunidade*). On a third level the exploitation of the* favela *as a touristic space is analysed critically based on guided interviews with tour operators, guides and participating tourists. The results show that 'favela tourism' in Rio de Janeiro has reached mass tourism dimensions and is characterized by an almost exclusive dominance of external agencies but little participation of the local population as well as scarce interaction between locals and tourists, who are bonded by the search for the 'authentic' other.*

Introduction

The *favela* has been an issue for public discussion since the very beginning of its historic origins in the early twentieth century. Throughout more than 100 years it has predominantly been perceived as a synonym for poverty, violence and social problems. However, since the early 1990s a growing market of tourism has evolved in a few particular *favela*s and developed into a major segment of the touristic exploration of Rio de Janeiro. The evident contradiction at first sight and the popularization of similar kinds of tourism phenomena – which have been embraced by the term 'slum tourism' – motivated an increasing number of scholarly productions in recent years. This article is set in the context of growing academic interest and the occasional media debate on the ethical boundary these specific forms of tourism seem to transcend. The focus of research is the *favela* as a particular spatial entity that is produced and consumed as a touristic attraction. Taking a social-constructivist perspective, it is presumed that the *favela* has undergone various processes of transformation in order to become a touristic sight. This paper aims at defining these processes and at finding out which variables made such a development possible before analysing how the *favela* is produced and consumed touristically.

As a first step the *favela* is defined on a theoretical level as a particular 'spatially identified community' (Cardoso *et al.* 2005: 1), which is suitable due to its qualities of being relatively autonomous and localized in certain parts of the city. The theoretical construction allows an analysis on three sub-levels, which are based around a very general framework derived from a sociology of space. The course of analysis of these levels will be as follows: for a starting point the *favela* is treated as a social space, whose historical development has been influenced by numerous political actors. As a discussion of the *favela* cannot be restricted to material spatial matters, different representations that label public discourse about the *favela* are investigated on a second level. Finally, the third level examines how the *favela* is commodified into a touristic product and presents three characteristics of a 'touristic space *favela*': the development from a niche status into a mass tourism product; the Western origin of most '*favela* tourists' and their desire for real, 'authentic' experiences of a perceived 'other'; the marginal participation of the local population and little interaction between tourists and *favela* residents. This research is based on a review of the literature on *favela*s and tourism, which is reflected in all three analytical levels, as well as a series of guided interviews with tourists, tour operators and tour guides, which constitute the basis for the elaboration of the characteristics of a 'touristic space *favela*'.

Theoretical Background

Unlike time, space has long been neglected by sociological interest. Only since the spatial turn in the late 1970s (Urry 1995: 2) have sociologists been discovering space as category worth researching and been recognizing the scientific potential at the intersection point of geography and sociology. Consequently, sociological concepts of space have been influenced principally by other fields, such as philosophy and physics, that have produced basically two main positions regarding space: the absolute concept, represented mainly by Isaac Newton, and the relative concept, represented mainly by Gottfried Wilhelm Leibniz (Schroer 2006: 29–44). Whereas the absolute idea conceives space as a 'container', i.e. static, fixed and independent from external influences, for representatives of the relative position space is generated only by physical objects that relate to each other. The differentiation between absolute and relative concepts can also be observed in sociological examination of the topic (Schroer 2006: 44). An absolute perspective assumes that social processes occur in a certain confined spatial entity and that these processes can be distinguished from those in other spatial entities. The sociological equivalent of the relative position does not perceive space as a given condition but as a result of social relations. Both concepts do have their advantages and problems and the appropriateness of each depends on the specific research question. Consequently, I will seek to combine the two concepts and to consider both – i.e. the impact of the *favela* on tourists but also the way the particular touristic experience of the *favela* is constructed or produced by the three participating groups.

Similarly to sociology in general, space had a rather marginal significance in scientific debate on tourism until the 1990s, when the spatial dimension was introduced most notably by Edensor (1998). He is concerned with the construction and regulation of tourist spaces, putting special emphasis on the symbolic representation of places and the possibilities of multiple interpretations, an aspect that has also been emphasized by Pott (2007: 131). Based on the assumption that tourist spaces are increasingly regulated, Edensor presents a dualistic approach, which distinguishes between enclavic and heterogeneous tourist spaces. Enclavic tourist spaces are exclusively designed and organized for tourism and purified from any irritating circumstances (Edensor 1998: 45–49), whereas 'heterogeneous tourist spaces accommodate tourism as one economic activity but are not dominated by it' (Edensor 1998: 54). Although his analysis is built on a binary opposition, Edensor admits a co-existence of both spaces and a hybridity of most tourist spaces in social reality. Following Edensor, academic interest in the subject grew and, especially in recent years, various publications (amongst others Terkenli 2002; Shaw & Williams 2004; Pott 2007; Saarinen & Kask 2008) have been released which apply a wider notion of space. In particular, Pott (2007: 26) has been influential with German-speaking academics by grasping tourism as a spatial phenomenon and further developing Luhmann's approach to interpret reality as a construction based on observation, which has also been adapted to township and slum tourism by Rolfes *et al.* (2009) and Meschkank (2011). These theoretical considerations of a social-constructivist perspective constitute the tool for the following analysis of the *favela* as the object of research.

Removal or Urbanization – The *Favela* as a Social Space and Sociological Category

Looking back at the history of the *favela* in Rio de Janeiro two aspects stand out that are essential for understanding its significance in Brazilian society and later on also for understanding the very existence of tourism. The first aspect is the consolidation as a particular social and geographical space with its population forming a specific social group, whose collective identity is based on their housing condition. The second aspect is the manifestation as international sociological category and subsequently the globalization of the *favela* as trademark (Freire-Medeiros 2009a: 580) through mass media as well as information and communication technologies (Figure 1).

Roughly speaking, the historical development may be described as a process departing from an originating genesis at the turn of the nineteenth to the twentieth centuries, passing a period of varying growth with peaks in the 1950s and 1970s, and finally reaching consolidation in the early 1980s. In order to understand this

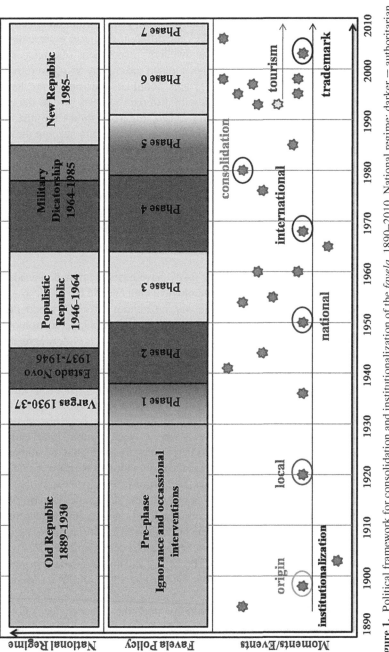

Figure 1. Political framework for consolidation and institutionalization of the *favela*, 1890–2010. National regime: darker = authoritarian, lighter = democratic. *Favela* policy: darker = relocation, lighter = urbanization. *Source:* compiled by the author.

process the *favela* needs to be interpreted as a contested field with numerous political agents trying to achieve their intentions. The most important actors have been the State, the Catholic Church, the social sciences and different groups of representatives from the *favela* population – especially the dwellers' associations (*Associações de Moradores*). These traditional actors have been joined recently by non-governmental organizations (NGOs), popular religious groups, multinationals and – not least – tourist agencies. Just the number of actors with different interests reveals the complexity that characterizes the contemporary *favela*. Figure 1 shows the historical development of the *favela* during the twentieth century, taking into account three dimensions: the national political framework, several phases of *favela* policies (based on Valladares 2005: 23) and a range of very different specific moments and events (foundation of *favela* dwellers' associations, internationally successful movies like City of God, the first *favela* tours in Rocinha ...). Beside the two aspects mentioned above, Figure 1 should also illustrate the growing complexity and increase of (political) agents in recent years, among which tourism plays an important role, and that go hand in hand with an increasing production of images and discourses on the *favela* (Jaguaribe 2007: 126).

Two prime sources for the genesis of the *favela* have been mentioned in academic literature: (a) the war at Canudos – the mythological element and (b) the destruction of the *cortiços* – the realistic element. The war at Canudos (1893–7) was depicted by Euclides da Cunha in his epic *Os sertões*, which shaped public perception of the *favela*s as rural enclaves in the city hills (Valladares 2005: 28). It is widely agreed that parts of the winning troops engaged in the war settled on a hill close to the city centre, which became known as the first *favela* in Rio de Janeiro – the Morro da Providência. Nevertheless, the destruction of the central *cortiços* – the major housing type of the urban poor in the nineteenth century – may be seen as the realistic element in the formation of the *favela*, as the displaced population started to build shacks on the uninhabited hills. As early as 1902 the *favela*s were subject to public intervention – although on a small scale – when Francisco Pereira Passos conducted the first major initiative of urban planning, which resulted in the designation of Rio as a 'wonderful city' (*cidade maravilhosa*). In the 1920s the *favela*s grew to such an extent that they were perceived as a problem for the whole society. At the same time the term *favela* underwent a first institutionalization by becoming a local category for the settlements of the urban poor on hills. However, it was not until 1937 that the *favela* actually became central to public attention, when the Building Code (*Código de Obras*) first recognized their very existence in an official document and thus marked the beginning of explicit *favela* policies (Valladares 2005: 52; Burgos 2006: 48; Freire-Medeiros 2009a: 581).

By means of the following political actions from the State or local governments various periods can be identified based on the national political regime (authoritarian/democratic) and the predominant strategy of intervention (relocation/ urbanization). As a fundamental pattern one can argue that in authoritarian regimes the dominant policy was the destruction of the *favela*s and a relocation of its population, whereas in democratic periods the *favela*s were mostly accepted and the prevailing strategy was to urbanize them primarily with a focus on basic infrastructure measures. This distinction needs to be seen more as a general tendency than an absolute fact, because there have been urbanization policies during the military dictatorship as well as efforts to remove *favela*s in recent (democratically governed) years. In any case, all these interventions during the twentieth century – especially the relocation policies – have strengthened the political organization of the *favela* population in their quest for better living conditions and social rights. Consequently, a strong spatially defined identity and communal spirit emerged based on the common housing form.

The first proposition during the totalitarian Estado Novo state (1937–46) was the proletarian parks (*parques proletários*) built by the government at the beginning of the 1940s, where relocated *favela* dwellers should have been morally educated and transformed into decent workers. The second major relocation plan was carried out mostly during the military dictatorship from 1962 to 1978. In this period – known as *Remocionismo* – many *favela*s in the richer southern zone were destroyed and their inhabitants transferred to simple public housing complexes (*conjuntos habitacionais*) at the remote ends of the city. During democratic eras the policies toward the *favela* have been much less antagonistic for its dwellers. In particular, the 1950s are remembered as a flourishing period of Brazilian populism and clientelism, when votes were exchanged for little personal favours. It is also the decade that saw a massive increase in *favela*s and their population, which partially caused the relocation policy that was about to follow. Since the opening of the military dictatorship (*abertura*) in the late 1970s, the relocation policies gave way to a predominance of the urbanization strategy. The most prominent public intervention was the city's *Favela-Bairro* programme, which has been running since the early 1990s and intends to transform *favela*s into formal quarters (*bairros*) through investments in basic infrastructure (Burgos 2006: 48). Since 2007 another programme – the *Programa de Aceleração do Crescimento* (PAC) – has benefitted a number of large *favela*s with a similar approach as *Favela-Bairro*, only patronized by the federal State.

The second aforementioned aspect – the manifestation of the *favela* as international sociological category has not been such a complex process as the *favela* policies. However, its impact on the global popularity of the *favela* cannot be underestimated. When the interventions from local and federal governments sought to control a social problem, the social scientists opted for a deeper understanding of the social phenomenon of 'favelization' and the supposed particularities it produced. A major mark in scientific preoccupation was the census in 1950, when the *favela* was first treated as a separate category (Valladares 2005: 198). During the 1960s the topic definitely entered wider sociological discussion with the landmark study published by *Sociedade de Análises Gráficas e Mecanográficas Aplicadas aos Complexos Sociais* (SAGMACS), the international bestseller *Child of the Dark* by *favela* dweller

Maria Carolina de Jesus and the *favela* as cover story in the journal *America Latína* in 1969 (Valladares 2005: 102–117). In recent years the production of material has grown immensely so that it has become an up-to-date topic. Still the popularity of the *favela* is not limited to social science by far. The international success of films such as *City of God* (2004) and *The Elite Squad* (2008), as well as the concept of *favela* Chic, the *favela* Funk music or the multitude of *favela* images in global circulation, are examples of a phenomenon that Freire-Medeiros (2009a: 580) has described as the *favela* as 'global trademark'. The following section will analyse how this 'trademark' *favela* is represented in public discourse.

Favela or *Comunidade* – The Rich Symbolic Potential of the *Favela* and Public Discourse

Valladares (2005: 151) has pointed out three dogmas stemming from scientific research of the *favela* and which are maintained by different groups for various reasons. Those are: (a) its particularity – i.e. the emphasis of difference to other city areas, (b) its unity – i.e. the treatment as a homogeneous phenomenon by using '*favela*' in the singular; and (c) the characterization as *the* urban space of poverty *per se*. The widespread reading of the *favela* as a synonym for poverty as such builds the backbone when analysing the representations in public discourse, because it is the dominant qualitative attribute. Besides, the *favela* has traditionally been interpreted as a place that possesses a constructed 'otherness' due to a dominance of external definitions – by the state or social sciences – which can be identified by the approaches that stress the aspects the *favela* is lacking compared to an idealized conception of its respective counterpart, mostly the formal city (Silva & Barbosa 2005: 24). The practice of comparing to and distancing oneself from others was originally termed 'othering' by Spivak (1985) and adapted to slum tourism research by Pott and Steinbrink (2010). In their essay they describe, how 'othering' is used to construct the 'other' in tourism and subsequently how this construction is spatialized in the slum. However, the *favela* is not only a place of the 'other' contrasted to the 'self', it has also frequently been understood as a place of the 'authentic'. Authenticity is a very complex concept and has been discussed in different ways by various authors in tourism and is a key issue in slum tourism research. As the question for the authenticity of an object, a person or an idea cannot be answered from a social-constructivist perspective, a touristification of the *favela* needs to be analysed through the conceptualization of a constructive authenticity, which focuses on the authenticity perceived by the tourist (Shaw & Williams 2004) and has been distinguished from objective and existential authenticity (Wang 1999).

As previously stated, Edensor (1998: 10–40) and Pott (2007: 131) have already emphasized the possibility of multiple interpretations of places, while Jaguaribe (2007: 126, translated by TF) has identified a proliferation of images of the *favela*, in which the *favela* stands as a focus point, where 'ideas and imaginations of modernity fail and are reinvented'. This analysis undertakes a condensation of the vast symbolic potential of the *favela* to two main discourses – the problem-centred and the idealized discourse – in order to structure different ideas and make the representations more understandable. The problem-centred position is currently dominant and concentrates on all negative associations with the *favela*, such as drug trafficking, violence, precarious housing etc. The idealized position is currently subordinate and can be seen as a reaction to the problem-centred position, which highlights the positive aspects connected with the *favela*, such as community or popular culture. Both discourses focus on the same phenomenon – the *favela* – but represent two opposing perspectives. Both perspectives are also manifested in language, as *favela* predominantly stands for a problem-centred viewpoint, whereas the frequently used term *comunidade* (community) refers to an idealized approach.

The most prominent examples of the problem-centred representation are the denomination of the *favela* as a social problem, a cultural problem and a security problem. As the various interventions by federal or local governments show, the *favela* has always been depicted as a social problem – almost exclusively based on housing conditions – that needs to be tackled in some way or another, i.e. either relocation or urbanization policies. The most extreme version of this representation could be found during the *Remocionismo* period, when the *favela* was deliberately identified as a 'social disease' (Lima 2005: 175). However, a similar rhetoric has been observed recently, when taking into account the statement of Governor Sergio Cabral, who spoke in 2007 of the *favela* as 'literal fabrics of the marginalised' (Birman 2008: 99, translated by TF). Similarly, the *favela* has been understood as a cultural problem since its very beginning. Its dwellers have been depicted as culturally inferior, an assumption often combined with explicit racism (Zaluar & Alvito 2006: 13). Whereas open racism has become unacceptable, the *favela* is still prominently seen as a place where amoral ways of living – like promiscuity, alcoholism, contempt of laws – dominate social life (Lima 2005: 172).

The interpretation as a security problem is probably the foremost representation of all. The relationship between dominant social classes and the poor in Rio de Janeiro has always been ambiguous. On the one hand the former benefits from a cheap labour force for various formal and informal occupations; on the other hand the presence of the latter is seen as uncomforting, disruptive or even threatening. However, a continuous trend of self-segregation of the upper classes has been documented particularly since the 1990s (Lago 2000; Ottaviano 2006), which leads to an increasing homogenization and privatization but also to a segmentation of urban space. This retreat into the *condomínios fechados* – the Brazilian form of gated communities – has been driven largely by a socio-psychological status of fear (Zaluar 2006: 212–227) and is both a consequence and enhancement of an existing rupture between the classes, which has characterized their relationship since the late 1980s (Burgos 2006: 41–42). The process has been associated primarily with an increase in violence and the militarization of drug trafficking. The fact that drug trafficking has got totally out of control had the important side effect of a criminalization of poverty. The prevailing identification of organized crime with the *favela*s favoured the acceptance of repressive police actions, which are carried out there, so that the *favela* dwellers became victims between two sides – the drug traffickers and the police (Silva 2008).

Due to the heavy dominance of the problem-centred position the idealized representation works on a much narrower range and is mostly restricted to relativizing the mentioned problem-centred aspects. In particular the depiction as social problem and as symbol for existing inequalities seems to be hard to idealize and is not useful for any societal group. When, in a problem-centred perspective, the *favela* was seen as a problem of housing for the poor population, the idealizing position understands it as a solution to the housing problem by emphasizing the advantages of the *favela* compared to other poor neighbourhoods in peripheral locations, such as proximity to work and leisure activities. The security problem has been relativized by romanticizing drug trafficking groups as social movements, expressed by the euphemistic term *'movimento'* for describing their activities. The ruling factions around a 'good don' (Leeds 2006: 242, translated by TF) have actually taken over functions that were supposed to be provided by the State, such as the financial support of the population for medical treatment, transport or food. However, the most important function is a security-political one by incorporating the monopoly of legitimate violence. At this point the perceptions of the different societal groups are drifting apart in the most extreme way. Whereas for the dominant social classes the *favela* represents the synonym of violence and fear, the dwellers often describe their homes as quiet and safe.

The most important element for an idealized identity of the *favela* is its rich cultural potential. If media reports speak of the *favela* in an idealized tone, it has almost exclusively been formulated via this thread of discourse. Many forms of popular culture originated in the *favela* or are primarily associated with the *favela*. Among the most significant examples are the carnival of the samba schools, different musical styles (*samba*, hip hop, *funk carioca*) popular religious phenomena (*umbanda*, protestant groups), the Afro-Brazilian mixture between martial arts and dance (*capoeira*), football – still the most popular sport in Brazil – or specific art forms such as recycling art and street art. Besides, the term *comunidade* has functioned to describe a particular way of living that is characterized by affective neighbourhood relationships and a distinct valuation of public space – aspects that are supposed to have gone missing in the majority of the population (Silva & Barbosa 2005: 98).

The Commodification of Poverty – the *Favela* as Touristic Attraction

It has been shown that the *favela* possesses rich symbolic potential, which can be interpreted in different ways. The touristic exploitation of the *favela* takes up this symbolic potential and both depends on and contributes to the existing discourses.

The existing representations are central for a wider understanding of *favela* tourism, because the commodification process – the way in which the *favela* is commercialized into a product – depends excessively on its sign value, as has been emphasized by Watson and Kopachevsky (1996: 283) or Edensor (1998: 13) amongst others.

In scientific debate '*favela* tourism' is discussed in the wider context of 'slum tourism' or 'poverty tourism'. We are only at the very beginning of establishing a new research field – highlighted by the uncertainty that surrounds the appropriateness of the terminology used to define this particular tourism phenomenon (Rolfes *et al.* 2009). However, there have been several valuable contributions, most notably by a number of German writers. On the one hand, they have outlined the changing character of 'slumming' in different historical periods (Pott & Steinbrink 2010) and, on the other, they have outlined the similarities and differences between various forms of slum tourism in South Africa, Mumbai and Rio de Janeiro (Rolfes 2010; Meschkank 2011). The most interesting similarity, according to the latter authors, is an assumed image change from the very negative semantics of poverty before undertaking a slum tour towards a more positive one after the tour. Apart from this socio-political objective, Rolfes (2010) has described differences with regards to the content at the respective places/cities where slum tourism has evolved. Whereas in the townships of South Africa – the most visited form of slum tourism – the focus is put on political issues and the history of ethnic segregation during the apartheid regime, slum tours in Mumbai focus on the economic productivity of slum dwellers as opposed to a certain cliché of a passiveness, stagnation, crime or educational deficits (Meschkank 2011).

The Rio de Janeiro case has been examined by a number of academics, in addition to the aforementioned Jaguaribe (2007), most importantly by Freire-Medeiros. She relates the emergence of *favela* tours to the rise of alternative forms of travelling, which can be interpreted either as a reaction against discontent with mass tourism or as a further differentiation of the tourism market. Freire-Medeiros (2006; 2009a; 2009b) has analysed the *favela* tours in Rocinha with reference to what she calls 'reality tours', thus tours that promise an authentic, realistic and interactional contact with the foreign 'other'. Furthermore she concludes that *favela* tours are particularly interesting because they combine aspects of both major subcategories of the reality tours – 'social' and 'dark tours' (Freire-Medeiros 2009a: 582). 'Social tours' are educationally orientated and primarily address people with an interest in supporting social projects in less developed regions. 'Dark tours' – a form of 'dark tourism' (Lennon & Foley 2002) – take place at destinations that are connected with death or tragic events or, in the case of the *favela*, produce similar emotional responses, such as fear, doubt or concern.

The curiosity to visit areas associated with poverty is not a new phenomenon, but was a frequent practice in Victorian England, as well as in certain immigrant neighbourhoods of New York in the late nineteenth and early twentieth centuries (Freire-Medeiros 2009a,b; Pott & Steinbrink 2010). However, the growing popularity of recent 'global slumming' (Pott and Steinbrink 2010: 268) differs from the nineteenth century 'slumming' in three aspects: the commodification and incorporation into the logic of the market; the shifting from the limitation of practices within city borders to practices of long-distance travelling to destinations in the global south; and the existence of a globally circulating 'touristic poverty' through a multitude of images on the internet produced by a new generation of frequent travellers (Freire-Medeiros 2009b: 6)

The growing popularity in recent years has led to intensive discussions in media and academic circles on the moral questionability of touristic exploitation of poverty areas. Critics of 'slum' and *'favela* tourism' concentrate mostly on two distinct aspects: (a) the voyeuristic motive and behaviour practised by affluent tourists 'gazing at the poor' (Freire-Medeiros 2009b: 1); and (b) the postcolonial appropriation of foreign spaces by Western tourists for egoistic reasons. Selinger and Outterson (2009) have theoretically examined the accusation of voyeurism associated with forms of 'negative sightseeing' (MacCannell 1999: 40) and conclude that an undifferentiated, categorical rejection is not justifiable, although they admit that empirical studies would probably observe moral reprehensibility of most of 'slum tourism'. A much more critical view is held by Salazar (2004: 85), who carried out an empirical study on 'development tourism', a particular form of a social tour, where tourists take part in social projects in less developed regions for a limited time. According to Salazar the neo-colonialist aspect was confirmed, as tourists are more interested in their own development than in the one of the area visited. In fact, he documented that tourists deliberately blind out indications of modernity and frequently express concern about the preservation of authenticity – and thus under-development – of the particular region. Accordingly, one could argue for a projection of colonial ideas and an exotic idealization of the authentic 'other' that reveals more about the self than about the supposed 'other' and is thus just another self-referential form of 'othering'.

Tourism in the *favela* – the Rio de Janeiro version of the localized 'other' – has already existed for nearly two decades, as self-declared pioneers of *favela* tourism date its origins to around the Rio Conference in 1992 (Freire-Medeiros 2009a: 584). Short, guided tours remain the predominant form of touristic exploration, despite the emergence of other offers, such as guesthouses or the visit of *baile funk* parties. Although there have been experiences with tourism in a number of *favelas* (Freire-Medeiros 2006) and an expansion to other *favelas*, organized tourism concentrates almost exclusively on one particular *favela* – Rocinha. Consequently, these guided *favela* tours in Rocinha are the subject of the following empirical case study.

Distinctive Qualities of the 'Touristic Space *Favela*'

Rocinha is situated in the richer southern zone, where only a small minority of Rio's *favelas* is located. In fact, Rocinha ceased to be a *favela* in legal terms in 1993 (Freire-Medeiros 2009a: 583), when it was declared the status of a formal city quarter (*bairro*). However, in public opinion it is still perceived as a *favela* (Jaguaribe 2007:

145) and probably also as the most prominent one. Besides, Rocinha is surrounded by the myth of being the largest *favela* in Latin America, an aspect that tour operators also like to emphasize by exaggerating the number of its inhabitants. Nevertheless, Rocinha reaches the dimension of a medium-sized city (100,000–150,000 people) and is better described as a complex of 13 different sub-quarters and also has various different stakeholders because of pronounced income and wealth variation. Although it had long been affected by rural characteristics and isolation from other city areas, Rocinha faced massive growth from the 1950s onwards, primarily associated with the city expansion to the area of Barra da Tijuca. Due to heavy migration from states such as Ceára or Bahia during this period, its population is predominantly of northeastern Brazilian descent. Unlike many other *favelas*, Rocinha has attracted the attention of a range of external agents since its immense growth (the State, Catholic Church, NGOs and others) and has been subject to various projects of intervention. Among the most important actors are also the social scientists, as Rocinha has been the most popular of all *favelas* for researchers (Valladares 2005: 147). While Valladares (2005: 163) criticizes that many of these confound the *favela* with poverty and explain those phenomena associated with poverty as distinctive phenomena of the *favela*, the present article seeks to avoid this misinterpretation by examining the *favela* not as an explanatory force, but as a constructed object that requires further understanding. As stated previously, the *favela* is treated rather as a category that is produced and consumed touristically and thus has evolved a series of characteristics, which are depicted in the following three preliminary results.

These qualities of a 'touristic space *favela*' are based on a series of semi-structured, guided, in-depth interviews with five representatives of tour operators and ten '*favela* tourists', carried out in Rio de Janeiro between March and April 2008. A qualitative method was chosen in order to avoid pre-categorization on behalf of the researcher and due to the explorative character of the research design. Consequently, the part of the interviewer was reduced to little intervention, primarily confined to keeping up the conversation flow and specifying questions when necessary. Additionally the author accompanied tours of three different operators, made various informal visits to Rocinha and kept a research diary throughout the fieldwork for documenting and self-reflexive purposes. All of the seven officially recognized tour operators at that time were contacted, of whom five – four owners and one tour guide, who was also a resident – agreed to do an interview. The tourists were all questioned after they took a *favela* tour and they participated in tours from three different operators. Unfortunately, the perspective of the *favela* residents could not be considered due to the need for mediating contacts which require established mutual trust, a relationship that could not be accomplished in the short research period. The evaluation of the data derived from the interviews was made in five steps: a complete transcription according to major transcription norms; a general evaluation of each interview; a one-page summary of each interview; comparative thematic coding – based on the approaches of Froschauer and Lueger (2003) and Flick (2007) as well as a

computer-assisted approach with MAXQDA software – separately for the two interviewee groups; and, finally, a derivation of a working hypothesis based on general-
ization and selection of the most frequent and significant themes and topics.

1.   Favela Tourism: from a Niche Status to a Mass Tourism Product

Organized as well as informal tourist exploration of the *favela* has emerged very
early compared to similar forms of slum tourism in other countries. However, the
proportions were low until the turn of the millennium. Since then a moderate increase
could be observed, which has been promoted extensively by the international success
of the 2004 film *City of God*, a similar development to what has been observed in
Mumbai with the 2008 motion picture *Slumdog Millionaire* (Meschkank 2011). This
is also reflected in scientific productions on the topic, which only then started to
gain a wider attention. Although it is still far from being an enclavic tourist space
(Edensor 1998), and despite there not being as sophisticated a touristic infrastructure
as in South Africa (Rolfes 2010), many indications can be observed that argue in
favour of denominating '*favela* tourism' as a mass tourism travel form.

(a)   The simple dimension of visitors – estimated to be 3,000 to 4,000 tourists per
      month, without those informal tours provided by private people and taxi drivers
      (Freire-Medeiros 2009a). One of the interviewees even stated that 40 percent of
      the tourists who visit Rio de Janeiro go on a *favela* tour, be it in an organized or
      informal way.

(b)   There is an increasing segmentation of the '*favela* tourism' market and a diversi-
      fication of products aimed at distinctive target groups. Even though short guided
      tours in small groups remain the most common form of '*favela* tourism', various
      other products have been launched in recent years. Among them are several ac-
      commodation facilities – mainly the bed and breakfast type – in different *favelas*,
      visits of a famous *baile funk* club and the efforts of local and federal governments
      to promote tourism in *favelas* with a focus on their cultural heritage. Also within
      the field of guided tours in Rocinha, tour operators deliberately aim at different
      target groups, as the owner of a tour company stresses:

      > I started six and a half years ago, because the other operators do a tour with
      > a jeep or a van, inside a car. So, it was because of that that I decided to do
      > a tour for a young audience, backpackers, walking inside [of the favela]
      > (Agency 3).

(c)   There is an established, commission-based cooperation of tour operators with
      local agencies, hotels and hostels – which, however, does not account for all
      operators to the same extent – as one of the interviewees states: 'In fact, the
      Jeep Tour does not sell; the Jeep Tour is sold by hotels and by travel agencies.

Sometimes someone enters our site but normally it is other people, who sell for us, travel agencies, hotels ... ' (Agency 2).

(d) There is an increase in the number of competing operators of *favela* tours. Originally, there were three *favela* tour pioneers, but several other operators emerged along with the growing popularity, so that the *favela* tour market has become an established field of highly competitive players, who try to achieve their share of visitors. Freire-Medeiros (2009a) speaks of seven operators, who are registered with the local tourism institution Rio Tur. However, the number is definitely larger due to the emergence of new operators and several unregistered and informal providers.

(e) There has been formal recognition of '*favela* tourism' by local tourism institutions (Rio Tur) as well as local governments since around 2006 (Freire-Medeiros 2009a). Recently, this included the former president Luiz Inácio Lula da Silva, who introduced in 2010 a government-funded tour through the *favela* Santa Marta, which became famous when Michael Jackson filmed one of his music videos there in 1996 (*Der Standard* 2010).

2. Favela Tourists Share their Western Origin, a Desire for a Real, Authentic Experience of the 'Other' as the Dominant Travel Motive and a Common Interpretation of the Favela as a Place of the 'Other'

Favela tourists do not share many common socio-demographic characteristics apart from their Western origin and are thus a quite homogeneous group. Although the interviewed tourists have different ages, professions and travel forms (individual/ organized), it has become quite clear that the affiliation to a supposed Western culture group is the prime characteristic of the *favela* tourist, an aspect that has also been documented with visitors of South African townships (Rolfes *et al.* 2009). As an example, when one operator was asked about his audience, he said 'Americans, Australians, South Africans, Israeli, Canadians. But South Americans little, Latin Americans little like 5% or at most 10%, possibly less ... Europeans and North Americans they make about 75–80% [of my customers]' (Agency 1).

The second typical quality of the *favela* tourists is one principal underlying common motive for visiting the *favela*. This motive is best described as a combination of two attracting aspects – the 'other' and the 'real'. Both aspects are attributed to the *favela*, which assures an authentic, real experience of the 'other'. This interpretation as a distant and foreign place ties in well with the earlier mentioned construction of the *favela* as a place of the 'other'. The fact, that many parts of the city do not differ much from any large Western city favours locating the 'otherness' in the *favela*. A quote from a Swedish tourist illustrates this perceived attraction of 'otherness' and the process described earlier as 'othering' in (Steinbrink & Pott 2010: 267): 'Well, we actually discussed it before. Why is it so interesting to go to places where people suffer? I don't know. I think it's just because you are so far from our reality' (Sonja, Sweden).

The second attraction – the curiosity to see what a *favela* is *really* like – draws upon the massive global circulation of images and associations connected with the *favela* as trademark. Although foreign and distant, all of the tourists have heard about the notorious *favelas* before, mostly through media reports, films or stories from other people, and thus have exclusively negative associations with the *favelas*. Paradoxically, this stimulates the interest in doing a tour:

> The *favelas* of Rio are possible the thing that it's probably the most famous for, notoriously famous for, in a negative sense. And I think that doing a tour there is, we sort of wanted to put it in perspective and see what it was really like, if it's as bad as everyone said it was (Jason, England).

Another commonality among the tourists has been their similar interpretation of the *favela* as a space of the 'other'. Before their visit, the tourists who were interviewed had exclusively negative associations that can be assigned to the problem-centred discourse. Thus, their imaginations before the travel experience are characterized by the perception of the *favela* as a social and security problem and as a foreign, hostile place. Their statements after the *favela* tour clearly show a tendency of relativizing their preconceived associations, which is, however, unsurprising due to the extremely negative character of their preconception:

> You know, *City of God* the movie, and so when you think of that and then you think of what we saw today, it's quite different. You know, and not that there's not violence or problems but I guess what today really taught me and where I thought our guide was really good at doing, is saying that you know things are not always black and white. There's a lot of grey. And every situation and that's, you know, that's what I got out of the *favela* tour (Victoria, USA).

Nevertheless, the *favela* persists as a foreign place of the 'other', which they do visit in the protected manner of a guided tour, but where they would still not feel at ease. Thus, the image transformation from the very negative to more positive semantics of poverty, which has been documented for slum and township tours in Mumbai and South Africa (Rolfes *et al.* 2009; Rolfes 2010; Meschkank 2011), should not be overestimated in the case of *favela* tourism and is probably best termed as a relativization. The missing indications for a romantic reading of the *favela* – in terms of an idealized discourse – are probably rooted in the missing participation of, and little interaction with, the local population.

3. Participation of the Local Community in Tourism is Marginal, Contact and Interaction with Tourists Scarcely Exists

The empirical study has shown that participation of the local community in tourism is marginal, an aspect which discerns '*favela* tourism' from '*township* tourism', where tour guides are residents of the respective township at the same time (Rolfes *et al.* 2009). The tour operators as well as the tour guides in '*favela* tourism' are primarily people from outside the local community with the intention of marketing it for touristic purposes. For this reason the status quo of '*favela* tourism' cannot be understood as socially responsible and sustainable (development) tourism, although some of the operators would like to define themselves in that way. Indeed, parts of the *favela* population benefit – mostly children – from the presence of tourists indirectly via social projects, supported by some tour operators, but not all of the operators pursue a policy of shared revenue with the local population, a fact that some agencies use for distancing themselves from their competitors:

> Another difference [to other operators] is that there is – from my part – a continuously financed project, a local school ... and I do this relative to the market, depending on how many tourists make a tour, a representation of this goes into the project ... And other agencies don't have this policy. They think that it is enough to bring the tourist there, who buys something or makes a donation. This is enough for them (Agency 1).

Furthermore, external people are almost exclusively in charge of arranging the tours and selecting the relevant information. Those residents that benefit in one way or another from tourism (souvenir shops, bakeries, art studies etc.) do not participate actively in the symbolic production of the 'touristic space *favela*', but do depend passively on the benevolence of the tour operators, who decide on bringing tourists to the *favela*. The questioned agency owners are also not *favela* residents, nor do many of the tour guides live in Rocinha or another *favela* – the latter because of the alleged inadequate qualifications of the residents: 'At the moment of the guides that we have, nobody lives there [in Rocinha] ... I would employ them, but at the moment I don't have qualified labour for that' (Agency 3).

Exchange between tourists and residents is restricted to a minimum during the actual tour, although all parties questioned would welcome a more intensive involvement with their respective counterpart. A series of factors have been responsible for a lack of interaction between tourists and residents. The primary obstacle is the existing language barrier, which can hardly be overcome and defines the framework for possible approximation. Due to the presence of tourists in Rocinha over a long period, one can observe a 'habituation effect' on the residents' side, which reflects a state of resignation because of the lack of possibilities of communication and active participation:

The people want to communicate with the tourist, but they don't speak any languages. That is normal. With me, because I'm known here, they go and say: Tell me where he is from. Hey, how are you? Do you like it? But he [the *favela* dweller] doesn't manage to communicate. Soon he stays quiet. Well, he will let it happen; it is already daily routine in the community (tour guide and Rocinha dweller).

Finally, the short actual presence in the *favela* and the tours' typically standardized schedule prevent a more thorough relationship between tourists and residents.

Conclusion

Although tourism can be seen as a rather recent phenomenon, which takes part in the global production and circulation of the *favela* as a 'trademark' (Freire-Medeiros 2009a: 580), it is still dependent on existing discourse. It has been shown that initially the problem-centred discourse supersedes completely the idealized reading of a 'touristic space *favela*', as *favela* tourists exclusively have negative stereotypes of the *favela* before their visit. Thus, the popularity of the tour feeds upon the contradiction between the tourists' 'terrible' imaginations and associations concerning the *favela* and the fact that it is being sold to them as a touristic product. Ironically, the pre-conceived stereotypes are momentarily relativized shortly after the tour, even if the permanence of the experience is questionable and needs further investigation. The tourists' primary motive – the personal, authentic and real experience of a constructed and commercialized 'other' – might be seen as the most interesting aspect on the side of the consumption of the *favela*.

When thinking of the production of the 'touristic space *favela*' the most important aspect and also major point of critique has been the dominance of external agents and little participation of the local community in positions that would allow an actual involvement in the process of tourism exploration. In this sense it is still more appropriate to speak of a touristic *exploitation* of the *favela*, as tourism stays a primarily exogenous phenomenon. Basically, an ethical questionability of *favela* tourism does not exist *a priori*, but depends on the way touristic activities are carried out. As long as the *favela* residents are not reduced to plain objects of the 'tourist gaze' (Urry 1995; 2002) and the relationship is based on mutual respect, a worthwhile exchange between tourists and residents is possible and perfectly acceptable. A categorical moral denunciation would therefore fail its yet noble intention, as it reflects a paternalistic attitude, which denies the residents from being thinking, independently acting subjects. However, until their 'genuine participation' in the production of the 'touristic space *favela*' is achieved, '*favela* tourism' will not go very far beyond being a form of the much criticized 'negative sightseeing' (MacCannell 1999: 40) with a bitter, voyeuristic aftertaste.

Acknowledgements

I kindly thank Fabian Frenzel and Ko Koens for inviting me to take part in the Special Issue on 'slum tourism' and everyone involved in supporting my research for this project.

References

Birman, P. (2008) Favela é comunidade?, in: L. A. Machado da Silva (Ed.) *Vida sob cerco – violência e rotina nas favelas do Rio de Janeiro*, pp. 99–114 (Rio de Janeiro: FAPERJ/Nova Fronteira).

Burgos, M. B. (2006) Dos parques proletários ao *Favela*-Bairro – as políticas públicas nas favelas do Rio de Janeiro, in: A. Zaluar & M. Alvito (Eds) *Um século de Favela*, pp. 25–60 (Rio de Janeiro: FGV).

Cardoso, A., Elias, P. & Pero, V. (2005) Spatial Segregation and Labour Market Discrimination – The Case of Rio's Favelas. Paper presented at the IER Conference, Coventry.

Der Standard (2010) Slum schaun' als Touristen-Attraktion, 31 August 2010. Available at http://derstandard.at/1282978544923/Rio-de-Janeiro-Slum-schaun-als-Touristen-Attraktion (accessed 28 January 2011).

Edensor, T. (1998) *Tourists at the Taj – Performance and Meaning at a Symbolic Site* (London: Routledge).

Flick, U. (2007) *Qualitative Sozialforschung: Eine Einführung* (Hamburg: Rowohlts Enzyklopädie).

Freire-Medeiros, B. (2006) *A construção da Favela Carioca como Destino Turístico* (Rio de Janeiro: CPDOC).

Freire-Medeiros, B. (2009a) The favela and its touristic transits, *Geoforum*, 40, pp. 580–588.

Freire-Medeiros, B. (2009b) Gazing at the poor: Favela tours and the colonial legacy. Available at http://www.sas.ac.uk/fileadmin/documents/postgraduate/Papers_London_Debates_2010/Freire_Medeiros__Gazing_at_the_poor.pdf (accessed 28 January 2011).

Froschauer, U. & Lueger, M. (2003) *Das qualitative Interview: zur Praxis interpretativer Analyse sozialer Systeme* (Wien: Facultas).

Jaguaribe, B. (2007) *Favela Tours*: o olhar turístico e as representações da 'realidade', in: B. Jaguaribe (Ed.) *O choque do real – estética, mídia e cultura*, pp. 125–151 (Rio de Janeiro: Rocco).

Lago, L. Corrêa do (2000) *Desigualdades e Segregação na Metropole – O Rio de Janeiro em tempo de crise* (Rio de Janeiro: Revan).

Leeds, E. (2006) Cocaína e poderes paralelos na periferia urbana brasileira: ameaças à democratização em nível local, in: A. Zaluar & M. Alvito (Eds) *Um século de Favela*, pp. 233–276 (Rio de Janeiro: FGV).

Lennon, J. & Foley, M. (2002) *Dark Tourism: The Attraction of Death and Disaster* (London: Continuum).

Lima, M. Hélio Trindade de (2005) *Exclusão Social – Representações Sociais da Pobreza Urbana no Brasil* (Vitória: Edufes).

MacCannell, D. (1999) *The Tourist: A New Theory of the Leisure Class* (Berkeley: University of California Press).

Meschkank, J. (2011) Investigations into slumming in Mumbai – poorism and the tensions between different constructions of reality, *GeoJournal*, 76(1), pp. 47–62.

Ottaviano, M. Camila Loffredo d' (2006) Condomínios Fechados na Região Metropolitana de São Paulo: fim do modelo centro rico versus periferia pobre? Paper presented at the XV Encontro Nacional de Estudos Populacionais, Caxambú, 18–22 September. Available at http://www.abep.nepo.unicamp.br/encontro2006/docspdf/ABEP2006_590.pdf (accessed 28 January 2011).

Pott, A. (2007) *Orte des Tourismus: Eine raum- und gesellschaftstheoretische Untersuchung* (Bielefeld: transcript).

Pott, A. & Steinbrink, M. (2010) Global Slumming. Zur Genese und Globalisierung des Armutstourismus, in: K. Wöhler, A. Pott & V. Denzer (Eds) *Tourismusräume – zur soziokulturellen Konstruktion eines globalen Phänomen*, pp. 247–270 (Bielefeld: transcript).

Rolfes, M. (2010) Poverty tourism – theoretical reflections and empirical findings on an extraordinary form of tourism, *GeoJournal*, 75(5), pp. 421–442.

Rolfes, M., Steinbrink, M. & Uhl, C. (2009) *Townships as Attraction – An Empirical Study of Township Tourism in Cape Town* (Potsdam: Universitätsverlag). Available at http://opus.kobv.de/ubp/volltexte/2009/2894/pdf/pks46.pdf (accessed 28 January 2011).

Saarinen, J. & Kask, T. (2008) Transforming tourism spaces in changing socio-political contexts: The case of Pärnu, Estonia, as a tourist destination, *Tourism Geographies*, 10(4), pp. 452–473.

Salazar, N. B. (2004) Developmental tourists vs. development tourism: A case study, in: A. Raj (Ed.) *Tourist behaviour: A psychological perspective*, pp. 85–107 (New Delhi: Kanishka Publishers).

Schroer, M. (2006) *Räume, Orte, Grenzen – Auf dem Weg zu einer Soziologie des Raums* (Frankfurt am Main: Suhrkamp).

Selinger, E. & Outterson, K. (2009) *The Ethics of Poverty Tourism*, Boston University School of Law Working Paper No. 09-29. Available at http://www.bu.edu/law/faculty/scholarship/workingpapers/documents/SelingerEOuttersonK06-02-09.pdf (accessed 28 January 2011).

Shaw, G. & Williams, A. M. (2004) *Tourism and Tourism Spaces* (London: Sage).

Silva, J. de Souza e & Barbosa, J. L. (2005) *Favela – alegria e dor na cidade* (Rio de Janeiro: Senac).

Silva, L. A. Machado da (2008) Violência urbana, sociabilidade violenta e agenda pública, in: L. A. Machado da Silva (Ed.) *Vida sob cerco – violência e rotina nas favelas do Rio de Janeiro*, pp. 35–46 (Rio de Janeiro: FAPERJ/Nova Fronteira).

Spivak, G. C. (1985) The Rani of Sirmur – An essay in reading the archives, *History and Theory*, 24(3), pp. 247–272.

Terkenli, T. S. (2002) Landscapes of tourism: Towards a global cultural economy of space?, *Tourism Geographies*, 4(3), pp. 227–254.

Urry, J. (1995) *Consuming Places* (London: Routledge).

Urry, J. (2002) *The Tourist Gaze* (London: Sage).

Valladares, L. do Prado (2005) *A invenção da favela – Do mito de origem a favela.com* (Rio de Janeiro: FGV).

Wang, N. (1999) Rethinking authenticity in tourism experience, *Annals of Tourism Research*, 26(2), pp. 349–370.

Watson, G. L. & Kopachevsky, J. P. (1996) Interpretations of tourism as commodity, in: Y. Apostolopoulos, S. Leivadi & A. Yiannakis (Eds) *The Sociology of Tourism – Theoretical and Empirical Investigations*, pp. 281–300 (London: Routledge).

Zaluar, A. (2006) Crime, medo e política, in: A. Zaluar & M. Alvito (Eds) *Um século de Favela*, pp. 206–232 (Rio de Janeiro: FGV).

Zaluar, A. & Alvito, M. (2006) Introdução, in: A. Zaluar & M. Alvito (Eds) *Um século de Favela*, pp. 7–24 (Rio de Janeiro: FGV).

Notes on Contributor

Thomas Frisch studied Sociology, English and Portuguese in Salzburg and Rio de Janeiro and was graduated in Sociology from University of Salzburg in November 2010. His major academic interests are urban sociology, social inequality as well as tourism and intercultural exchange. The article 'Glimpses of Another World' is a based on his master thesis 'Die *Favela* Carioca: vom sozialen Problem zum Ort der authentischen touristischen Erfahrung' and was first presented at the 'Destination Slum' conference in Bristol, England on 11th December 2010. He currently lives in Hamburg and Salzburg.

Encounters over Garbage: Tourists and Lifestyle Migrants in Mexico

EVELINE DÜRR

Institute for Social and Cultural Anthropology, Ludwig-Maximilians-University, Munich, Germany

ABSTRACT *This article explores a tour to the garbage dump in the city of Mazatlán, northern Mexico, as an alternative to mass tourism. The tour, conducted by an evangelical North American church, is conceptualized as a non-profit, eye-opening experience for affluent tourists. I frame the tour as a particular kind of slum tourism, which is embedded in Christian values and promises a meaningful tourist experience by helping the poor. Drawing on an ethnographic approach, I argue that the interplay of globalization processes and local conditions in Mazatlán produces a particular framework in which slum tours emerge and work. The analysis reveals that this tour is a consequence of revised forms of tourism, transnational lifestyles and global forces at work in the North American–Mexican relationships. I stress that research needs to draw further attention to slum tourism's positioning in wider structural and historical contexts in order to understand its idiosyncratic features.*

Introduction

Slum tours figure increasingly in the tourist agenda world-wide, stirring a public controversy on ethical issues that links into debates on the relationship between tourism and poverty as either exploitation or support of the most vulnerable urban dwellers (Hall 2007; Weiner 2008; Foster 2009; Odede 2010; Scheyvens 2011). As a result, slum tours have recently experienced a surge of research interest which has revealed different kinds of tours in diverse localities, from township tours in South Africa (Rolfes 2009), through *favela* tours in Brazil (Jaguaribe & Hetherington 2006; Freire-Medeiros 2008; 2009) to slum tours in India (Meschkank 2010). Touring slums, however, is not a recent activity but dates back to the nineteenth century, when poor urban neighbourhoods were touristified as sites for adventure. 'Slumming' referred to the exploration of the life of the poorer classes by affluent ladies and gentlemen, who stepped out of their comfort zones and the safety of their own spaces (Heap 2009: 103).

In the USA, immigrant and racial dimensions figured prominently in these practices and played a key role in the exotic and erotic appeal of underprivileged urban districts. These activities produced new commercialized leisure spaces by transgressing racial and economic boundaries, generating new forms of social encounter and mixing (Koven 2006; Dowling 2009; Heap 2009).

In this article, I investigate a particular form of slum tourism conducted on a garbage dump in Mazatlán, an established tourist town located at the Pacific coast of northern Mexico. This tour, carried out by an evangelical US-based church, is explicitly non-profit orientated and free of charge. While it has no commercial competitor in Mazatlán, it challenges entrepreneurship and business-like slum tours as they take place in many other cities around the globe. Further, this tour is embedded in philanthropic and Christian ideals, which intertwine lifestyle migration, charity, urban poverty and tourism. In some ways, the ideological approach of this tour echoes the missionary work of protestant clergymen who, from early in the nineteenth century, were pointing to social inequality associated with urbanization and industrialization (Dyos 1967; Schwartz 2000). Philanthropy and charity are deeply rooted in US-American traditions of missionary service shaped by a range of religious ideologies and values (Friedman & McGarvie 2003). I follow the historical trajectory of charity-orientated missionary work but also place current responses to urban poverty in the context of globalization and economic imbalances. Furthermore, I seek to understand the underlying assumptions of charity and missionary services by inquiring into the motives and meanings that generate social action. This perspective requires a re-conceptualization of both charity and slum tourism so that they take on new meanings. I argue that this lens also helps us to unravel significant differences between earlier forms of charity-inspired activities in urban poverty districts and today's ambitions as they take place in Mazatlán.

The tour to the garbage dump is inextricably linked to revised forms of tourism, transnational lifestyles and globalization processes which frame the North American–Mexican relationships. Power imbalances and uneven economic conditions are crucial in this context and impact immensely on local politics and social realities on each side of the border. I argue that it is precisely the nexus between global forces and local conditions that generates a particular framework in which slum tours operate and by which their distinctive forms are stamped. The dynamic and constantly changing interplay between the global and the local impacts on the ways poverty issues and, consequently, slum tours are displayed, conceived of and conducted. Thus, global and national contexts as well as specific local politics, representation strategies and social conditions set the stage for slum tours and need to be taken into consideration in order to adequately understand their idiosyncratic features.

In this vein, I situate the slum tour in Mazatlán in its wider context and highlight the entanglement of socio-political dimensions with global economic forces that finally produce a particular perception of and response to urban poverty. Specifically, I examine how religious ideas are formed by and intersect with a range of globalized phenomena, such as transnational mobility, lifestyle migration and the quest for alternatives to mainstream and mass tourism. The tour to Mazatlán's garbage dump promises a less-commodified and more reciprocal, beneficial, enlightening, meaningful and engaging experience. These aspects are also identified as key in more recent tourism concepts and feature prominently in volunteer tourism and pro-poor tourism (Wearing 2001; Stebbins & Graham 2004; Hall 2007; Keese 2011). Taking part in social projects is seen as both rewarding and mutually beneficial: it contributes positively to both personal development and to the local community (Wearing 2001: 2; Stebbings 2004: 2; McIntosh & Zahra 2007). However, it has been argued that, if not carefully managed, these approaches may also lead to the reinforcement of stereotypes and preconceptions (Raymond & Hall 2008).

This article is guided by an integrated anthropological approach which explores the effects of globalization processes on individuals' life-worlds by considering the interweaving of cultural, social, political and economic dimensions. Accordingly, I follow the anthropological quest for small-scale research, but always situating it in a wider contextual, interconnected and historically informed framework. Drawing on an ethnographic approach using participant observation, local narratives, discursive accounts and in-depth interviews conducted in 2009, this article makes an empirical contribution to the multiple ways slum tours are conceived of and operate. I attended tours to the garbage dump during the high and low seasons, spent time with the garbage collectors on the dump with and without tourists and took part in the activities of both church members and tourists. Also, I scrutinized the tour's visual, virtual and printed promotion material, thus considering the representational forms in which both Mazatlán's poverty issues and the tour to the garbage dump are advertised and circulate in global networks. This research was possible because the church members, tourists and dump workers were prepared to support it by sharing their experiences.

Tourism and Lifestyle Migration in Globalized Mazatlán

Mazatlán, located in the state of Sinaloa in northern Mexico, has a population of 438,434 (INEGI 2010) and is one of the country's most prominent tourist destinations. As the 'Pearl of the Pacific', the city hosted a total of 1,861,658 visitors in 2008 (Secretaría de Turismo del Estado/Departamento de Enlace Tecnológico). In addition to tourism, the fishing industry is economically important, providing a range of job opportunities. The city's social fabric has been strongly shaped by commercial activities. Prestigious nineteenth-century buildings can still be seen in the historical city centre, where they now host restaurants, museums and art galleries. As part of Mazatláns's tourist appeal, the city administration has invested in this area to make this a picturesque tourist zone by restoring historic buildings and the *plaza*. This redevelopment increased the property value and created new jobs in the service industry. Some 8 km further north, the *Zona Dorada*, the Golden Zone, hosts luxury tourist resorts and draws seasonal migrants from rural regions to the city. Migrants often settle at the urban fringe where they seek affordable housing in poorer areas which lack the most basic infrastructure. Consequently, some of the city's underprivileged neighbourhoods have emerged out of and are inextricably linked to upmarket beach resort tourism and the revitalization of historic districts.

In Mazatlán, the globalized tourist industry had unintended consequences. More and more North American tourists decided not only to spend their holidays in this beach resort, but chose the city as their retirement destination. Subsequently, Mazatlán developed into a favourite place for affluent North American seniors. Lizárraga Morales' study (2008: 96, 97) reveals the close linkage between tourism and retirement migration, as the overwhelming majority (95%) of the elderly he interviewed had visited the city before while they were on vacation. He also points out that the overall number of US-national migrants to the state of Sinaloa is steadily rising from 3,431 in 2005, to 5,000 in 2006 and 6,100 in 2007 (Lizárraga Morales 2008: 98). This rapid increase is an effect of networks and information systems made available to those interested in relocating to Mexico and thus facilitating further migration flows. It is impossible to obtain precise numbers on North American migration to Mazatlán as many migrants stay six months and then cross the border either just to renew their permit or to re-enter the country some months later. Only a small proportion of these seasonal migrants register with their embassies or with the Mexican immigration office. Estimates suggest that 20,000 US nationals visit the state of Sinaloa on a monthly basis, with an increase to 35,000 during the high season in the winter and spring months (Zamora 2007; Lizárraga Morales 2008: 99).

The transnational movement of North Americans to Mexico is situated in an emerging and rapidly growing migratory pattern sprawling from affluent and politically powerful countries to less potent nations. It is tied into globalization processes and unbalanced economic forces between the Global North and the Global South that play out and become manifest in specific ways at the local level. This form of mobility is conceptualized as lifestyle migration (Benson & O'Reilly 2009) and gained new momentum in Mexico when the country became part of the North American Free Trade Agreement (NAFTA). The agreement facilitates an easy flow of products and services between the trading partners. As a consequence, multinational corporations emerge and North American products are widely available in Mexico. There are indications that this process alters both the volume of the migratory flow and the kind of migrants (Truly 2002). Some of the new arrivals seem to be unwilling to embrace the local culture. They are instead set on 'importing a lifestyle' (Truly 2002: 268, 270, 273; Sunil *et al.* 2007).

Furthermore, this mode of migration adds a new dimension to the politically contested and symbolically charged border that divides a powerful globalized economy and a less developed country. In countless representations and discourses, Mexico is constructed as a nation not capable of providing adequate living standards and services to its citizens and unable to control violence and drug trafficking (Patenostro 1995; Domínguez-Ruvalcaba & Corona 2010). There is also the widespread perception that the only way for Mexicans to achieve social mobility is by moving to the USA (Vila 2005: 119). But for those crossing the border southward, this perspective is turned around and Mexico is represented as an attractive destination of residence for North American citizens, one that actually benefits from the economic disparity between the two regions. The Mexican government welcomes the new migrants as they are expected to bring in economic resources and potentially increase the country's prosperity. The consequences of this process, however, are not limited to economic advancement and regional development, but are also expressed in the promotion of specific values, worldviews and practices. Being far from passive observers, some retired migrants tend to take on leadership roles by engaging deeply in local affairs. Even though retirement migrants are still low in numbers with regard to Mexico's overall population, their impact on the local level is significant and felt in the social, political and economic realms. This phenomenon is increasingly observed and addressed in recent studies from a range of disciplines (Stockes 1990; Otero Young 1997; Palma Mora 2000; Truly 2002; Banks 2004; Sunil *et al.* 2007; Lizárraga Morales 2008; Croucher 2009a; 2009b; Janoschka 2009).

The effects of the North American migrants' presence are mixed, but there are some similar patterns reported from prime destinations, such as the Pacific Coast, Baja California and Lake Chapala Rivera, where former tourists settle as senior migrants. While the local economy is stimulated and job opportunities increase, new delineations are drawn, producing various forms of social exclusion and disadvantage for the local population, such as increased prices, gentrification and an alteration of the built environment that matches primarily the needs of the retirees. They also contribute to the city's spatial and social fragmentation by creating new urban enclaves in the forms of gated communities, condominiums and hotel complexes (Truly 2002; Lizárraga Morales 2008; Croucher 2009a; 2009b; Janoschka 2009).

While most retirees point to economic advantages in their decision to move to a less developed country, some stress their appreciation of the 'Mexican way of life' and of 'Mexican culture' as significant factors (Banks 2004; Sunil *et al.* 2007). They perceive the pace of life as more pleasant than in North America and embrace Mexican 'culture' as less profit-orientated, less interested in consumerism and far more welcoming than the North American one. Simultaneously, they articulate critiques of some Mexican attitudes which they perceive as resentful, needy and lazy. As a consequence, friendliness and helpfulness is rendered superficial, making relationships instrumental rather than close friendships (Banks 2004: 374). Few retirees command Spanish and are able to converse with non English-speaking Mexicans. They rather maintain tight social networks amongst themselves, live close to each other and, according to their interests, socialize in particular restaurants, clubs, leisure activities, sporting events and church services. They also sustain information networks by using internet blogs and local newsletters published in English. Furthermore, they tend to maintain close linkages with their places of origin and take advantage of numerous and inexpensive flights between Mexico and North America. In spite of these tendencies, it is important to note that the retirees are not a closed, primarily inward-orientated community. Quite the contrary, as many migrants aspire to create a 'better Mexico' by promoting charity work and social welfare (Stokes 1990; Croucher 2009a: 67f.).

The wish to better the living conditions in Mexico according to their own values and worldviews seems to be ubiquitous among affluent retirement migrants. In their perception, they bring the 'first world' to the 'third world' while still appreciating the 'Mexican way of life'. This attitude, along with negative outcomes of this migratory flow, such as urban gentrification and fragmentation, is critically discussed in both newspapers (Davis 2006) and scholarly literature and tentatively assessed as a kind of '"post-colonial" behaviour' (Janoschka 2009: 4) or as 'perhaps something more akin to imperialism' (Croucher 2009b: 484) or, with regard to the more recent retirees arriving at Lake Chapala Riviera, as '"importing a lifestyle", rather than adapting to the community's established culture' (Truly 2002: 268).

While all these notions rightfully point to the tendency to impose 'western' values and reveal a sense of superiority and paternalism, they also, and implicitly, draw on a dichotomist, one-dimensional relationship between colonizers and colonized. More importantly, the retirees themselves challenge this classification and do not see themselves as being 'colonizers'. This is certainly evident from the self-perceptions of retirees in Mazatlán as socially engaged citizens. Many seniors are involved in a range of social organizations, community service and support networks. These charitable endeavours take up social issues with an emphasis on educational schemes and medical assistance. Some of these organizations are religiously motivated, others not, such as the American Legion, Friends of Mexico, Hands Across the Borders, the Rotary Club or the Cancer Society, just to name a few. There are so many organizations in the city that they even duplicate their services in some cases (Fortney 2007) and some seniors are members in several organizations at once. According to the retirees, their charitable work witnesses to their non-colonial practices and attitudes. They are mainly middle-class men and women who 'are keen to contribute to a better world' as one retiree told me. As a former successful professional, he still wishes to apply his knowledge and 'deliver some skills' which he feels are 'desperately needed here'.

It is important to note that the North American retirees in Mazatlán are not a homogeneous group, but rather divided by class, religious denomination, regional provenance and nationality as there are perceived differences between US-Americans and Canadian citizens. Although most of the elderly have backgrounds as middle class professionals, some reside in luxury real estate, while others live in far more modest housing, even in trailer parks. Accordingly, retirees choose Mazatlán for a retirement destination for a variety of reasons, ranging from its excellent fishing and golfing facilities, through the demand for a warmer climate for health reasons, to a more affordable lifestyle. Regardless of their individual motivations, the migrants all benefit from the fact that their currency has more spending power in Mexico than in North America, where real estate, health care and living costs are far more expensive. Thus, globalization processes create a complex web of relationships and identities in

Mazatlán. In what follows, the focus is on a specific segment of the affluent North American migrant group, that is, middle-class retirees involved in an evangelical charismatic church. Analysis reveals the meanings associated with their most salient project: a tour to the city's garbage dump.

Christianity, Charity and Poor Relief

In 1996, a US-American pastor founded an evangelical charismatic church and mission, La Viña, in Mazatlán (Collom 2004). The Vineyard churches were born out of missionary work amongst the Hippie-movement in California and established a world-wide network (Watling 2008). Financially, the church depends on the donations of particular individuals, charity-minded marketing companies and its home church in the USA, the Vineyard Christian Fellowship of Champaign, Illinois. La Viña in Mazatlán, suitably located on the main tourist avenue in the resort zone and offering services in Spanish and English, aims at reaching both local professional-class Mexicans and North Americans. The church is open to all Christians and does not require an official membership because of the high fluctuation of its clientele. The majority of the English language service attendees are transnational retirees and some tourists who visit Mazatlán during their holidays and take the opportunity to participate in a Sunday service. While the church service might be attended by 200 or more individuals during the high season, only 20–30 persons attend during the low season.

The church has a strong social commitment, which is embedded in the principle of reaching out to the people in need. This approach is enacted by the volunteer and charity-minded retirees who are particularly concerned with helping the poor, as the pastor states in his book describing the vineyard community (Collom 2004: 113). Religiously inspired charity and philanthropy have long-standing histories in North America and some of the retirees have been engaged in these activities before relocating to Mexico. While charity involves the individual in concrete actions motivated by compassion, philanthropy may be seen as a mainly institutionalized form of social service, promoting public good and reforming society (Gross 2003; Bornstein 2009). The church in Mazatlán combines both approaches by being concerned with improving social conditions in terms of educational and medical assistance on a more general level but also by offering concrete action to alleviate poverty on an individual basis. This mission is intertwined with moral categories and works on various levels resonating earlier protestant parish officials who reacted to urban poverty in the eighteenth and nineteenth century. Charity activities were perceived as signs of duty to God and donors hoped for salvation, thus benefiting both the urban poor and the donor's spirituality (Porterfield 2003; Lloyd 2009: 27). Charity was also seen as an effective tool encompassing both a transformative and redemptive power that brought moral improvement and profane benefits that helped to construct a modern society. In this vein, clergy and missionaries functioned as voices articulating social critique and promoting urban reform. Having noticed unsanitary housing and exploitive labour conditions of the urban poor, some of them emerged as social reformers calling for changes in the wider society (Dyos 1967: 17; Gross 2003: 44). In the USA, there were also racialized hierarchies and paternalistic discourses involved when members of the white elite were concerned with the politics of poor relief. Whiteness was equated with endowment, giftedness and privilege, reflecting a sense of cultural superiority toward non-white individuals. This became evident when some missionary groups were seeking to uplift darker races by introducing them to both 'civilization' and salvation (Gross 2003: 45; Rosenberg 2003: 246).

The church in Mazatlán wants to keep social service and missionary work separate in order to avoid criticism (Collom 2004: 94). Their philosophy is to serve the poor without expecting bible study in return as their aim goes beyond faith-based charity activities. Rather, they strive to raise awareness of urban misery by connecting affluent tourists with the most vulnerable urban poor, ultimately hoping that individuals engage in these issues and take action. In my discussions with leading church members they referred to the parable of the Good Samaritan as a model of an altruistic, selfless service to one's fellow human, but also indicated a desire to increase tourists' attention to misery as a key incentive for their engagement in social projects. The tour to the garbage dump is not about voyeurism or profit but about a selfless social service. This is expressed in the following quote from a church official:

> Our mission is to change this place. We show tourists the real face of Mazatlán. We confront them with poverty and dirt, but our tour is not about 'poorism'. We want to contribute to a better world by opening the tourists' eyes and by pointing to the misery here ... We get them out of the tourist bubble ... Many of our volunteers are skilled professionals and keen to be actively involved in fighting poverty. They provide assistance in a range of projects and help with medical assistance, teaching materials, scholarships, building skills.

This statement shows that the garbage tour is not intended to be a leisure or commercial activity in the first place, but is meant to address and raise awareness of social inequality and to alleviate poverty, 'to inspire people to do stuff they have never done before', as the minister is quoted in one of the promotion videos for the tour (Harvey 2006). By showing tourists the garbage dump, the church also hopes that local officials and Mexicans will be faced with the responsibility to respond to the city's poverty issues. The tourists are promised to experience 'authenticity' in a space not made for visitors. Thus, the artificially created resort environment with its glamorous hotel spaces is juxtaposed with the garbage dump as a unique vernacular landscape rarely seen by outsiders. However, the tour to the dump is also an instrument to market the church's philosophy and mission. In this vein, charity is used to compete for attention in a city almost overloaded with offerings, distractions and advertisements.

152

Even though the church leaders intentionally try to keep charity separate from missionary work, this is almost impossible in practice as the charity activity is deeply rooted in the Christian tradition and in Protestant values. For instance, satellite churches in the city's disadvantaged districts help to promote charity programmes but are obviously associated with the church, thus endorsing charity and a Christian philosophy at once. Currently, the Vineyard Church has a dozen centres in Mazatlán, each of which is a base for some kind of social work. Many church attendees actively support these projects which range from educational programmes to mobile feeding centres and medical clinics. The most prominent project, however, is the tour to the city's garbage dump, intertwining charity, tourism and the promotion of the church's philosophy and success.

The Garbage Dump as Tourist Site

The tour to the city dump is conducted once a week during the low season (April–October) and three to four times a week during the high season. The tour is advertised in local magazines, flyers, in a tourist guide book and on the website of the ministry and draws tourist from the various resort zones and even from the cruise ships stopping in Mazatlán. Others receive notice of the tour while attending a Sunday service in the church. It is labelled as a 'life-changing experience' and as a 'unique opportunity to see the real face of the city', which is otherwise inaccessible to tourists. A range of promotional videos are available on the internet, as well as reports from tourists who took part in this tour (Collom 2007; Davis 2008; Weiss 2010).

The half-day excursion starts at the church where the tourists are asked to prepare sandwiches and bottled water for the dump workers. The tour guide, usually one of the retirees, instructs the participants on the tour's protocol and ideology. He teaches the tourists how to greet in Spanish and advises them not to hand out cash to the dump workers. A promotional video is shown which addresses general poverty issues in the city, discrimination against 'darker' individuals and finally records living conditions at the garbage dump. The garbage collectors are construed as struggling for a better life by working hard and being active. They are portrayed as 'amazing people', full of hope, with an exceptional 'will to survive' and 'resilience', as well as 'eager recipients' of the church's benevolent activities. This representation links into the concept of the 'deserving poor', who are unable to find suitable employment and require assistance for reasons beyond their control and, therefore, deserve social support and sympathy. They stand in moral distinction to the unworthy poor, who are idle and lack discipline and, therefore, are poor through their own fault. The latter category does not deserve public aid and poor relief. This distinction has been very influential and reflects nineteenth-century assumptions that slums are the consequences of failings in the inhabitants, who are disorderly and dangerous, possibly a threat to society at large (Gaskell 1990: 5; Gross 2003: 34; Lloyd 2009: 26). This perception still resonates today in the notion of the 'lazy Mexican', a stereotype and prejudice that the church dump tour seeks to challenge.

The representation of Mazatlán's poor as morally deserving enhances the tourists' conception that charity is the appropriate way to make a positive difference and create a better world. This is sustained by visually contrasting the city's most expensive resort zones with the garbage dump. By accentuating the disparity between the dump workers and tourists, the deprived and the affluent, the church mirrors the North American–Mexican border narratives as delimiting between an underdeveloped/weak and a developed/strong nation. This dualist, racialized conception may add force to feelings of exceptionalism and cultural superiority while simultaneously evoking compassion for the poor. Thus, some tourists reflect on their own life circumstances and express relief, while others state they feel 'blessed' or 'lucky' to be born in more comfortable conditions. These emotive responses neatly fit the framing of the encounters at the dump as charity. They, however, do not address the structural reasons generating disparity between rich and poor. Nevertheless, the promotional material both advertises the Christian message and displays the church as a successful actor fighting poverty and injustice as a responsibility before God. This creates further distinctions between those who have been evangelized and those who are unevangelized, still in need of the gospel. Thus, religious and economic wants are displayed and Christianity is presented as a possible route out of both spiritual and material poverty.

The tourists are mostly North American citizens and are drawn from all age groups. Local Mexicans and Mexican tourists hardly ever participate. The motivational factors for the tourists to take part in this tour are manifold and comprise a mixture of curiosity to step into an unknown life-world and to see what it is like to live in a dump. Major incentives also include a quest for experiencing the 'authentic', something that is actually not made for tourists and, therefore, not 'artificial'. While this is also the case in slum tours in other cities, the tour in Mazatlán goes beyond this by showing how the tourists can do something useful by supporting efforts to alleviate poverty. The tour's alternative ideological approach certainly promises a more meaningful experience than mass tourism products but also aims to stir self-awareness and -reflection in ways different from other slum tours. In this vein, the tourists' active involvement in a strongly felt good cause is intertwined with discovering the personal and social rewards available in community work. Participants seek new travel experiences beyond the mere leisure activity by engaging in a process in which the self is challenged. It reflects a desire for altruism and self-reflection that extends beyond the actual tourist excursion. This effect is promised in the dump tour's advertisement as 'an experience that will change your life'.

After the introduction in the church building, the tourists are driven in an unpretentious vehicle through some of the city's underprivileged districts where the church undertakes social projects. When approaching the dump, the guide provides some information on the business of garbage sorting and highlights the importance of the dump workers in this context. He explains that roughly 200 male and female garbage collectors are experts in the recycling of rubbish and make an enormous contribution to the reduction of the city's waste. They collect and sell the non-organic rubbish, such as plastic, glass, copper or cans. None the less, their activity and their often unhealthy working conditions, not to speak of prestige and dignity, receive scant attention. The tourists' presence on the dump, however, increases the garbage collectors' visibility in the overall context in the city and draws attention from the municipality. One effect of the dump's touristification is a stronger police presence and the prohibition of children as dump workers. The church interprets this as a success of their efforts to increase awareness of social issues and to better the living conditions of the garbage sorters.

Having arrived on the dump site, the tourists get in close contact with the dump workers by delivering sandwiches, fruit and bottled water. The exchange of food and water, in particular bread, is symbolically charged with Christian virtues and values of solidarity. This links into a long-standing history of charitable undertakings to which food was integral, such as serving breakfasts and dinners to urban poor in the context of almsgiving (Lloyd 2009: 219). Drawing on these practices, however, also reaffirms hierarchies of recipients in need and privileged donors – and places the tourists in the position to give or to withhold.

During this interaction, there is a physical closeness of individuals with extremely disparate life chances which is an idiosyncratic feature of this tour. This encounter is accompanied by the attempt to exchange some words. While the tourists try to communicate in Spanish, applying some sentences they have learned from the guide, such as '*Dios te bendiga*' (God bless you), the dump workers reply in English 'thank you'. In some cases, however, the tourists command Spanish and try to have a more profound conversation with some individuals helping to recycle rubbish by asking them about their living conditions, how much money they make on the dump, how many children they have, how old they are and so on. In any case, this interaction, which lasts for roughly twenty minutes to half an hour in the midst of trash, stench and squalor, leaves a deep emotional impression on the tourists. Social distance and racial barriers seem to be bridged in these very moments.

At the same time, there are diverse and contradictory agendas at play on the dump site. Some garbage collectors invite the tourists to visit their homes which are located close to the dump site. By doing this, they take charge of the programme using the tour to advance their own goals and articulate their needs. Alternatively, a few tour guides have agreements with dump workers to visit their shacks on the way back to the city. However, it is important to note that these practices are contested. Neither all garbage collectors nor all tour guides approve. Some dump workers reject the idea of letting tourists enter their homes and further object to the touristification of their workplace. They perceive the tourists' presence as inappropriate and prefer not to be seen while sorting rubbish. These workers will not approach the bus on the dump and also mostly avoided contact with me. As a researcher of European descent, I am different but still similar to and at times identified with either members of the church or the tourist crowd.

Nevertheless, some dump workers do embrace the tourists' interest in their conditions and try to communicate with them. They even express a sense of pride that international visitors pay attention to their situation. Just as the tourists are keen to get, literally, in touch with individuals who work on the dump, some garbage collectors are curious to get close to individuals from luxury resorts. The garbage actually creates a link between these seemingly opposed living environments. Dump workers perceive the garbage not just as recycling material and income, but also as an indication of particular living habits and social contexts. The kind and size of the rubbish bag gives them a clue to its social origins. Further, they imagine the social life that goes along with the garbage from the bags' contents and can identify particular lifestyles, such as food habits, hobbies, preferred cosmetics, even diseases and use of drugs. This competency may contribute to their curiosity to meet affluent tourists, whose garbage is considered to be the most valuable.

On the journey back to the resort zone, the bus drives through other poverty and red light districts. This part of the tour resembles more a sightseeing tour, even though it is broken up by some more stops where the tourists hand out food to children in underprivileged neighbourhoods. The focus is now on the achievements of the church's charity programmes, such as child sponsoring programmes, scholarships for around 230 students and other projects that are financed by donations. Ultimately, the church provides around 22,000 meals per year for disadvantaged individuals in the city of Mazatlán. The slum tour is only the most visible part of a broader range of projects.

Many tourists experience the tour as an opportunity to get in touch with and to learn about other people's environment, an endeavour which entails a transforming power. This becomes apparent on various levels and affects all individuals involved. The tourists feel more knowledgeable and are convinced that the visit to the dump helps to develop the self and to improve the world. They gain a different personal experience than other tourists by having interacted closely with the poor, even if only for less than half an hour. Thus, the tour to the garbage dump is a creative way to provide a meaningful tourist experience by conveying the feeling to have accomplished something significant and useful, for others and for themselves. In contrast to commodified encounters, this experience transforms them from irresponsible tourists into socially conscious explorers who have documented their encounter by picture taking. This is pertinently expressed by a middle-aged woman who took part in the tour:

> After a week or so, I was bored in my resort Hotel. My husband is enjoying the marvellous golf course, but I got tired of it ... I attended the church service on Sunday at the Vineyard and heard of the tour to the garbage dump. I would never go to a poverty district on my own, but I was intrigued hearing about the

charity work of the church. And I wanted to do an unselfish thing on a selfish trip. I think that this tour was the most valuable experience of my holidays and helped me to put my life into perspective.

The tourists understand the dump dwellers in interesting ways. Some see the garbage collectors as coping with devastating and pitiful life circumstances. They turn from marginalized poor into deserving poor, and are thus cast as positive and valuable individuals who struggle with unfair conditions. Others admire the garbage dwellers' efforts and creativity. In accord with critical discourses on consumer practices and the environment, some tourists even perceive the dump workers' few material possessions as signifying modest environmental footprints. The dump workers turn from 'scavengers' into 'real ecologists' as garbage recycling is conceived of as a sustainable, ecologically positive and 'modern' activity. This shows also a sense of awareness of the tourists' own environmental behaviour while tentatively ennobling the deplorable living conditions in the dump. My own role as a researcher is transformed into a messenger, interpreter and witness. Also, this role contributes to a revised conception of dump workers and garbage as not only an attraction for tourists, but also as a field for charity and for missionary activity.

Simultaneously, the tour guide is confirmed in his role as an expert who made a successful transition from an unaware and ignorant tourist to a socially responsible and knowledgeable person, now able to lead into the mysterious world on the garbage dump. He embodies morally ideal values, dedicating his efforts to create a better world. This transformation is a rewarding experience for the retirees who develop from tourists to retirement migrants to social activists and advisers as they discover the garbage dump as a new field of engagement. Their achievement is confirmed and expanded when they display a more intimate relationship with some individual dump workers. Because of the regularity of the trip, some tour guides, as well as the bus driver, develop a closer and more personal relationship with the garbage collectors, so that they know each other's names, biographies and life circumstances. This is also the case for other congregation members who accompany the tour on a more regular basis and connect to urban poor in a more personalized way rather than a de-personalized mode. In these cases, durable social relationships are established and result in a more complex connection between the retirees' and the dump workers' lives. This becomes apparent when some of the retirees sponsor individual families, be it by supporting them with additional food, by providing scholarships for their children, assisting with health care, school supplies or housing material. The sponsoring of individual families, however, is not a straightforward practice as the dump is also a site for contestation. Jealousy and envy is fomented amongst the garbage collectors because it is not possible to distribute the goods equally to all families living in this area. As a heterogeneous group comprising migrants from all over Mexico, the dump workers often compete for scarce resources. While charity can bridge social, racial and national divides, it may simultaneously evoke envy, distrust and resentment.

Long-lasting relationships prove to be far more intricate than brief encounters. Some retirees told me that they perceive a lack of gratitude over time and feel disappointed to receive demands and queries, asking for more support instead of reflecting thankfulness. The recipients are more likely to articulate critique in durable relationships, but they cannot claim rights. This hierarchy is hardly questioned, but rather taken for granted because of the obvious discrepancies in the economic, social and cultural resources of the actors involved. Nevertheless, some recipients challenge the role of being mere beneficiaries by refusing respectful compliance.

The retirees' individual impact is noticeable and confirms a reciprocal relationship between donor and recipient. Donors feel successful when recipients of their generosity are grateful. Their status is elevated when they are seen to be effective. Power and prestige can be generated from their efforts to improve the world. In their own interpretation, they provide a selfless service to one's fellow human being, serving the spiritual and material needs of both Mazatlán and their own community members. Thus, they are of service to others and to the common good. However, there may be risks attached to thinking that their works are the will of God.

Conclusion

This research shows that the global–local nexus is key for the understanding of the idiosyncratic features of slum tours, which are proliferating around the globe. Globalization processes reconfigure each local community in particular ways and stimulate local responses. The tour of the Mazatlán dump offered by the Vineyard Church clearly reflects the underlying forces shaping the relationship between North America and Mexico. It reveals an intricate engagement with urban poverty through the interweaving of lifestyle migration, tourism and charity. In the tour, the tourists and retirees demonstrate their power to explore the most peripheral parts of Mexico and on terms of their own making, however well meaning. Charity not only helps to distinguish the tour to Mazatlán's garbage dump from other slum tours but also takes on specific meanings in the Mazatlán context.

The tour is an opportunity to articulate religious viewpoints and moral convictions, and to call for political action in order to create a better world. It is also a form of missionary work entailing conscience-salving acts that are seen as blessing for the donor and the recipient at once. Charity is conceptualized as a form of self-realization, self-transformation and personal renewal. This potential is key in promising a meaningful tourist experience that goes beyond altruism, but rather constitutes an inquiry into self and mirrors the quest for the 'authentic'. These features are also salient in the retirees' activities as a means of value-adding and creating a meaningful evening of life. Migration often coincides with specific events in individuals' lives and reflects a search for meaning and an opportunity to recast one's identity. In this process, the retirees become socially useful and the distinction between tourists, social reformers and clergy is blurred. Furthermore, these practices are tied into the American Dream of personal achievement, underpinned by the commitment to creating a more tractable society. This aspiration, however, is contested and could be seen as imposing a vision of a good society on others. It is a political aid, involving power issues and generating discourses on new forms of imperialism with multiple effects. The tour activities affect marginalized urban spaces in Mazatlán against the backdrop of a particular set of globalization processes, thus producing a distinctive response to urban poverty, that is, a tourist experience of poverty, framed by discourses of charity.

References

Banks, S. (2004) Identity narratives by American and Canadian retirees in Mexico, *Journal of Cross-Cultural Gerontology*, 19(4), pp. 361–381.

Benson, M. & O'Reilly, K. (2009) *Lifestyle Migration. Expectations, Aspirations and Experiences* (Farnham: Ashgate).

Bornstein, E. (2009) The impulse of philanthropy, *Cultural Anthropology*, 24(4), pp. 622–651.

Collom, F. C. (2004) *The Dumb Gringo. How not to be one in Missions* (o.O.: Xulon Press).

Collom, F. (2007) The Other Mazatlán. Available at http://www.youtube.com/watch?v=9QlIEGU76PY (accessed 20 January 2011).

Croucher, S. (2009a) *The Other Side of the Fence: American Migrants in Mexico* (Austin: University of Texas Press).

Croucher, S. (2009b) Migrants of privilege: The political transnationalism of Americans in Mexico, *Identities: Global Studies in Culture and Power*, 16(4), pp. 463–491.

Davis, M. (2006) Invasores de Fronteras, La Jornada, 23 Spetiembre 2006. Available at http://www.jornada.unam.mx/2006/09/23/ (accessed 13 January 2001).

Davis, M. (2008) La Viña: Mazatlán Dump Water Distribution. Available at http://vimeo.com/3922854 (accessed 20 January 2011).

Domínguez-Ruvalcaba, H. & Corona, I. (2010) *Gender Violence at the U.S.–Mexico Border. Media Representation and Public Response* (Tucson: University of Arizona Press).

Dowling, R. M. (2009) *Slumming in New York. From the Waterfront to Mythic Harlem* (Urbana Champaign: University of Illinois Press).

Dyos, H. (1967) The slums of Victorian London, *Victorian Studies*, 11(1), pp. 5–40.

Fortney, V. (2007) Loving orphans make his heart sing: Troupe founder 'the gringo of the hood', *Calgary Herald*, February 5, p. A9.

Foster, J. (2009) 'Slumdog Millionaire puts slum tourism in the spotlight', *Asia Development. A Publication of the Asian Development Bank*, No. 3, April. Available at http://development.asia/issue03/feature-01.asp (accessed 30 November 2010).

Freire-Medeiros, B. (2008) And the favela went global: the invention of a trademark and a tourist destination, in: M. M. Valenca, E. Nel & W. Leimgruber (Eds) *The Global Challenge and Marginalization*, pp. 33–52 (New York: Nova Science Publishers).

Freire-Medeiros, B. (2009) The favela and its touristic transits, *Geoforum*, 40, pp. 580–588.

Friedman, L. J. & McGarvie, M. D. (2003) *Charity, Philanthropy, and Civility in American History* (Cambridge: Cambridge University Press).

Gaskell, M. S. (1990) Introduction, in: M. S. Gaskell (Ed.) *Slums*, pp. 1–16 (Leicester: Leicester University Press).

Gross, R. (2003) Giving in America. From charity to philanthropy, in: L. J. Friedman & M. D. McGarvie (Eds) *Charity, Philanthropy and Civility in American History*, pp. 29–48 (Cambridge: Cambridge University Press).

Hall, C. M. (2007) *Pro-poor Tourism* (Clevedon: Channel View).

Harvey, C. (2006) *The Two Sides of Mazatlán*. DVD, Promotion Video of La Viña, Mazatlán, México.

Heap, C. (2009) *Slumming: Sexual and Racial Encounters in American Nightlife, 1885–1940* (Chicago: University of Chicago Press).

INEGI, Instituto Nacional de Estadística Geografía e Informática (2010) Información Demográfica. Available at http://www.mazatlan.gob.mx/modules.php?name=News&file=article&sid=1634 (accessed 10 January 2011).

Jaguaribe, B. & Hetherington, K. (2006) Favela tours: Indistinct and maples representations of the real in Rio de Janeiro, in: M. Sheller & J. Urry (Eds) *Mobile Technologies of the City*, pp. 155–166 (London: Routledge).

Janoschka, M. (2009) The contested spaces of lifestyle mobilities: Regime analysis as a tool to study political claims in Latin American retirement destinations, *Die Erde*, 140(3), pp. 1–20.

Keese, J. R. (2011) The geography of volunteer tourism: Place matters, *Tourism Geographies*, 13(2), pp. 257–279.

Koven, S. (2006) *Slumming: Sexual and Social Politics in Victorian London* (Princeton: University Press).

Lizárraga Morales, O. (2008) Immigration and transnational practices of U.S. retirees in Mexico. A case study in Mazatlán, Sinaloa and Cabo San Lucas, Baja California Sur, Vol. 18. Available at http://estudiosdeldesarrollo.net/revista/rev11ing/t5.pdf (accessed 9 December 2011).

Lloyd, S. (2009) *Charity and Poverty in England, c.1680–1820. Wild and Visionary Schemes* (Manchester: Manchester University Press).

McIntosh, A. & Zahra, A. (2007) A cultural encounter through volunteer tourism: Towards the ideals of sustainable tourism? *Journal of Sustainable Tourism*, 15(5), pp. 541–556.

Meschkank, J. (2010) Investigations into slum tourism in Mumbai. Poverty tourism and the tension between different constructions of reality, *Geojournal*, DOI: 10.1007/s10708-010-9401-7.

Odede, K. (2010) Slumdog tourism, *International Herald Tribune – The New York Times*, 11 August.

Otero Young, L. M. Y. (1997) U.S. retired persons in Mexico, *American Behavioral Scientist*, 40(7), pp. 914–923.

Palma Mora, M. (2000) La immigracion en México en la segunda mitad del siglo XX: un estudio intorductorio, *Estudios Migratorios Latinoamericanos*, 15(48), pp. 551–586.

Patenostro, S. (1995) Mexico as a narco-democracy, *World Policy Journal*, 12(1), pp. 41–47.

Porterfield, A. (2003) Protestant missionaries: Pioneers of American philanthropy, in: L. J. Friedman & M. D. McGarvie (Eds) *Charity, Philanthropy and Civility in American History*, pp. 49–69 (Cambridge: Cambridge University Press).

Raymond, E. M. & Hall, M. C. (2008) The development of cross-cultural (mis)understanding through volunteer tourism, *Journal of Sustainable Tourism*, 16(5), pp. 530–543.

Rolfes, M. (2009) Poverty tourism: Theoretical reflections and empirical findings regarding an extraordinary form of tourism, *Geojournal*, DOI 10.1007/s10708-009-9311-8.

Rosenberg, E. S. (2003) Missions to the world: Philanthropy abroad, in: L. J. Friedman & M. D. McGarvie (Eds) *Charity, Philanthropy and Civility in American History*, pp. 241–257 (Cambridge: Cambridge University Press).

Scheyvens, R. (2011) *Tourism and Poverty* (New York: Routledge).

Schwartz, J. (2000) *Fighting Poverty with Virtue: Moral Reform and America's Urban Poor, 1825–2000* (Bloomington: Indiana University Press).

Secretaría de Turismo del Estado/Departamento de Enlace Tecnológico (2008) *Mazatlán: Afluencia Turística según procedencia, 2004–2008* (Mazatlán, Sin., México: Secretaría de Turismo, Gobierno del Estado).

Stebbins, R. A. (2004) Introduction, in: R. A. Stebbins & M. Graham (Eds) *Volunteering as Leisure/Leisure as Volunteering. An International Assessment*, pp. 1–12 (Wallingford: CABI Publishing).

Stebbins, R. A. & Graham, M. (Eds) (2004) *Volunteering as Leisure/Leisure as Volunteering. An International Assessment* (Wallingford: CABI Publishing).

Stokes, E. M. (1990) Ethnography of a social border: The case of an American retirement community in Mexico, *Journal of Cross-Cultural Gerontology*, 5(2), pp.169–182.

Sunil, T. S., Rojas, V. & Bradley, D. E. (2007) United States' international retirement migration: The reasons for retiring to the environs of Lake Chapala, Mexico, *Ageing & Society*, 27(4), pp. 489–510.

Truly, D. (2002) International retirement migration and tourism along the Lake Chapala Riviera: Developing a matrix of retirement migration behaviour, *Tourism Geographies*, 4(3), pp. 261–281.

Vila, P. (2005) *Border Identifications. Narratives of Religion, Gender, and Class on the U.S.–Mexico Border* (Austin: University of Texas Press).

Watling, M. (2008) *Natürlich übernatürlich. Die Geschichte der Vineyard-Bewegung* (Witten: Brockhaus Verlag im SCM-Verlag).

Wearing, S. (2001) *Volunteer Tourism. Experiences that Make a Difference* (Wallingford: CABI Publishing).

Weiner, E. (2008) Slum visits: Tourism or voyeurism?, *New York Times – Travel*, 9 March.

Weiss, R. (2010) The discarded people of the Mexican Riviera. Available at http://vimeo.com/12283364 (accessed 10 January 2011).

Zamora, L. (2007) Eligen extranjeros a Mazatlán para residir, *Noroeste*, October.

Notes on Contributor

Eveline Dürr is a Professor at the Institute for Social and Cultural Anthropology, Ludwig-Maximilians-University in Munich. She has conducted fieldwork in Mexico, the USA, New Zealand and Germany on topics ranging from patterns of cultural change to migration and the formation of cultural identities. Her research projects and publications reflect her interests in urban anthropology, spatiality, representation and globalization, and take into consideration the historical trajectories that have formed present conditions.

Index

Note:
Page numbers in **bold** type refer to figures
Page numbers in *italic* type refer to tables

For Product Safety Concerns and Information please contact our EU
representative GPSR@taylorandfrancis.com Taylor & Francis Verlag GmbH,
Kaufingerstraße 24, 80331 München, Germany

Printed and bound by CPI Group (UK) Ltd, Croydon, CR0 4YY

01/05/2025

01858422-0013